AUTOPSY

an element of realism in film noir

by
CARL RICHARDSON

The Scarecrow Press, Inc.
Metuchen, N.J., & London
1992

British Library Cataloguing-in-Publication data available

Library of Congress Cataloging-in-Publication Data

Richardson, Carl, 1950-
      Autopsy : an element of realism in film noir / by Carl
Richardson.
            p.   cm.
      Includes bibliographical references and index.
      ISBN 0-8108-2496-5 (alk. paper)
      1. Film noir—History and criticism.   2. Realism in motion
pictures.   I. Title.
PN1995.9.F54R5   1992
791.43'655—dc20   91-44181

To My Father

CONTENTS

LIST OF ILLUSTRATIONS

ACKNOWLEDGMENTS

The author gratefully acknowledges the following institutions for granting permission to use their materials:

The Albert Maltz Collection, Mugar Memorial Library, Boston University, Boston, Mass., for quoted material.

The Mark Hellinger Collection and The Universal Collection, University of Southern California Cinema-Television Library and Archives, Los Angeles, for quoted material.

The Museum of Modern Art, New York City, for photographs.

Oral History Collection, Columbia University in the City of New York, for quoted material.

Warner Bros. Archive at Princeton University Libraries, Princeton, N.J., for quoted material.

Warner Bros. Archive at the University of Southern California Library, Los Angeles, for photograph.

I AN ELEMENT OF REALISM IN CINEMA

We are in a film morgue and lying on a stretcher is a corpse, tagged *film noir*.

Autopsy is a probe that cuts into its tissue, beneath its pale skin, constituting everything that is already known and appreciated about the departed. It is necessary to scrape away widely held beliefs that have attached themselves like maggots to the deceased organism, but were not originally a part of it to begin with. From the looks of it, *film noir* appears to have been a vigorous cycle of films, making a vital contribution to the American cinema, and exerting a strong posthumous influence on many subsequent films. But it was relatively young when it disappeared, not much more than twenty. What killed it?

Autopsy will suggest that an element of realism infused *film noir* with the breath of life. Separated from its support-system, *film noir* became lifeless, decayed, and finally went under. It was fantasy that killed *film noir*. Fantasy could sustain the comedy film, the adventure film, westerns, and melodramas, but it was venomous to *film noir*. *Films noirs* may well have been conceived as wholly detached cinematic hyperbole, but they were not severed from all that was real. They were never mere shadowy reflections. They depicted life in odd ways, distorted for the sake of entertainment, but they also allowed for a certain reading of life, articulated in twisted, unconventional cinematic terms. In their collectively dark view of life they touched on an aspect of reality—the very fact that it *is* dark—that is as constant as it is perpetually ignored by Hollywood.

A word of warning is in order. *Autopsy* is not a nostalgic

study, lavishly stuffed with praise for the way movies used to be made. Furthermore, it is not success, but failure, that is of concern. *Autopsy* is about the failure of *film noir* to assimilate an element of realism into its voluminous corps of films. *Films noirs* were not just stories, but stories that retrospectively solidify into a fairly coherent philosophy. This philosophy dealt with a world that was unmovielike, where the hero didn't always wind up with the girl, and was sometimes better off if he didn't. *Film noir* curiously foregrounded pessimism and existentialism, albeit American style. It addressed a slew of feelings, human conditions, and predicaments that seemed at first to have no business on the screen. It boldly debunked pre-depression optimism and like a one-dish menu, served up post-war doom, take it or leave it. It also dealt with the alarming growth of resignation, suddenly cropping up in a dynamic land of opportunity. Lack of faith in the future was especially shocking to a nation unmolested by the shellings and bombings that ripped Europe apart. *Film noir* rendered this bleak situation in an elaborate, artistic fashion, somewhat softening the blow. But by doing so, *film noir* in effect underscored the difficulties Americans experienced in having to give up unrealizable dreams in deference to harsh truths.

Although it is unfair to assign a teleology to a rather loose aggregate of films, the *film noir* trajectory is noticeably bisected by a totally different use of film, the documentary. Both *film noir* and the semi-documentary, an off-shoot of the documentary movement, reached a peak at the same time. The approach toward a union between the two—*film noir* and the semi-documentary—the union itself, and then the rupture that tore the two forms of expression apart, define the whole *film noir* cycle. The documentary movement had its pure, uncommercial expressions, but attracted more spectators and won more advocates grafted onto other genres in what has come to be known as semi-documentaries. The *film noir* semi-documentaries that proliferated during the middle period of its cycle aspired to a level of cinematic realism that transcended the meager standards of realism that informed the great majority of Hollywood films of the time. The documentary movement in feature films was not confined to *film noir*, yet found in *film noir* some of its best, most lyrical expressions. The landmark semi-documentary, *The Naked City* (Jules Dassin, 1948), is an example which serves herein as one of three primary studies. *Films noirs* released before the documentary influence took root are represented by a film sometimes cited as the first *film noir*, *The Maltese Falcon* (John Huston, 1941). More fanciful, latter-day *films noirs*, emerging on the heels of *The Naked City* and its semi-documentary ilk, are represented by *Touch of Evil* (Orson Welles, 1958). The years during which the films selected for textual analysis were released are 1941, 1948, and 1958, dates which coincide with the beginning, middle, and end of the *film noir* cycle.

There is no way one can precisely state the years *film noir* began and ended. But it is reasonable to say that it was phased in around 1940, gathered momentum until about 1950, and was pretty much phased out by 1960. Similarly, none of the unavoidably loaded terms essential to a discussion of *film noir* should be too rigidly defined. Like cinema, *film noir*'s "existence precedes its essence."[1] Why be concerned about discrepancies in the existing studies of *film noir* pertaining to parameters, definitions, and lists of films? Despite the various dispositions of a markedly heterogenous collection of scholars, critics, historians and theoreticians, all articles, essays, and books address the same phenomenon.

There is enough agreement about the fact that *film noir*, if not a *bona fide* genre, at least constitutes a cycle of sorts. It was produced sporadically throughout the 1940s and 1950s. Almost every listing of *films noirs* that has thus far been generated has included *The Maltese Falcon*, *The Naked City*, and *Touch of Evil*. Raymond Borde and Étienne Chaumeton call *The Naked City* a *documentaire policier*, but the distinction is suspect.[2] Their classic study, *Panorama du film noir américain*, was published before the dissolution of *film noir* in the late 1950s. Their assessments are necessarily premature, since their account of *films noirs* comes to a halt in 1953. Even as late as 1953 it was still possible to view *films noirs* as a single, homogeneous entity. But hindsight demands that a history of *film noir* remark upon its evolutionary and mercurial character. And ethics demand that the scholar emphasize *film noir*'s poetic relevancy to modern society. To be specific, *films noirs* addressed the question of violence as a persistent feature in American life. Now, more than ever, the entrenchment of violence as something more common than a desperate action in the nature of a last resort has made this country a dark place. A thousand points of light are not enough to illuminate the perniciousness that sponsors homicides several times that number. Both directly and indirectly, *films noirs* confronted this crisis. Although they were stylized, contrived, and even tame (by today's outlook), this confrontation made *films noirs* more realistic than other kinds of films before and during the 1940s and 1950s.

The use of the term "realism" poses some very knotty problems that would take space at least equal to the size of another book to resolve. But the best, most concise guide to its use hereafter is to be found in an understanding of the distinction that André Bazin proposed between "the aesthetic" and "the psychological." Since today's leading film theories dovetail with leading psychoanalytic theories, aesthetic realism has been eclipsed by psychological realism. Yet, according to Bazin, it is the former, aesthetic realism, that is the "true realism." It alone fulfills "the need . . . to give significant expression to the world both concretely and [in] essence."

Bazin called the latter, psychological realism, counterfeit. It is "the pseudorealism of a deception aimed at fooling the eye (or for that matter the mind)."[3] Psychological realism lulls the spectator into an unquestioning, mindless state of passivity, as do sedentary theories of art that appeal to psychology for authority. Bazin sought to educate the spectator, bestowing upon him an appreciation of aesthetic realism, which the spectator, in turn, should demand of the filmmaker. Our definition of realism

will run counter to the grain of contemporary connotations
relating to this elusive term. In the pages that follow, there
are few allusions to the works of Sigmund Freud, Jacques
Lacan, Christian Metz, Michel Foucault, Roland Barthes,
Jean-François Lyotard and many of the other charismatic
intellectual figures whose thoughts continue to shape
contemporary scholarship and the latest critical methodol-
ogies. When it is invoked, reality will refer to empirical,
experiential externality.

External reality is indifferent to minds that aspire to
know it. It is as unmoved by the incantations of the
psychology-driven shamans who seek to master it as
economic cycles are unaffected by the heroic efforts of the
most gifted economic wizards. The whole advantage of
cinema over its sister artistic practices lies in its blindness,
its dumbness, and its brainlessness. It merely records, at
once, its vice and virtue. Whereas in other media the
human face of a creator shines forth, in cinema it is the face
of technology that is always aglitter and aglow. Again,
according to Bazin, "All the arts are based on the presence
of man, only photography derives an advantage from his
absence."[4] Cinema is derived from photography, and its
"aesthetic qualities . . . are to be sought in its power to lay
bare the realities."[5] Everything else depends upon the
exertions of filmmakers who are as often as not bent on
manipulating an audience and thereby depriving it of the
freedom to interpret.

Cinematic exaggerations and distortions occur, not
under a cloak of darkness but in full view, lit up by the
artificial light of projection. Because of its verisimilitude,
cinema almost always appears real enough to audiences. If
it were not, massive numbers of people would not sit
motionless for ninety-minute stretches or longer in front of
plain rectangles. Yet, verisimilitude is not the better part of
realism. A distillation of Bazin's comments on the subject
of realism would invariably yield one most essential
ingredient—restraint. Realism for cinema has to do with
not using glamor-ridden lighting, cloying make-up, constructed sets, and implausible scenarios. It means *not*
overusing gauzes, filters, and narrow lenses. It also means

not commissioning an art department to simulate locations. Lack of realism results from the deliberate deployment of these and other excesses. Lack of realism is aimed at a spectatorship that is assumed either not to know or not to care about the differences involved. The classic American cinema is primarily identified by, even celebrated for, its excessiveness. Its stories are jammed with incredulities and its images succeed one another with merciless, pre-MTV speed. They are peopled by photogenic men and women whose characters have been defined by careful, intertextual crafting. Before the documentary influence changed filmmaking strategies— and the expectations of spectators—these living, legendary personae appeared on sets that were not infrequently gaudy, unrealistic, and extravagant.

Location shooting provided a much needed release, but over time it began to mirror studio filmmaking in terms of the degree of control exerted over the location. Filmmakers today routinely cordon off city blocks that have been scouted, inspected, and scrubbed clean. They negotiate the use of these streets and sidewalks, and firm up their control by complex legal documents. They can disrupt the normal course of life in any given locale, arrange and re-arrange automobiles, and, if necessary, touch up the leaves of trees with a brighter verdure. During a shoot, they direct passersby as much as their actors, letting them know just where they are allowed to walk—usually on the sidewalk across the street. The resultant films ordinarily have as little to do with the common people who actually live there as the common people have to do with the making of the films. In general, they show nothing of what the local inhabitants experience because what the people undergo has been surgically removed to allow for the filmmaker's vision.

With rare exception, except to draw them into the movie theatre or inveigle them into renting cassettes, filmmakers have pretty much abandoned real people in their representations. Instead, they favor dreams, collective and private, and devil-may-care fiction. In other words, films are not bigger but smaller than life. They are miniatures, artistically speaking, that are blown all out of proportion with visual and aural mechanisms. Re-recording credits confirm the fact that ultimately, location shooting notwithstanding, films are made behind the insulated barricades of studio filmmaking mentalities. Films are more a mirror of backroom deals than of life.

The historic move beyond the secure borders of the Dream Factory opened up the possibility that real life as it is truly lived could influence the content of films as much as the inventiveness of screenwriters, directors, and actors. But this was by no means a universal goal. Executives in front offices were fearful, knowing that audiences wanted not to see, but to escape, ordinary life. They wanted to see stars, not their next-door-neighbors. And they wanted stories that did not repeat, reiterate, and re-create the real life dramas that already saturated everyday life. But were the executives right?

The answer is, we'll never really know. The semi-documentary never fulfilled its promise. Its natural cycle of waxing and waning interest was truncated, cut short by two kinds of fears. One originated from within the filmmaking community, the other from without. First, filmmakers so feared the wrath of the establishment that they bungled the opportunities that semi-documentaries had to offer. Second, the establishment's watchdog committees so feared the potential of the film medium to incite the masses that they interfered with production. Needless to add, resistance to experimentation in Hollywood was already powerful enough without additional incentive.

Not only the semi-documentary movement but government interference bisects the *film noir* cycle. According to George A. Huaco, realistic film waves require "a political climate which is either in harmony with or at least permissive of the ideology and style of the wave."[6] What was "the ideology and style" of the *film noir* "wave"? A good guess is that it had none, that it was neither left nor right, certainly not communist, and for the most part not particularly anti-communist. Yet, it is equally true that questions of ideology lurked in the background, for many of the hearts and minds that shaped *film noir* were schooled in rhetoric more radical than the conservative principles that informed the age of conformity. *Films noirs* somehow bridge the transformation of the 1930s into the 1960s, of a decade characterized by a flurry of intellectual activity into a basically anti-intellectual era, overshadowed by a strong, military-industrial complex. In each of the selected films, unpleasant truths or assumptions about contemporary life are brought to light. *The Maltese Falcon* shows (in a roundabout way) how the exigencies of a mercantile society can thwart a passionate love affair. *The Naked City* harps on both the chronicity and banality of urban-based murder. *Touch of Evil* illuminates some of the disparities between law and law enforcement. Of course, each film is much more than what any of these encapsulated statements state or imply. But they do impart to us a sense of willingness to face the brutal facts of life that most films before the advent of *film noir* try so ardently to conceal. It is, therefore, not surprising that the semi-documentary and *film noir* could find common ground and form a viable joint partnership. Both were bold enterprises that sought out places, conditions, and situations in contemporary life that movies customarily shunted off their canvases.

Sometimes a movie, like *The Naked City*, turned out to be successful despite the cynicism, ridicule, and lack of support of the distributor. Because of the stigmatized reputations of Jules Dassin, the director, and Albert Maltz, a co-writer, as leftwing activists, Universal treated them and the film with disdain. Dassin was refused the final cut, and because of Maltz's misfortune as one of the Hollywood Ten, the film was unreasonably scrutinized to weed out "subversiveness" and, ultimately, was butchered. Some of this arrogant disregard by the front office for the creative talent of a film already earmarked for box-office success was directed against Malvin Wald. The chief screenwriter of the film, who also wrote the story upon which it was based, was refused a ticket for the first press review of *The Naked City*. Although Wald was nominated for Best Story because of his efforts and originality, the studio did not

rehire him. In such a situation, with an Oscar at stake, a studio would usually reward the writer.[7]
In addition to analyses of the films themselves, *Autopsy* delves into the production behind the films, the stories behind the stories. No film exists in a vacuum or in a state independent of its makers and their fondest dreams and aspirations. Behind *The Maltese Falcon*, there is the personal victory of an aging actor, Humphrey Bogart. Warner Bros. unfairly confined his career to the repetitious portrayal of stick-figure bad guys. In the role of Samuel Spade he broke free.
Behind *The Naked City*, there is the triumph of individuals over an uncooperative studio. Owing to the fickle vicissitudes of commercial destiny, Universal created a hostile filmmaking climate. Like the story behind *The Maltese Falcon*, the story behind *The Naked City* is one of unprecedented success. In both cases, there are influences and forerunners, but these films themselves became the prototypes.
Behind *Touch of Evil*, there is the heroic story of a talented director who returns to feature filmmaking after a period of decline. Welles's work on *Touch of Evil* was preceded by a self-imposed exile, steeled by an ostracism more or less decreed by the Sanhedrin of the moviemaking community. Like the story behind *The Naked City*, the story behind *Touch of Evil* highlights some of the more pathetic goings-on behind Hollywood's shield of glamor. In both cases, a major studio proved recalcitrant, inflexible, and unenthusiastic. In the end, Welles abandoned *Touch of Evil*, but his film went on to become a classic.
Studio filmmaking, McCarthyism, blacklists, increasing costs, and the star system are some of the burdensome problems that *film noir* filmmakers had to dodge, manage, and sometimes surmount. In reality, the problems themselves dictated most of the solutions and agreements; as a result, the problems curbed ambitions, diminished wills, and sometimes ended careers. It is not surprising that in the mirrored, compensatory world of art, filmmakers who felt or witnessed the attrition produced a peculiar breed of

hero. Unlike the genres, with their established narrative patterns and stock characters, protagonists in *films noirs* don't always succeed in winning the girl, getting the money, or even keeping their lives. They are caught in a spider's web of certain failure, but they achieve a measure of heroism in their attitude of defiance against it.

No-account drifters like Frank Chambers in *The Postman Always Rings Twice* (Tay Garnett, 1946), or Al Roberts in *Detour* (Edgar G. Ulmer, 1945), fight the system and lose. But in their resignation to a bleak fate they find the tranquility that eluded them in life. In one *film noir* after another, main characters, sometimes villainous, sometimes heroic, are foiled (*Strangers on a Train, In a Lonely Place, Sweet Smell of Success, Force of Evil*), beaten (*Murder My Sweet, The Set-Up*) and killed (*Out of the Past, Night and the City, Double Indemnity, Underworld U.S.A.*). Often they pay the ultimate price, but they purchase a safe passage for their most cherished dreams.

Some of these dreams are surprisingly simple. In *The Asphalt Jungle* (John Huston, 1950), Dix Handley boyishly dreams of a horse farmer's life. After he is fatally wounded in a bungled bank heist, he drives to a rural spot where horses graze. There he dies, his life in shambles, but his dream pristine, undefiled, and unpolluted.

In general, *films noirs* were much more pessimistic than other films of the time. As a direct consequence, there are passages in many *films noirs* that rival the realism of foreign cinemas. Pessimism freed these films from the prison bars of cheery optimism and made them more in tune with a world much darker than movies could ever approximate. In the context of pessimism, an element of realism was integrated into *film noir*. The realism is spotty, sporadic, inconsistent, but unapologetic. If the world is prone to violence, cupidity, and immorality, it is not the fault of movies with moody, philosophical underpinnings. *Film noir* is identifiable on the basis of its pessimistic view of the world and its more realistic portrayal of this selfsame world. Indeed, often enough, realism and pessimism are indistinguishable.

The division of *film noir* into three successive stages of

development is a little pat, but it provides us with a logical—and largely justifiable—tool of analysis. There is a great deal of overlapping among the categories, but to lump all *films noirs* together without distinction is to obscure a certain, distinguishable evolution. In his unpublished dissertation, *The Dark Age of American Film*, Robert Porfirio chronologically divides *films noirs* into four categories: "(1) the early period of 'experimentation' (1940–1943); (2) the 'studio-bound' period of the private-eye (1944–1947); (3) the 'location' period of the semi-documentary and social problem film (1947–1952); (4) the final period of fragmentation and decay (1952–1960)."[8] For the sake of convenience, *Autopsy* collapses the first two categories into a single category. Both are "studio-bound," and both involve the exploits of private-eyes. *The Maltese Falcon, The Naked City*, and *Touch of Evil* represent the three phases of this tripartite division, respectively.

Moreover, this categorization is useful in that it shows an approach toward semi-documentary filmmaking followed by a retreat away from it. This movement does not hold true with each, individual film; there are dozens of exceptions. But a macroscopic view confirms this perception. In the long run, it is always the primary trend that prevails.

-2-

Film noir benefited from the disintegration of the studio system. Filmmakers gained greater freedom in the selection of projects, greater control over production, and more authority in the final, post-production stages. In this respect, *film noir* conformed to an industry-wide pattern. Not just *film noir* filmmakers, but American filmmakers across the board, were gradually liberating themselves from autarchical studios. The Paramount decision of 1948 effectively destroyed studio hegemony. Independent companies multiplied in response to this court action, which dismantled the vertical integration of movie production, distribution, and exhibition.

It is noteworthy that not all independent filmmakers chose to emulate the Hollywood paradigm. Instead of competing against Hollywood's fancifulness and flightiness, they adopted a less inventive strategy. Instead of steeping their work in cinematic rhetoric—the imagistic counterpart of literary, poetic license—they brought their cameras to real streets, sidewalks, bus stations, subways, stores, construction sites, highways, a variety of public arenas, and private houses. Instead of tinsel and hokum, they foregrounded commonplace urban eyesores in the context of stories that did not sacrifice credibility to the promotion of idealistic familial values.

This one hundred and eighty-degree turnaround became especially prevalent during the middle period of *film noir*, throughout the late 1940s. The French film critic, Nino Frank, coined the term *film noir* in 1946, after screening predominantly studio-bound *films noirs*.[9] Raymond Borde and Étienne Chaumeton published their early, now classic, study of *film noir* in 1955. They relegated semi-documentaries to a special category, separate from studio-bound *films noirs*, which they perceived as more genuine representations of the cycle. But in order to be fully appreciated and understood, the *film noir* phenomenon has to be perceived in its entirety.

In fact, the *film noir* movement in its entirety has also to be seen against the much larger background of cinema. Darker crime stories, greyer characters, and the failure of people to cope and coexist in a rapidly changing twentieth century were always ripe for the picking. *Film noir* harvested some of the strange fruits that a modern industrial world drifting into madness readily produced. Instead of a hoe, cinema uses a mirror to garner a fresh crop. The inaccuracy of the mirror, compressing three dimensions into two, relies on the compensatory judgment of the viewer. It is in the viewer's mind that the world's natural contours are restored. After all, if films are to be perceived as realistic, they have to be projected before the eyes of informed spectators who already have some inkling of what is going on in their lifetime.

Mimetic realism is the film medium's legacy; as such, it

is the natural heir to all the preceding movements that flourished in the name of realism. Yet, from the beginning, filmmakers have heaped scorn on their birthright. Cinema is the most realistic medium, but is stigmatized—and rightfully so—by a reputation for wanton fabrication. Realism is possible in cinema only when filmmakers exercise restraint and desist from intervening and manipulating. Realism is possible only when the power of the image is unleashed with naked honesty. Distortion, doctoring, and the exaggeration of subject material make realism impossible.

The ability of cinema to intensify visual matter and magnify the microscopic encouraged great egos to ruin some of the most ingenious early experimentation in realism. Erich von Stroheim made one of the greatest of metaphysical leaps when he came to suggest, by means of a number of directorial commands, that every interjection into the proto-filmic event registers on screen. It is well known how he insisted—to the horror of his crew, artistic collaborators and business associates—on strict standards of realism. He transported moviemaking machinery and personnel to distant, out-of-the-way locations. He forced a full orchestra to play with precise accuracy on a silent filmmaking set. On another occasion he was critical of certain details on undergarments which were invisible to the spectator's eye. Stroheim was so tyrannical in his filmmaking practice that he jealously guarded against the intrusion of any influential force that competed with his own. It was not realism, but a kind of *personalism* that he sought.

Robert Flaherty, the pioneer documentarist who traveled to the Arctic to document a way of life still unaffected by industrialization, was a less commercial director. His subject material focused attention on exotic lifestyles, not fictional dramatizations. His lyrical films are testimonies to forgotten hardships and extinct ways of life. His work is more reverential than egotistical, but he was also dictatorial when it came to the formation of images. He shot thousands and thousands of feet of film, out of which he selected only a fraction to be projected. Moreover, like

Hollywood filmmakers, he faked action sequences and manipulated objects put before the camera. But his best camerawork—in *Nanook*, at any rate—disavows the stamp of creative mediation.

In the 1930s, rather than self-effacement, directorial interpolation became an industry-wide standard. The experiments in the direction of realism begun by Stroheim and Flaherty received little notice, support, or further development. For writers, the hypothetical held more interest than the actual. For actors and actresses, career personae took precedence over the creation of real people. For producers, fantasy was the ticket, not the penetration into unmovie-like reality.

According to Erik Barnouw, in the midst of the Depression, "films from Hollywood were in an opulent phase of Busby Berkeley choruses, and were beginning to seem as remote to many Americans as to Asians and Africans. And its 'non-fiction' product, the newsreel, was perhaps even more irrelevant and bizarre."[10] To radical filmmakers in the 1930s, these newsreels reported on pet shows and beauty contests, but "carried no word of breadlines and evictions or of strikes in the coal mines, in the textile mills, and on the waterfront."[11] Such remarks having to do with films and newsreels made over half a century ago are still valid for many of today's movies and news broadcasts. Of course, then as now, there are some notable exceptions. Throughout the 1930s, contrarians tried to reverse irreversible trends leading away from gloomy realism and toward brighter works of fiction.

In an early effort to counter Hollywood's roseate vision of contemporary life here and elsewhere throughout the globe, the *Workers Film and Photo League* was formed in 1930. This rebel organization was the brainchild of a handful of discontented, abrasive, and idealistic young men. They were frustrated by the fact that their ideas mustered little sympathy, acknowledgment, or representation on the silver screen. They retaliated against the neglectfulness of feature films by making small budget documentaries. At first they hoped to proselytize others, but the religion of patronizing Hollywood films proved an insurmountable obstacle.

In their films, they informed the public about political and social injustices. They reminded their spectators of the omnipresence of hunger, famine, disease, pestilence, oppression, unjustifiable wars, and natural disasters. Their audiences were small, not nearly enough to chip away at Hollywood's massive following. But if they could not come up with a competitive product, at least they proved that there were viable alternatives to Hollywood's homogeneous output. However, a compromise was essential. In terms of commerce—which is to say, survival—the *Workers Films and Photo League* met with mixed results, as did *Frontier Films*, another progressive, artistic filmmaking unit that formed in the mid-thirties.

Despite their lack of commercial success, such filmmaking projects helped initiate an effective, adversative force. This force would continue to pit informative, newsworthy and ideologically-hued types of films against Hollywood's resistance to change. Movieland's fairy-tale imaginativeness, nursery-school naivete, and inert Panglossian philosophy was under attack. The *Workers Film and Photo League* and *Frontier Films* were belligerent groups, without power, prestige and popularity. But they gave a voice to a significant minority that wanted to stem the tide of escapism manufactured in Southern California. Furthermore, they gained a foothold in the doorway leading to the public arena. Americans accepted the documentary image and even developed a passion for it. At the same time, they rejected the political shading and heavily laden social consciousness that seemed to coincide with the image.

Around 1935, *The March of Time* serial began. It provided a journalistic forum that played to the same audiences who attended Saturday afternoon matinees. The difference between *The March of Time* and its predecessors had to do with its more conservative and superficial orientation. Its purpose was not to stir up controversy but to entertain. Needless to add, it was far more successful. A parody of its concerns is apparent in the prologue to *Citizen Kane*. A journalist gets an assignment to find out the meaning of the last words of a tycoon, a human interest angle rather than a full-fledged news item.

-3-

Pare Lorentz was the first to bridge the gap between commercialism and documentary filmmaking. His government-funded *The Plow That Broke the Plains* (1937–8) attracted significant box-office attention. He followed up on this documentary with another, *The River* (1938), which earned a cool profit for its distributor, Paramount, one of the Big Five. No doubt, Lorentz's work added to the process of acculturation that eventuated. Documentary filmmaking was absorbed by feature filmmaking and a mutually beneficial, symbiotic relationship budded. Feature films necessarily tampered with the purity of the documentary image, but did not fully mutilate its autonomy. Feature films mitigated the subversiveness of documentary images, but in doing so, became less impervious to the political-social-economic matrix they once so skillfully avoided. Barnouw notes that by the end of the 1930s, "the atmosphere of cinema . . . changed. With such films as *The Grapes of Wrath* (1939), Hollywood was following where Lorentz and others had led."[12]

As a film reviewer, Lorentz persistently criticized the way "that Hollywood ruined talented actors, actresses, and directors with standard, cheap and unimaginative roles and scripts."[13] His crew concurred. It consisted of a contingent of radicals well versed in the apocalyptic rhetoric of the time. In the specific context of the 1930s, documentary "seemed the logical extension, in the medium of cinema, of the doctrine of social realism."[14] Lorentz hoped to convey to audiences a truer vision of prevailing conditions in America's hinterland. He sought to purge the screen of make-believe so that the backbone of the nation could occupy the center of the stage. Moreover, he had no need to mobilize professional actors to act in, or screenwriters to craft, a soapy script. The real-life drama was inherent in the subject, the struggle of impoverished farmers to survive. Stage sets would surely have been an absurd, diluted substitute for the actual rural settings, which consisted of abandoned farms and barren soil, parched by severe dust storms.

Works of fiction are not always devoid of controversy, but direct statements about real events are always more likely to stir up emotionally-tinged responses. Today there are all sorts of forums for debates and free expression: television talk shows, radio talk shows, numerous publications, and countless video and filmmaking companies. In the mid-1930s there were less opportunities to air minority as well as extremist viewpoints. Neutral, uncontroversial movies helped stalwart defenders of the status quo to maintain its mandate and defang the opposition.

That is why a rift pried Lorentz apart from the "young turks" he employed. They disapproved of the way he virtually cast the federal government in the role of hero in *The Plow That Broke the Plains*. Also, they felt betrayed by the way Lorentz excised from the final cut the most shocking visual material he captured on film. According to William Alexander, who researched in depth the leftwing documentary filmmaking movement of the 1930s, Lorentz had the rare opportunity to use very visceral material. However, the reason he decided against the incorporation of the more gut-wrenching shots taken was because he was beholden to his sponsor—the Department of Agriculture. He knew that "a government film could not show, and he did not want to apprehend, that things had gone so bad."[15]

Still, even in its final watered-down form, the film stirred up a great deal of acrimony. Conservatives abhorred Lorentz's depiction of infertile United States farmland. They did not challenge the veracity of his photojournalism, only the ethics of making a domestic problem so conspicuous. When it came to disseminating unpopular notions about unpleasant predicaments, documentaries were raw, abrasive, and graphic. Government officials also condemned the film. Although they could not argue with Lorentz's reportage, they questioned the wisdom behind a commercial product financed by Washington and pitted against Hollywood in the economic marketplace. They decried the government's production of a film that got second billing on marquees that silently hawked Hollywood features.

Today, after a protracted televised war, loosening F.C.C. regulations, and cable networks, audiences have gradually acquired cast-iron stomachs, enabling them to digest the most blood-soaked imagery. But half a century ago there was a much greater need for discrimination. Lorentz had shown that the same audiences would support both documentaries and fiction films. Rankled factions could injure studio chieftains, whose careers were based on an ability to deliver, time and again, inoffensive products.

Each method enhanced the other. Separately, they diverged widely, but together they achieved a viable union and a single purpose. As with any compromise, there were pluses and minuses, gains and losses, advantages and disadvantages. In the context of feature films, documentary footage lost its purity. It fell from grace, dragged down to a lower, more commercial level. In turn, fiction filmmaking lost it innocence. It rose to new levels. The more documentary and documentary-like passages appeared in features, the more likely it was that those films would hold themselves more than usually accountable to reality. Also, it was unlikely for those same films to develop ideas and attitudes that location work might contradict.

Each benefited and suffered from this merger at one and the same time. The negative side of the ledger contained several meaningful entries. For example, the intrusion of fiction could mar documentaries. Also, documentary and semi-documentary passages could ruin a feature film. Sensitive subjects could make filmmakers unusually timid. Voice-of-God narration in semi-documentaries underscore the reluctance of filmmakers to grapple with the ambiguity of government institutions, agencies, and bureaucracies. Furthermore, it was possible that factual matter would puncture the illusion of reality so essential to works of fiction. Conversely, fiction could destroy the credibility of documentary footage. But on the more positive side of the ledger, fiction diffused the controversy that documentaries evoked. In turn, documentaries lent credence to some works of fiction that were lacking in believability. Once documentary passages, including certain kinds of location footage, emerged in the format of fiction films, they never totally surrendered their autonomous status to the force of the narrative. They remain self-reflexive, independent of the exigencies of the diegesis. According to Marc Ferro, for instance, "films shot outdoors furnish much documentary information which resembles that found in reportage, even if the *function* of such information is not the same in both types of films."[16] Before movies could incorporate documentary imagery, they had to undergo a fundamental textural change. Specifically, they had to become philosophically darker.

Film noir was ideally suited to absorb documentary passages in the guise of location footage. To be certain, it was darker in a superficial, cinematographic sense. But *film noir*'s notoriously dim lighting schemes also served to delineate a taut, grim, existential atmosphere. Even periodic glimpses of the real world could not be forced to intermesh with the bright, evenly lit, artificial backlot settings of an MGM movie. MGM's traditionally soft, shadowless lighting schemes complemented an equally luminous philosophy, set aglow with unrealistic expectations.

Even before the semi-documentary phase, *films noirs* served to disabuse audiences of Pollyanna ideas that Hollywood studio filmmaking propagated. The *film noir* milieu was at first an unfamiliar one in the movie theatre. It was sometimes humorless and perverse. Judged in terms solely of entertainment, early *films noirs* were conspicuously different from standard Hollywood fare. *Films noirs* had little in common with exotic adventures, zany comedies, or dewy melodramas. There was something so unlike Hollywood about films that were faithful to the inner mechanisms of the real world. The real world *is* shadowy, crime-ridden, web-like, amoral, illogical. The Hollywood world is just the opposite. There, crimes are punished and virtue is rewarded. While not everything about *films noirs* contradicted classical Hollywood filmmaking, they did help shift moviemaking focus from the spit and polish of stages and sets to the grime of real, litter-strewn, spat-upon streets.

Indeed, the more *films noirs* changed to accommodate semi-documentary footage, the more realistic they became. The more realistic they became, the darker they grew. To Eric F. Goldman, "location shooting gave the postwar *film noir* a certain verisimilitude in portraying the dark, sinister, urban environment."[17] According to Alfred Appel Jr., "When the *film noir* went outdoors, its vision of America became more severe."[18] This severity was sometimes disturbing, producing a nostalgic backlash. Reviewers, representing sizable readerships, missed the silver screen, and the feeling of well being that accompanied such a comforting cinematographic aesthetic. Looking back almost fifty years later, their apprehension seems quaint. But at the time, they were jolted by the tenebrosity of the screen. Moreover, the copious lugrubrious scenarios and chiaroscuro cinematography that supplanted the older, sweeter vision was not the sole, exclusive handicraft of *film noir*.

One *Sight and Sound* journalist complained about the burgeoning multitude of "dim figures creeping along dimmer corridors, sinister shadows lurking in doorways, blinds pulled down hastily over lighted windows."[19] Another bemoaned the repetitive cheerlessness of "such prosaic subjects as factories, oil fields, bargain basements, pub-drinking and all the petty domestic and economic troubles which savour of 'mass observation.' "[20] This spontaneously generated debate was picked up by yet another British journalist who chose to join the fray. He wrote that it was better to see things in a clear light, whatever the cost. No matter how oppressively the screen portrayed the world, this was better "than to bury our heads in the sand and dream of Parnassus."[21]

Artists striving after realism in any medium automatically attack their predecessors' beliefs and principles. It is only natural that such assaults be met with defensive reactions. In an artistic practice as informed by compromise as cinema, movements regress at the same time they progress. As *film noir* evolved, numerous *films noirs* retreated to safer territory. They employed typical, Hollywoodian tactics, designed to bring about happy endings. But *film noir* is best remembered today for its foliage, not for the spaces between the leaves that let the sun shine through. In *films noirs*, shadows are ubiquitous, as are dark themes, shady characters, web-like plots. The darkness of *film noir* constantly shifts from aesthetic to moral, from symbolic to literal, from personal to universal. Vis-à-vis the status quo, *film noir*'s darkness is often critical and subversive. Yet, just as often, it casts its shadows inward, attacking radicalism, idealism, and subversion.

The tool of darkness in artistic practice relies heavily on an alliance with realism because otherwise it has no force in the marketplace of ideas. It enlists the aid of realism to disprove the self-aggrandizing optimism of the status quo. To perpetuate such a facade, the status quo has to conceal, ignore, or otherwise escape close scrutiny. It is not enough just to say that *film noir* owes a great debt to German Expressionism. The political, social and economic vectors that gave rise to both movements were worlds apart. Immigrant directors, writers, cameramen and actors helped Hollywood sharpen the techniques drawn upon to make *films noirs*. But *film noir* had its own wheels to turn and axes to grind. After all, it was an American phenomenon. Although Hollywood absorbed European talent, Hollywood never allowed itself to be colonized by it.

-4-

A century before, realist artists concentrated on themes that most artists until then considered unworthy. Instead of painting aristocrats, mythological creatures, and Biblical events, they used their skills to delve into the lives of oppressed peoples on an unprecedented scale. It was the darker, more unsavory elements of ordinary lives that appealed most to the realists of the 19th century, as is evidenced by the paintings and novels they produced. They shocked audiences inured to more acceptable material. Realists wanted to make spectators and readers see better, not just experience a mindless sensation. For example, according to Roger L. Williams, the novels of les frères Goncourt "were flowers of illness meant to sicken us with reality, in the hope that we might come to share the horror of life. . . ."[22]

Where realism in all pre-film fields of artistic endeavor failed was in the vainglorious attempt to create an illusion of transparency. No painting could escape its own artificial trappings; no work of literature could comprehend the exact nature of its topic of concern, no matter how closely observed. Émile Zola was skeptical of the term realism, used to describe "a theory as old as the world; only it is rejuvenated at each new literary period."[23] He criticized "the realism of 1856" as "exclusively bourgeois," the most widely-employed pejorative of the era. Yet his own novels were microscopically accurate in detailing *fin de siècle* France.

Still, it is hardly surprising that the era of supremacy of realism as the dominant movement in the arts was relatively short-lived. It embraced little more than a slice of the 19th century. It is revealing that a groundbreaking journal, *Le Réalisme,* which monitored the movement's emergence, began publication in November 1856 and by April/May 1857 had run out of funds. Realism itself declared bankruptcy when realist artists ultimately ran out of ideas. How long could they shock an increasingly resilient public? How much mileage could they get harping on the same, familiar themes of poverty, hardship, and all manner of disparities between dream and reality?

But these foolhardy alchemists of realism were redeemed by the advent of cinema, which effortlessly and mechanically satisfied the requisites of an unmediated, artistic perception. Les frères Lumière set their camera on a tripod, aimed and cranked it. The first kinds of film shot were like windows opening out onto infinity. However, almost from the beginning, the seeds were planted that would gradually undermine the unusual capacity of film to document life in all its variegated aspects.

At its inception, cinema promised to become the realist medium par excellence. This unique promise has always encountered stiff resistance, from both practitioners and commentators. Cynics, like Jean-Louis Comolli and others, disparage any equation between film and reality.[24] But to Bazin, cinema has the unique ability to fulfill the eternal quest for "an integral realism, a recreation of the world in its own image, an image unburdened by the freedom of interpretation of the artist. . . ."[25] Bazin conceived of cinema as an art in which the artist recedes from his work, which then follows a course all its own, contingent upon the emotions and intelligence of the spectator. Bazin invested a great deal of faith in the ability of the spectator to ascend to a level commensurate with that of the auteur.

Cinema came into existence as realism gave way to naturalism—at least in the realm of literature. Like realism, naturalism made optimum use of accurate observation and freedom in the choice of subject matter. In these respects, it was akin to realism. But unlike realism, naturalism held one of the most unflattering views possible about humankind. It went a step further than realism in its assessment of life as something bitter, vile, futile, and degrading. In fact, as an artistic movement, it was more scathing an attack on society than *film noir* would ever be. Naturalists were often psychotically obsessed with the repugnant underside of existence. Friedrich Nietzsche called Zola's work "delight in stinking."[26] Realists, too, were cast in a similar mold. According to Mario Vargas Llosa, to Gustave Flaubert "it was above all negative experiences that inspired literary creation."[27]

Both Zola and Flaubert wrote about very human situations. Many of the stories of *films noirs*, in contrast, are unlikely contrivances. Nevertheless, their artificiality often occasioned the employment of location footage containing faithful descriptions and authentic details hitherto seldom observed on the screen. This contradictory condition resulted in large part from the fact that so many of the films were derived from or inspired by tough-minded novelists. *Film noir* owes a great deal to the literature of Dashiell Hammett, Raymond Chandler, James M. Cain, W. R.

Burnett, Cornell Woolrich, Horace McCoy, and David Goodis—all of whom were perceptive observers. They focused on concrete details, created well-defined characters, and employed unambiguous wording. They honed in on the music of common, spoken vernacular and the activity of the street smart. They wrote with such precision and leanness that legend has it that John Huston's script of *The Maltese Falcon* was actually the book itself, broken down by a Warner Bros. secretary. The story goes that Huston went on vacation, asking his secretary to fragment the novel, and funnel it directly into a screenplay format. Having access to all secretarial work, Jack Warner looked at the outcome of this paraphrasing. Since it had Huston's name on it, he assumed that it was Huston's script. Warner liked it, okayed it, and assigned Huston to direct the film.[28]

Hammett knew his trade. A screenwriter who wished to adapt a work such as *The Maltese Falcon* was indeed fortunate. The novel rang true with crackling dialogue, intriguing characters, and scintillating imagery embedded within a brilliantly plotted narrative. Hammett had been well-schooled in the craft of mystery writing by Captain Joseph T. Shaw. Shaw was the editor of *Black Mask*, a pulp journal that gave several excellent writers their start. The best of Shaw's disciples learned to scrutinize the world from top to bottom. A good cross-section of American society is represented by mystery fiction. Its settings range from the Sternwood residence in Chandler's *The Big Sleep* (Howard Hawks, 1946) to the greasy roadside diner in Cain's *The Postman Always Rings Twice*.

Hard-boiled novels emphasized details gleaned from a cold professional observation of contemporary city streets. They incorporated both sybaritic and penurious cultures. They described urbanscapes filled with run-down flop-houses, dimly-lit bars, and shabby apartments. But they also included descriptions of vast estates with gardens and livery, and hotel suites with alacritous bellhops and nervous managers. In sum, hard-boiled novels presented a wide-angle view of contrasts in wealth and poverty. Many of the protagonists of these stories are borderline personalities, weaving in and out of criminal environs and socially acceptable milieux, just as psychotics might drift into and out of insanity. Hard-boiled novels did not just nibble on the crust, but took a healthy bite out of reality. For this reason, the writing in such books has a special lilt. The obsession of tough-guy novelists with a multitude of details that commented on contemporary existence set a precedent for *film noir*. According to Raymond Chandler, Hammett "took murder out of the Venetian vase and dropped it into the alley. . . ."[29] *Film noir* took the camera out of the studio and moved it through the dirty streets and commerce-ridden main thoroughfares of various localities. According to Penelope Huston, "The new thing in the cinema, in these years, became the location-made thriller."[30] Location work was more than just a passing fad; it captured the spirit of an era and shattered time-honored boundaries separating art from reality.

A century before, realist painters started a new trend in the selection of subject matter by depicting common people, seen in their native habitats. The simple, idyllic paintings that often resulted were denounced by guardians of *les beaux-arts* in France. For instance, Gustave Courbet was admonished for his *Young Ladies from the Village* (1851/2). The departure from an abstract, idealized view provided a major bone of contention. Courbet came under attack because his composition juxtaposed petty bourgeois maidens with a simple, barefooted peasant girl. The women were painted with common, ordinary features and the girl wore a rustic dress. Even more baffling to arbiters of good taste was the presence of cattle and a dog. These animals seemed not to serve any lofty, artistic purpose.

Exhibited in a prestigious Paris salon, Courbet's painting looked queer and eccentric. In addition, *Young Ladies from the Village* also came under condemnation as an unwelcome "reminder of class distinctions in the provinces."[31] But Courbet was not alone. Anton Mauve (Dutch, 1838–1888), Jean François Millet (French, 1814–1875) and Théodule Ribot (French, 1823–1891) were among his contemporaries who also painted unvarnished records of peasant life. All experienced the same resistance—a resistance as old as the realist tendency in art. The more political climates relegated reality to the public domain, the more artists freely partook of this largesse. Whether in mid-19th century French painting, late-19th century literature, or mid-20th century semi-documentaries, perceptive artists integrated truthful observations of life into their work. They couched reality, as best as they could reproduce or represent it, in their graphic compositions, literary narratives, and film imagery. It was only logical that such an orientation should come to focus on incongruities and contradictions. Favoritism in the dispensation of justice, bias, discrimination, disparities of wealth and poverty, superstitions, and objects previously regarded as superfluous to art provided a windfall in terms of subject material.

This is why it is not outrageous to look for some of *film noir*'s antecedents farther back than the tough-guy proletarian writers of the 1930s and early 19th-century German Expressionism. If one identifies *film noir* on the basis of its being more realistic than the films that preceded it, and even if it only exceeds the realism of its predecessors by a minuscule increment, then one has to include among its progenitors Zola, the Goncourts, Huysmans, Galdos, Gissing, and all the other novelists who plumbed the lower depths of society with an eye for detail and a stomach for poverty, cruelty, and meaninglessness.

In fact, as Erich Auerbach has shown in his classic study, *Mimesis: The Representation of Reality in Western Literature*, the realist tendency began very early. And with each new age, it remained a potent force. It adjusted and readjusted to survive changing temperaments and ideologies. Throughout, it constantly found new methods of expression. It remained elastic and durable throughout periods characterized by superstition, dogmatism, and elitism. And overall, it managed to expand, not contract.

Among the more significant changes in (relatively) recent times is the elimination of the double-tiered structure of storytelling. For a long while, most accurate depictions of the mundane were considered base and vulgar. In high art,

"the separation of the realm of the heroic and sublime from
that of the practical and everyday is a matter of course."[32]
Another literary theorist, M. M. Bakhtin, points out that
when realists reversed this aristocratic bias, they seized a
unique opportunity. Artists could virtually help themselves
to virgin territory, unmolested by previous artists. Instead of
being heirs to the great artists of the past, they stood a good
chance of becoming the father of artists yet to come. But to
do so they had to alter fundamental relationships between
art and reality. They had "to raise reality into a new and
heroic sphere."[33] Consequently, they altered the nature of
heroism.

In developing his thesis concerning *The Tainted Adam: The
American Hero in Film Noir,* Paul Bernard Plouffe speaks of
how "American realism documents the transition of society
from the optimism of the agrarian ideal to the dismay of
urban reality." Naturalism went a step further "in its
portrayal of the hero's increasing inability to turn the
American dream into reality."[34] Not long before the emergence of *film noir,* in the midst of the Depression, United
States literature dealt a great deal with bleak themes such as
isolation, failure, and resignation. But the same set of
circumstances also gave rise to a new tough-minded spirit.

Not only did artists face up to reality; their characters did,
too. *Films noirs* show how many characters came to face up
to unthinkable, unforeseen troubles. Sometimes they are the
architects of their own downfall. But usually, if only in the
last few seconds of their tattered lives, they own up. They
discover a way to halt the downward descent into absurdity,
if only by means of a premature, violent, self-destructive
death. For this to occur, not only did artists and, by
projection, their characters, have to face up to reality, but the
spectator had to as well. In this sense, *film noir* was the
mutual product of filmmakers and spectators.

-5-

Looking at the history of cinema, Bazin notes that "there
has been an evolution in the attitude of the general

public."[35] Part of the evolution of spectatorship coincides with the evolution of realism. Without the cooperation of spectators, film cannot shift in favor of greater realism. And greater realism entails greater negativity. Yet, one has to view the attraction to darker themes in a positive light (assuming the attraction does not go overboard—a strong tendency in *film noir*). While realism is no guarantor of cinematic virtue, distortion of reality and manipulation of the spectator are certainly vices. Leaving aside the question of using cinema to edify or reshape the spectator's ideological orientation, the question of cinema's obligation to be faithful to reality warrants some thought. According to Bazin, "The function of the cinema is to reveal. . . ."[36] Bazin is straightforward. Despite all his ferverish defense of film as the quintessential medium of expression, he seems to have felt that cinema has no higher purpose than to show things as they already are.

Bazin cited 1939 as a particularly stable year for filmmaking. He compared it to a river whose current no longer erodes the soil of its riverbed. According to Bazin, "By 1939 the cinema had arrived at what geographers call the equilibrium-profile of a river."[37] Looking back over a span of some fifty years, it is amazing how many classics were released then: *Gone With the Wind, Ninotchka, Stagecoach, Wuthering Heights, Mr. Smith Goes to Washington,* and *The Wizard of Oz,* to name a few. As is evident, most of these treasured films were products of wish-fulfillment, hyperbole, and nostalgia. Hollywood still remains stigmatized by *Gone With the Wind's* sugary rendition of slavery in the ante-bellum south.

That year would turn out to be a last hurrah for Hollywood's ostrich days; 1939 was also the year the Germans invaded Poland. During the winter of 1939–1940, the British released a propaganda film about the Royal Air Force, entitled *The Lion Has Wings* (Alexander Korda, 1939). Rudolf Arnheim, noted psychologist of art, was favorably struck by the way "the mere sticking to the facts produces . . . automatically more dignity and a keener human interest."[38] Drama that was more realistic than inventive was not necessarily less dramatic.

Although *film noir* had to do with crime rather than war, and personal destinies rather than the destinies of nations, there is a connection between war films and *films noirs*. Both indicate a change in the filmmaking climate. Both are more serious, more reliant on the use of facts and figures, and less inclined to fade on a kiss. If nothing else, the waving of the flag at least displaced the waving of Hollywood's magic wand. In its semi-documentary phase, *film noir* would also come to rely more on hard data—police files, case histories, and personal testimonies.

Because of cinema's inertia, any effective change has to have a great deal of force behind it. According to Alexander Korda's biographer and son, Michael, *The Lion Has Wings* was a low-budget film financed by Korda himself. Korda could not muster support from the staunch loyalists of cinema's *ancien regime*. Hollywood was even more resistant to change. Anita Loos, author of *Gentlemen Prefer Blondes* (1925), once remarked that in the thick of the Depression, she and her colleagues at MGM "were living in a Never-Never Land."[39] Filmmakers lived in sheltered environs and, in turn, sought to shelter ticket-buyers. There was something oddly conspiratorial in this arrangement. Even as late as 1941, *Screen Actor* reported that "despite the paralyzing war scare in 1940, Hollywood producers purchased 544 stories and plays for feature production, an increase of 50 over 1939."[40]

It has always been assumed that one of the reasons filmmakers avoided topicality was that their patrons had had enough of reality and needed an escape. Only those who lived during those turbulent years can say for certain. But almost everything about today's society negates this proposition. Addiction to drugs, high drop-out rates, and the infusion of large sums of money into high-risk junk bonds are some of the indications that paint a picture of people who already reject reality long before they enter a movie theatre. They show that from the high to the low, most people live at least a good half the time in worlds of their own device. There is not even much awareness of the present in general social, political, and economic terms. Even with media blitzes of major events, and expanded news coverage, ordinary people lack information in depth, hearing only the repetitious drone of headline material.

In the early 1940s, no one disputed the fact that Hollywood had little to do with anything—except in subtle, indirect, and symbolic ways that went largely unnoticed before the advent of film scholarship. But the prospect of war, followed by war itself, suffused critics, spectators, and filmmakers alike with a sense of responsibility and pause. So much is apparent from the sometimes naive but historically pertinent comments made by journalists of the time.

For example, early in 1942, *Variety* published a number of reflective articles focusing on the metamorphosis of a new Hollywood. *PM*'s film critic thought that in the long run, the war would change Hollywood for the better. Before the war, "the picture industry refused to look at the kind of world we were living in." Like "many big businesses, it didn't want to see what it didn't want to see."[41] Another critic condemned the perpetuation of Hollywood's "foolish greasepaint heroics that are arrogant and embarrassing and in every way fraudulent."[42] A progressive-thinking New York City civil liberties attorney disparaged Hollywood as "the sole remaining receptacle of cowardice in the fight against the censor in the American scene."[43]

Criticism came from within the filmmaking community as well, indicating a great deal of internal dissatisfaction. In 1941, before he became a screenwriter and author, Leo C. Rosten conducted a "Motion Picture Research Project." Interviews and surveys revealed that "most actors criticized the kind of story in which they were asked to appear. Nearly two-thirds commenting spoke unfavorably." Actors felt that movies "had been directed below the intelligence of the American box office." They lacked "the overtones and thoughtfulness of many foreign made pictures."[44]

It took a few years longer for the intelligentsia to realize that even films directed below the low common denominator of mass intelligence were not as arid as formerly believed. In 1947, a psychologist concluded from a study that "there can be no story, no moving picture, which is 'pure entertainment.' There is always the selection and presentation of some material, and with some goal, some value-system, in mind."[45] As the dream factory lost its thin outer lining of innocence, spectators began to become more discriminating, more selective. *Film noir* came into existence amidst a flurry of criticisms, like those in the Rosten report, and academic revelations, like the one cited above.

Nevertheless, there were always those to hang onto and defend cinema as a purely aimless, leisure-time activity. An executive for the distribution branch of Loew's Inc. declared at the outset of America's involvement in World War II that, "as Dr. Kildare might say, 'The role of the motion picture industry in times like these is to administer Vitamin E—entertainment to a public already jittery because of the emergency.' "[46] Larry Reid, editor of *Motion Picture*, concurred, promising his readers that reading his magazine will "take your mind off Hitler."[47] While Hitler was still winning the war, Americans at home could see films like *Blondie Goes to College* (Frank R. Strayer, 1942) and *Weekend in Havana* (Walter Lang, 1941) in movie theaters. In the latter, a musical, Alice Faye, Carmen Miranda and Cesar Romero sing "Romance and Rhumba" and "Tropical Magic." On the very day that the Japanese Air Force bombed Pearl Harbor, *The Denver Post* printed an article dealing with how giant cycloramas were "so realistic that studio visitors frequently walk right into them on film sets."[48] To veteran screenwriter Ben Hecht, cinema relied more on the technology of deception than on anything else. According to Hecht, "technicians were the men who made Hollywood—because all the other people were fakes."[49]

In the midst of all this friction, discontent, accusations, and recriminations, something was astir. Impresario Billy Rose, speaking about theater, said that "confections as 'Junior Miss' and 'Let's Face It!,' charming and bright as they are, will contribute little to the defeat of the Axis."[50] A new awareness was emerging, and members of the Screen Actor's Guild testified to the fact that new films were finally "telling about things that matter." Also, screen-writing was becoming "more adult in the past three years."[51] Will H. Hays, head of the Motion Pictures Producers and Distributors of America, stated in his annual report that 1940–1941 was "a period of supreme crisis in the history of the world." To Hays, "it is against this background, painted with huge black strokes, that the progress of our own, as of every industry, must be reviewed."[52] The following year, Hays deemed " 'Business as usual' . . . a counsel of complacency which everyone today rightly repudiates."[53] The false illusions, wishful axioms, and pipe dream philosophies of the 1930s were cast aside. The war jolted people out of what Friedrich Nietzsche called the "strange simplification and falsification" that informs everyday life.[54]

William Barrett summarized World War I and II as occurences that "characterize the age down to its marrow."[55] Of the two, the second world war is far more significant, and very possibly the single most important event of the century. No serious account of *film noir* can understate the immense influence of the war on the thinking of those involved in filmmaking. In a similar fashion, the Black Death of the Middle Ages struck down a trend in literature and painting that was unusually bright. Robert S. Gottfried refers to "a pervasive pessimism" that seeped into post-plague art. It established "the *ars moriendi*, the cadaver and death as major motifs in art and literature."[56]

Film noir also marks a radical shift in artistic practice. German expressionism, the influence of European immigrants on the American film industry, and the legacy of gangster films and hard-boiled pulp fiction cannot fully explain it. One must also take into consideration an element of realism which is fossilized in the films themselves. That *films noirs* are not wholly realistic should not preclude acknowledgment of the existence of a strong element of realism. In a unique period such as that during and following the second world war, the dark stylizing of *film noir* was perceived more as a realistic than a decorative device.

For this reason, it is important to note what reviewers, who wrote in the 1940s and later, in the 1950s, thought about what hindsight interprets as sheer embellishment. In a fast-changing century, semiotic codifications can have short half-lives. It is impossible for us to see *films noirs* the way they were originally received. Embalmed in the moribund commentaries of ancient film critics are the initial reactions to films released for contemporary audiences, not audiences of scholars half a century up the pike. *Autopsy* will rely upon the perspective inscribed by journalists who wrote in the 1940s and 1950s, rather than the biased perspective of post-1960s scholars, historians, and essayists—infused by more modern, ideological, and psychoanalytical concerns. *Autopsy* will first describe how the attenuation of typical Hollywood means of fabrication was accompanied by an expanded element of realism in *film noir*. Then, it will point out how this process of divestiture was curtailed, resulting in the demise of the cycle.

NOTES

1. André Bazin, "In Defense of Mixed Cinema" in *What Is Cinema? Volume I,* trans. Hugh Gray (Berkeley: University of California Press, 1967): 71. The quotation refers not to *film noir,* of course, but to cinema.
2. Raymond Borde & Étienne Chaumeton, *Panorama du Film Noir Américain (1941–1953),* (Paris: Les Editions de Minuit, 1955): 208.
3. Bazin, "The Ontology of the Photographic Image" in *What Is Cinema? Volume I:* 12.
4. Ibid.: 13.
5. Ibid.: 15.
6. George A. Huaco, *The Sociology of Film Art* (New York: Basic Books, 1965): 19.
7. Malvin Wald, Letter to Author, 23 September 1989.
8. Robert Gerald Porfirio, *The Dark Age of American Film: A Study of the American Film Noir [1940–1960],* unpublished Ph.D. dissertation, Yale University, 1979: 17.
9. Nino Frank, Un nouveau genre 'policier': L'aventure criminelle," *L'Écran Française* 28 August 1946: 8–9; 14.

10. Erik Barnouw, *Documentary, A History of the Non-Fiction Film* (New York: Oxford University Press, 1979): 111.
11. William Alexander, *Film on the Left, American Documentary Film From 1931 to 1942* (Princeton, N.J.: Princeton University Press, 1981): 19.
12. Barnouw: 121.
13. Alexander: 96.
14. Russell Campbell, *Cinema Strikes Back, Radical Filmmaking in the United States, 1930–1942* (Ann Arbor, Michigan: UMI Research Press, 1982): 1.
15. Alexander: 106.
16. Marc Ferro, *Cinema and History*, trans. Naomi Greene (Detroit: Wayne State University Press, 1988): 82.
17. Eric F. Goldman, *The Crucial Decade: America 1945–1955* (New York: Knopf, 1956).
18. Alfred Appel, Jr., *Nabokov's Dark Cinema* (New York: Oxford University Press, 1974): 202.
19. Elizabeth Cross, "Lighten Our Darkness," *Sight and Sound*, Summer 1945: 53.
20. Tudor Edwards, "Film and Unreality," *Sight and Sound*, Summer 1946: 59.
21. Adrian Cairns, "We Are Such Stuff As Films Are Made On," *Sight and Sound*, Autumn 1946: 93.
22. Roger L. Williams, *The Horror of Life, Charles Baudelaire, Jules de Goncourt, Gustave Flaubert, Guy de Maupassant, Alphonse Daudet* (Chicago: University of Chicago Press, 1980): 109.
23. Émile Zola, *The Experimental Novel and Other Essays*, trans. Belle M. Sherman (New York: Haskell House, 1964): 307.
24. See, for instance, Jean-Louis Comolli and Jean Narboni, "Cinema/Ideology/Criticism" in *Screen Reader I* (London: The Society for Education in Film and Television, 1977): 2–11.
25. Bazin, "The Myth of Total Cinema" in *What Is Cinema? Volume I:* 21.
26. Friedrich Nietzsche, *Twilight of the Idols*, trans. R. J. Hollingdale (Harmondsworth, Eng.: Penguin Books, 1984): 67.
27. Mario Vargas Llosa, *The Perceptual Orgy, Flaubert & Madame Bovary*, trans. Helen Lane (New York: Farrar, Straus and Giroux, 1987): 89.
28. Malvin Wald, Letter to Author, 24 October 1989. Wald heard the story from Allen Rivkin.
29. Raymond Chandler, *The Simple Art of Murder* (Boston: Houghton Mifflin, 1950): 530.

30. Penelope Huston, *The Contemporary Cinema* (Middlesex, England: Penguin Books, 1966): 44.
31. Linda Nochlin, *Realism, Style and Civilization* (New York: Penguin Books, 1971): 124.
32. Erich Auerbach, *Mimesis: The Representation of Reality in Western Literature*, trans. Willard R. Trask (Princeton, N.J.: Princeton University Press, 1974): 121.
33. M. M. Bakhtin, *The Dialogic Imagination, Four Essays*, ed. Michael Holquist, trans. Caryl Emerson and Michael Holquist (Austin: University of Texas Press, 1987): 40.
34. Paul Bernard Plouffe, *The Tainted Adam: The American Hero in Film Noir*, Unpublished Ph.D. Dissertation, University of California, Berkeley, 1979: 28.
35. Bazin, "The Virtues and Limitations of Montage" in *What Is Cinema?* Volume I: 51.
36. Bazin, "Theater and Cinema—Part One" in *What Is Cinema?* Volume I: 91.
37. Bazin, "The Evolution of the Language of Cinema" in *What Is Cinema?* Volume I: 31.
38. Rudolph Arnheim, "Fiction and Fact," *Sight and Sound*, Winter 1939–1940: 137.
39. Anita Loos, *Popular Arts Project*, Vol. I (1959), Oral History Research, Columbia University: 150.
40. *Screen Actor*, April 1941: 7.
41. Cecelia Ager, "Drama and Film Critics See the Stage and Screen's Function as Vivid in War," *Variety*, 7 January 1942: 25.
42. Richard Watts, Jr., "Drama and Film Critics See the Stage and Screen's Function as Vivid in War," *Variety*, 7 January 1942: 25.
43. Morris L. Ernst, " 'Fight and You'll Win': Meaning Hollywood, Which Meekly Bows to Censors' Dictation," *Variety*, 7 January 1942: 9.
44. *Screen Actor*, April 1941: 7.
45. Ralph H. Gundlach, "The Movies: Stereotype or Realities?" in *The Journal of Social Issues*, Summer 1947: 30.
46. William F. Rodgers, "Vitamins E and U for Post-War Pix," *Variety*, 7 January 1942: 16.
47. Larry Reid, Editorial, *Motion Picture*, January 1942: 98.
48. "How Giant Cycloramas Are Used in Pictures," *The Denver Post*, 7 December 1941: 6.
49. Ben Hecht, *Popular Arts Project*, Vol. III (1959), Oral History Research, Columbia University: 710.

utopsy

. Billy Rose, " 'Escapology' Not the Answer; Showmen Must Sell Aggressive Americanism to Everybody," *Variety*, 7 January 1942: 28.
51. *Screen Actor:* 7.
52. Will H. Hays, "Motion Pictures and Total Defense," *19 Annual Report of the Motion Picture Producers and Distributors of America, Inc.*, 31 March 1941: 1–2.
53. Will H. Hays, "The Motion Picture in a World at War," *20th Annual Report to the Motion Picture Producers & Distributors of America, Inc.*, 30 March 1942: 7.
54. Friedrich Nietzsche, *Beyond Good and Evil*, trans. R. J. Hollingdale (Harmondsworth, Eng.: Penguin Books, 1987): 37.
55. William Barrett, *Irrational Man, A Study in Existential Philosophy* (Westport, Conn.: Greenwood Press, 1977): 9.
56. Robert S. Gottfried, *The Black Death, Natural and Human Disaster in Medieval Europe* (New York: The Free Press, 1983): 89.

II FILM NOIR IN THE STUDIO: THE MALTESE FALCON

PRELIMINARY COMMENTS

The Maltese Falcon was conceived and written by Dashiell Hammett. When John Huston wrote the screenplay for the film, he adhered closely to the original work, retaining its structure, chronology of events, characters, dialogue, and settings. On May 22, 1941, Hal B. Wallis, an executive producer at Warner Bros., sent the chief casting executive a memo. It instructed him to send Huston's screenplay to George Raft as soon as it was completed.[1] Two days later, Huston finished writing and the script was sent to Raft. Raft read it, disliked it, and rejected it. He told Jack L. Warner that *The Maltese Falcon* was "not an important picture" and that he would not "perform in anything but important pictures."[2]

Through repetition over the years, faulty prognostications in Hollywood have become a cliché. Raft's miscalculation is a source of inspiration to anyone with an original idea that gets bogged down in the red tape of rejection. But Raft's judgment was not all that flawed. He was skeptical of "Huston, an untested director," overseeing "a property that had already bombed twice at the box office."[3] Raft also declined on the basis of a negative experience he had playing a part in *The Glass Key* (Frank Tuttle, 1935), another film based on a novel by Hammett. Stars have to protect their egos, and Raft seems to have sensed that somehow, in the special case of a Hammett story, the author—absent though he may be—would upstage the leading actor.

Back in 1930, Warner Bros. paid Alfred A. Knopf, Hammett's publisher, a flat sum of $8,500 for *The Maltese Falcon*.[4] Warner Bros. acquired exclusive rights to this artistic property and exercised them periodically in their

three versions of it. In the late 1940s, following the success
of Huston's film, Warner Bros. sued CBS for using the
character of Sam Spade in a radio serial. The show got into
trouble when, in 1948, it broadcast an installment of "The
Adventures of Sam Spade" called "The Kandy Tooth." It
clearly plagiarized *The Maltese Falcon*.[5] With its colorful
repartee and memorable one-liners, the story was irresist-
ibly and intrinsically tailored for radio.

When the question of ownership of the character of Sam
Spade arose, Hammett insisted that Spade was his alone.
He claimed that Spade was a personal invention, a product
of artistic vision. But in addition, Hammett declared that
he was a character extracted from real life. He maintained
in an affidavit that Spade "was a figure originated and
created from my imagination as well as my personal
experience with private detectives garnered during the
period from 1915 to 1922, when I was myself a Pinkerton
[private] detective."[6] Despite being the undisputed creator
of this lucrative piece of commercial and artistic property,
Hammett received no further compensation beyond the
initial payment of $8,500. But one has to include the
satisfaction of living to see his work achieve unprecedented fruition, durability, and longevity.

In 1931, Roy del Ruth directed the first version, also
entitled *The Maltese Falcon*, at a cost of about a quarter of a
million dollars.[7] That is to say, it was designed to be an
average moneymaker, producing a modest profit. The
financiers never envisioned Hammett's story as providing
anything more than a routine investment. A fairly popular
Valentino spin-off, Ricardo Cortez, was given the role of
Sam Spade. The name of the leading female protagonist
remained Miss Wonderly throughout, not changing first to
Leblanc and then to O'Shaughnessy, as in the novel and
the Huston film. Bebe Daniels played the notorious *femme
fatale* who reluctantly winds up as her own victim. Cortez
was smooth and oily, more at ease in the bedroom than in
the office, the iconographic center of the private-eye's
universe. At the end of the film, he confesses his love for
Miss Wonderly and, at the same time, lets on that he had
tumbled to her murderous crime from the start. Near the

scene of the crime, an Oriental tells Spade "whodunnit" in Chinese. Being a San Franciscan, the movie's Sam Spade is fluent in Chinese. Huddled in a doorway, the eye-witness's presence—a Hollywood convenience added to Hammett's streamlined work—both solved the riddle of the murder of Spade's partner and also brought to the film a demographic "touch."

Overall, the original adaptation is a denatured version of Hammett's more resonant mystery. Del Ruth kept things simple. There is nothing of the knotty, gut-wrenching inner conflict that Bogart's Spade undergoes. One does not listen to a tortured enumeration of the pros and the single, pathetic con—"maybe you love me and maybe I love you"—having to do with the issue of sending Brigid O'Shaughnessy to prison, possibly to hang. The original *Maltese Falcon* is by now nearly forgotten. Still, at least one anthologist of films from the 1930s preferred the del Ruth *Maltese Falcon* to the one directed by Huston. According to John Baxter, the del Ruth film had "far more verisimilitude than the Huston film." Among other reasons, "the sets, especially of Spade's spacious office, far out-distance those of later efforts."[8] In both cases, one deals with a depiction of San Francisco via Los Angeles.

More significant differences had to do with the treatment of the original text. The first *Falcon* sacrificed it to better conform to typical standards of contemporary Hollywood craftsmanship. Ignoring the subtext, it concentrated on the romantic thrusts and parries of a debonair hero and a sexy heroine. The machinations surrounding the jewel-bedecked statuette act to catalyze this ill-fated romance. Huston's version sought to redress these transgressions against the true, unsentimental spirit of the novel, which is braced by a coldly observant eye and an ear sensitive to the mellifluous-ness of hard-boiled vernacular. Huston's version restored Hammett's ingrained pessimism, too.

The second version, *Satan Met a Lady* (William Dieterle, 1936), had a comical intonation. It also exercised a great deal of latitude with Hammett's original intent. In this regard it paralleled the approach adopted by MGM for *The Thin Man* (W. S. Van Dyke II, 1934), which was based on another of Hammett's works. Earning Hammett nearly three times as much as *The Maltese Falcon, The Thin Man* proved to be an ideal vehicle for the talented, comic team of William Powell and Myrna Loy.[9] As Nick and Nora Charles, they launched a very successful series. Huston's re-make of *The Maltese Falcon* also contains a great deal of comic relief. But ultimately, a sense of gravity takes over, in deference to the true nature of the book.

Wallis felt that *The Maltese Falcon* had qualities and values that the first version either overlooked or left untapped. It was Hammett's best novel and the film had used it only in a sketchy fashion. Wallis urged Harry Joe Brown to read it. Brown once directed silent westerns and was now a producer. Wallis told him that "in the picture version we only touched on the story contained in the book."[10] Furthermore, "we can get another screenplay out of it by actually making the book."[11] Dieterle's use of the novel for the sake of a Bette Davis vehicle did not diminish Wallis's interest in a more faithful rendition. In 1939, a writer by the name of Charles Belden submitted to Warner Bros. an unfinished screenplay entitled, *Clock Struck Three,* loosely based on Hammett's *Falcon.*[12] However, it failed to attract notice.

This roundabout history of Huston's directorial debut is important because it is also the history of *film noir.* One can only speculate as to whether or not Wallis had something close to *film noir* in mind when he persistently promoted a two-time loser. One can say with some certainty that when it finally came about, the third *Maltese Falcon* emerged as a more accurate response to the troubled emotional climate of the times. John Howard Lawson, one of the Hollywood Ten, distinguished this film on the basis of its "awareness of evil which cannot be identified or fought."[13] True enough, the times had changed substantially so that the cinema—as conservative and reactive as it was—had to follow suit.

But before the war there was a depression, and there was also a sense of dissatisfaction at the way films skirted the issues of the day. However, it never fully impacted against the studio's ingrained reticence. In their morose tones, *films noirs* of the 1940s matched the mood of a society disrupted by the advent of war. The moodiness of this new cinema, still made within the confines of studios, indicated that it was vulnerable to the outside, and hence, inclined to manifest this vulnerability in the form of greater realism. At this point in time, the greater realism that ensued registered mostly in an emotional component that relied more on the help of expressionist techniques than on documentary. There were few visual innovations, but heavier atmospheres pregnant with anxiety amounted to a declaration of independence from the lighter intonation of the preceding decade. When it came into a full-fledged existence with *The Maltese Falcon, film noir* was more than just "a mutation in the practice of 'classical narrative.' "[14] The idea of a classical cinema was not yet in the consciousness or vocabulary of any of these filmmakers. The idea of films being re-directed toward the vital concerns of the times was.

Evidence suggests that Jack L. Warner wanted nothing more than the usual product that would acquit itself honorably in the black. Every outward aspect of the genesis of *The Maltese Falcon* was perfectly normal. Studio professionals and workers simply tried to produce good, if routine, matinee fare. In doing so, they dealt accordingly with the ordinary, traumatic events that always accompanied such endeavors. In this light, Raft's scorn for the Sam Spade role was nothing new. After rejecting the "Mad Dog" Roy Earle role in *High Sierra* (Raoul Walsh, 1941), Raft envisioned playing Sam Spade as something paltry and inconsequential. Actors were often particular about the roles they filled. The man who benefited most from these blunders, Humphrey Bogart, was himself suspended for refusing to appear in *Bad Men of Missouri* (Ray Enright, 1941).[15] But Raft's aversion to two prototypical *film noir* protagonists is illuminating. *Film noir* rarely attracted big-name celebrities who were more interested in padding their own legendary personae than in assuming the personality of an individual dogged by failure and misfortune.

Not only did *films noirs* eschew star mythologies, they were also opposed to the kind of lavishness that sundered movies further from connections to reality. Nothing extra went into *The Maltese Falcon*. It was a bare bones operation all the way through. It cost no more than the first version ten years before.[16] This is important because in the context of a studio, extravagance tends to diminish an element of realism in the final product.

While not a large film, *The Maltese Falcon* was not a "B" film either. Its thriftiness also illustrates the fact that "Warner Bros. employed a producer-unit system with relatively rigorous attention to cost-efficiency production."[17] Moreover, everyone involved in the production had a distinct niche. As a reward for his writing ability and friction-less cooperation, Huston was given an opportunity to direct. As associate executive in charge of production, Wallis answered only to Jack L. Warner. As associate producer on *The Maltese Falcon*, Henry Blanke answered only to Wallis. No *enfant terrible*, Huston reported to both Blanke and Wallis, and was anxious to please his older and more powerful superiors. Thus, the production of the film upheld the traditional hierarchy of producer-oriented filmmaking. Furthermore, it is important to see that *film noir* was not the brainchild of an isolated, rebellious individual. It was instead a unified, collective rebellion.

The advertising campaign was also in keeping with company policy. It emphasized sex and violence. *The New York Herald Tribune* referred to " 'killer' Bogart, a guy without a conscience," who "moves in on Mary Astor, a dame without a heart!"[18] Typecast as a hardened gangster alongside stars of greater magnitude like Cagney, Robinson, or Raft, Bogart was invariably depicted with a scowl. Usually, he brandished a gun or two. *The New York Sun* showed a pistol-packing Bogart "as fast on the draw . . . as he is in the drawing room!" Familiar journalistic hyperbole billed Bogart and Astor as "a new team! Watch the sparks fly!"[19] A picture of Bogart in *The New York Daily News* recalled the uncivilized look of Duke Mantee in *The Petrified Forest* (Archie Mayo, 1936). Below his ill-shaven, hunched-over figure, sporting a maniacal expression, a caption stated: "He's a killer when he hates and even more dangerous when he loves."[20]

The real difference in the production of *The Maltese Falcon* has to do with its cooler, aesthetic constitution. Rather than a "mutation," its style amounts to a threat against the naive innocence of Hollywood make-believe. The somber conclusion of the film punctures all the levity that precedes it. Indeed, critics who reviewed *The Maltese Falcon* after its release on October 3, 1941 saw in the film a glimmering of the bleakness that later *films noirs* would intensify.

Eileen Creelman of *The New York Sun* observed that "*The Maltese Falcon* is not a story of likable people. There is not a pleasant character in the tale, nor one who would not cause you to shudder if suddenly encountered in a dark alley. Even the central figure, perhaps most of all the central figure, is a frightening creature." After the murders of Miles Archer and Floyd Thursby, "the audience has reason to believe he [Spade] may be guilty. Spade's actions are at least suspicious. His partner's widow is in love with him. He is making love to a handsome woman."[21]

Creelman was disturbed by the ambiguity of the protagonist, who qualifies as neither hero nor anti-hero. Balanced neatly between good and evil, law and crime, human warmth and aloofness, the Sam Spade character casts doubt on the social matrices that give rise to such complexity. As a result, the overall movement of this *film noir* is centrifugal, directed outward, alluding to forces beyond Hollywood's control and jurisdiction. One misses the point if the film is viewed as though it takes place inside a dollhouse with no real correspondence to the outside world.

The promotional hoopla over sex and violence could not have prepared the spectator to experience the existential mistiness of the film's sentimental yet unromantic ending. *Variety* called it a "surprise finish."[22] But critics sensed that there was something more at stake than a twisted resolution. Creelman's description above intimates the recognition of an inherent, sinister quality, more oppressive than usual for a mystery-thriller. Howard Barnes of *The New*

York Herald Tribune also acknowledged in his review the presence of "a brutally realistic romance." The harshness to which both reviewers refer owes a great deal to the duplicitousness of the murderess, Brigid O'Shaughnessy. Mary Astor may have underplayed the part and censorship may have toned it down even further, but spectators got the idea nonetheless. To Barnes, Astor was "not tough enough for the tough treatment given the Strand offering."[23] Richard Dyer speaks of Astor's "superb plausibility,"[24] but writers at the time saw through her, just as Wallis feared they would. In a memorandum to Blanke, Wallis expressed reservations about the way Astor was "speaking her lines." He disliked her manner of "playing it just a little too coy and *ladylike*."[25]

It may have been difficult for Astor to find herself in a kind of role that did not exist when she began her career. The change in the portrayal of women that *film noir* helped initiate is an element of realism that prefigures the greater visual fidelity of semi-documentary *films noirs*. Indeed, Astor's Brigid O'Shaughnessy starts a trend that enables *film noir* to be interpreted as "one of the few periods of film in which women are active, not static symbols, are intelligent and powerful, if destructively so, and derive power, not weakness, from their sexuality."[26]

Borde and Chaumeton note that destructive female protagonists in *films noirs* are often self-immolating: "la femme fatale l'est aussi pour elle-même. Frustrée et criminelle, mi-dévoreuse, mi-dévorée, désinvolte et traquée, elle tombe victime de ses propre pièges."[27] She is a liberated yet censured character. As a free and equal agent acting on her own behalf, she comports herself comfortably enough with cutthroats and knaves. But she also shoulders the burden of condemnation that is their lot. Hammett's conception of O'Shaughnessy is of a woman so devious that "if Spade ever acts foolishly in the novel, it is because he agonizes over his final decision to hand Brigid over to the police."[28] The innate goodness of women— which establishes an unattainable standard—is a persistent mythology in western culture that Hammett's novel punctures.

Instead of the more familiar portrayal of femininity as an anchor of domestic tranquility, *film noir* depicts spidery women answerable to a host of misdeeds and misadventures. Women connive, steal, and murder. They are not "fallen women," victimized by patriarchal exploitation. They are fully responsible for their actions. They are ambitious exploiters, whose misdeeds merit punishment (in accordance with the Production Code), doled out in disappointment, grief, and sometimes—as is the case in *Dark Passage* (Delmer Daves, 1947)—death. The paradigmatic role of the Brigid O'Shaughnessy character is evident in the proliferation of similar female protagonists who appear regularly throughout the *film noir* cycle. Some of these include Phyllis Dietrichson (Barbara Stanwyck) in *Double Indemnity* (Billy Wilder, 1944); Kitty March (Joan Bennett) in *Scarlet Street* (Fritz Lang, 1945); Kathie Moffett (Jane Greer) in *Out of the Past* (Jacques Tourneur, 1947); Elsa Bannister (Rita Hayworth) in *The Lady from Shanghai* (Orson Welles, 1948); Anna (Yvonne DeCarlo) in *Criss Cross* (Robert Siodmak, 1949); Annie Laurie Starr (Peggy Cummins) in *Gun Crazy* (Joseph H. Lewis, 1950); Vicki Buckley (Gloria Grahame) in *Human Desire* (Fritz Lang, 1950); and Nancy (Rhonda Fleming) in *Cry Danger* (Robert Parrish, 1951). In one of the first semi-documentary *films noirs*, *The House on 92nd Street*, the chief Nazi fifth columnist is a crafty German woman, Elsa Gebhardt (Signe Hasso). In *Kiss Me Deadly* (Robert Aldrich, 1955), one of the last *films noirs*, it is a greedy, deceptive woman who stupidly opens the "Pandora's box" containing an atom bomb.

Critics found all the characters in *The Maltese Falcon* to be *bêtes noires*. Louise Levitas of *PM's Weekly* took note of "a rich assortment of scoundrels, such as you rarely meet in a movie, each trying to outsmart the others for possession of the gem-studded falcon. They're not the polite penthouse crowd of *The Thin Man*; they all carry guns."[29] Indeed, almost every major character in the film makes some use of a gun. John Hobart of *The San Francisco Chronicle* observed that "the people you meet in *The Maltese Falcon* are not exactly the kind you would choose to share a week-end with." Hobart was chilled by O'Shaughnessy, who, "while attractive to the eye, represents a woman of no morals at all."[30] Barnes complimented Sydney Greenstreet for "carving out a new type of sinister villain."[31]

Bogart's unprecedented success in the role of Sam Spade amounted to a great deal more than personal accomplishment. In being able to forge a new, more versatile acting persona for himself, he struck a blow at the whole process of stereotyping. In the artificial, black and white binarism of Hollywood typecasting, Bogart until then had always been black. The greyish hue of *film noir* restored to character portrayals the element of ambiguity, allowing for more complicated portraits. It is difficult to pass judgment on many *film noir* characters. They defy easy categorization because the films in question incorporate few absolute standards. Spectators require their own means of assessment to reach their own conclusions. Goodness and badness are left undetermined by the reductionism of pre-*film noir* movies.

Critics lauded the transformation of Bogart. Milton Meltzer of *The Daily Worker* commended Bogart for his performance. At the same time, he excoriated the way "Hollywood had gotten down to typing him as the cold killer." Meltzer relished the fact that the "tough and tender" character of Sam Spade was more human than a "Clark Gable cliché." As a consequence, the film was more believable. If anything, the ending seemed most "un-movie-like." That final mixture of sentimentality and harshness was "not what you'd expect after a lifetime of Hollywood conditioning, but you know that's just the way it is where you come from."[32] Audiences, too, were undismayed by a hero described by Borde and Chaumeton as "loin du superman."[33]

All across the nation, critics came to the same conclusion. To *The Denver Post*, "the famous screen bad man gives the best performance of his career."[34] In Milwaukee (where the film played on a rather mismatched double bill with *Appointment for Love* [William Seiter, 1941], a Charles Boyer-Margaret Sullavan comedy), *The Milwaukee Journal* stated: "Bogart has usually portrayed sinister roles, but here we have the heartless Humphrey Bogart on the side of law and order."[35] Bogart's performance created a fissure in the foundation upon which classical Hollywood cinema had been carefully layered, with its dense distribution of stars, supporting actors and extras.

It was evident even then that Bogart's personal triumph was at the helm of a wider, burgeoning movement. William Boehnel of *The New York Herald Telegram* was so impressed by the initial impact of *The Maltese Falcon* that he immediately envisioned the imminence of "a new cycle of tough screen melodramas." He reasoned that "cycles inevitably follow a good picture." In addition to being a tough, melodramatic feature film, Boehnel averred that *The Maltese Falcon* was also an "accurate and potent mirror of our era." To skeptics, he recommended that they "just read the papers."[36]

CAMERA

At Warner Bros., sets were built on a variety of different stages. Spade's apartment, Brigid O'Shaughnessy's apartment and the corridors leading up to them stood on Stage #3. The busy lobby of the Belvedere Hotel where Spade blows smoke into Wilmer's face was assembled on Stage #18. Gutman's posh suite at the Alexandria Hotel and the District Attorney's Office were constructed on Stage #19. The apartment complex on Geary Street where Spade guilefully eludes Wilmer was located on Stage #2. A special New York City set was used as the San Francisco bus terminal, where Spade temporarily stashes the falcon. The New York set also provided the space for the Union Square Theatre, where Spade goes to shadow Joel Cairo. A billboard in the background displays the latest show, *The Girl from Albany*. The exterior to Spade's apartment was shot on Warner Bros.' Brownstone Street set. The ship called the La Paloma was shot with controlled fires in the backlot.[37]

None of the scenes in the film were shot in San Francisco where the story takes place. The studio reproductions of the San Francisco environs are so modest and skeletal that they provide a realistic thrust. They are not as saturated with the stamp of Hollywood opulence as might have been the case. There are none of the gaudy trimmings that often appear in studio-made films. Although the murder sequence was originally shot with backscreen projection, Blanke ordered a re-take. Shooting took place on August 7, 1941 at the Warner Bros. Ranch with one Saul Gorse standing in as Jerome Cowen's double. This additional footage eliminated "the buildings we had shown in process."[38]

In the film, one sees heads peering out of windows as Spade moodily inspects the scene of the crime. The avoidance of process shooting and the sparse number of sets by-passed the need for trick photography and extravagance to cover moviemaking tracks. The number of sets built for the film was below the average of between twenty and thirty. Studios could be prodigal in their construction of sets. Warner Bros. used as many as one hundred and ten for *Anthony Adverse* (Mervyn LeRoy, 1936). During *The Maltese Falcon*'s release, Warner Bros. planned to employ some one hundred and fifty-eight for *Yankee Doodle Dandy* (Michael Curtiz, 1942).[39] Verisimilitude was easily sacrificed to artistic visions supported not by reality but by large budgets. The result would invariably be a veneer of spit and polish rarely encountered in the real world.

Like *Citizen Kane, The Maltese Falcon* was innovative in its use of a wide-angle lens. Hollywood ordinarily employed a narrow, forty- to fifty-millimeter lens. *The Maltese Falcon* was shot with a twenty-one millimeter lens.[40] This enabled the camera to incorporate substantially greater amounts of space into the frame. It was also practical, since the film was made with small sets. *The Maltese Falcon* required only a handful of sets, none of which was very sizable. The camera was necessarily placed in close proximity to the actors. Nevertheless, the inauguration of the wide-angle lens was an important step in the development of screen realism.

The topic of wide-angle cinematography in the historical context of classical Hollywood filmmaking has stimulated a great deal of scholarly interest. To Robert Porfirio, wide-angle lenses guided spectators of *film noir* "to a much deeper perceptual involvement."[41] Deep-focus composed images were more compelling than those shot with a shallower focus. In general, deep-focus expanded the perceptual dimensions of the spectator's field of vision. The scopic drive attained greater satisfaction. Deep-focus shots led logically to longer takes, since it took a longer period of time to digest them. As a result, deep-focus obviated the necessity for frequent cuts.

Huston himself did not venture very far into the as yet uncharted realms of deep-focus and long takes. As a novice, he was preoccupied by matters of pacing, an essential factor in action-filled American cinema. His editing style is extremely perforated, helping to move the narrative along at a fast clip. *The Maltese Falcon* does contain several long takes that periodically arrest the film's choppy suturing. These occur several years before Hitchcock's experimentation with takes averaging 925 feet in length in *Rope* (1948)[42] and "a three-and-a-half minute continuous take for *The Paradine Case*" (1948).[43] Here, however, Huston's main contribution toward the development of an element of realism in *film noir* was by and large the sheer introduction of a wide-angle lens. It would be put to much more elaborate use in semi-documentaries and other, later *films noirs*.

The film industry took to wide-angle cinematography accompanied by deep-focus and long takes like fish to water. The bait was *Citizen Kane*, released about half a year before the release of *The Maltese Falcon*. The film was a disappointing ordeal for RKO, which granted Welles unprecedented freedom protected by a reverential shroud of secrecy. Ultimately, the film failed to come close to commercial expectations and caused RKO considerable embarrassment because of its controversial subject matter. But filmmakers were drawn to its complex cinematographic and narrational strategems. Its profoundly sad tenor very probably helped set in motion the whole idea of *film noir*.

To Bazin, the cinematography of *Citizen Kane* was

nothing short of revolutionary. Patrick L. Ogle explains how wide-angle, deep-focus cinematography conveys a richer "sense of presence" than narrow-angle, shallow-focus shooting.[44] The general consensus argues that lenses do make a difference and that *Citizen Kane* represented an incremental advance in terms of visual realism. Arthur Edeson, A.S.C., Huston's cinematographer, shot *The Maltese Falcon* with a wider-angle lens than Gregg Toland used for *Citizen Kane*. Barry Salt points out that by surpassing Toland, Edeson deliberately sought to emulate the unique camera style of *Citizen Kane*.

However, Salt may be a little guilty of stretching the truth—elastic though it may be. Edeson lacked Toland's mobility and the spatially restrictive sets of *The Maltese Falcon* were nothing like the fancifully embroidered, picturesque backdrops for *Citizen Kane*. Moreover, Toland delighted in the use of foreshortening to achieve perspectives that seemed distorted and strange. He also relished Welles's propensity to embellish the film with swish pans and Vorkapich montage. Yet, technologically speaking, Welles introduced nothing new to cinema.

Citing selected statements made by James Wong Howe, A.S.C., Ogle describes how still photography and documentary film gradually acclimated spectators to wide-angle perspectives. Exposure to these perspectives in related media over a period of several years prepared the spectator for the reception of motion-picture images characterized by greater depth-of-field. Photographs were especially useful in this regard. According to Ogle, still cameras "take in an angle of view twice as wide as that taken in by a motion picture camera in filming the same event from the same distance."[45] Toland and Edeson alike engineered new strategies of feature-film cinematography by adopting and translating artistic practices from other visual media.

According to Jean-Luc Godard, not *Citizen Kane* but *Swamp Water* (Jean Renoir, 1941) "can be credited with having, over the long run, revolutionized Hollywood."[46] *Swamp Water* made use of remote exteriors such as shots of the Okefenokee Swamp in Georgia. At some point, the advances in cinematography ushered in by *Citizen Kane* and location shooting would come together. What is fairly certain is that in 1941 filmmakers began to grope for new means of expression. The year 1939 may have been a landmark one in the history of Hollywood classics, but film artists sought to launch new filmmaking strategies, sensing that certain kinds of success cannot be repeated.

In 1942, *American Cinematographer* noted that "without doubt the most immediately noticeable trend in cinematographic methods during the year was the trend toward crisper definition and increased depth of field." This formative change in the use of lenses and lighting opened the way for parallel changes in content. *Citizen Kane* inoculated the public, which could as a result brook a harsher look in visuals. Filmmaker and spectator alike were fortified by the trend "toward increased definition and realism, and strongly away from the softer style of photography popular a few years ago."[47]

Citizen Kane also popularized the use of ceilinged sets, a small but significant step in the direction of realism. Ceilinged sets compelled "the cinematographer to revise his system of lighting to a more realistic vein, lighting largely, if not exclusively, from the floor rather than from overhead."[48] Low-angle shots are also conspicuous throughout *The Maltese Falcon*. They help make Caspar Gutman's superciliousness seem all the more pronounced. Although low-angle designs were hardly novel— Pudovkin used them extensively in *Mother* (1926)—most classical Hollywood cinematography relied heavily on eye-level shooting with shallow focus. Aside from reinforcing personality traits, low-angle shots were rarely used to create a greater spatial sense of authenticity. By showing rooms replete with four walls and a ceiling, cinematographers eliminated some of the theatricality that results from a more proscenium arch style of shooting.

As with anything new, Toland's "pan-focus"—the current 1942 term to denote deep-focus—was a technique that stirred up some controversy. In opposition, Charles G. Clarke, A.S.C., defended standard, diffuse shooting as fully compatible with "the realist effect." Clarke explained

that when one looks squarely at a person and "your
attention is really centered on that person, you cannot be
aware of the details of the background. Your eye perceives
the general pattern, of course; but it is a soft, rather
out-of-focus pattern."[49]
Arthur Edeson differed, but also had serious reservations about the indiscriminate use of deep-focus cinematography. He felt that it was inappropriate except in the
context of a strong narrative. Deep-focus strengthened the
total cinematographic factor, but threatened the balance of
any given film, which consists of an interplay among
diverse elements. According to Edeson, "If the story or
characterizations are weak, he's [the cinematographer] got
to restrain himself or he'll weaken the picture. But if the
story is strong, he can let himself go photographically and
be sure he'll help the picture." Furthermore, "granting
equal story strength, a variety of different visual treat-
ments are possible. A picture like, say, 'Citizen Kane' or
'The Maltese Falcon' will call for strongly modernistic,
eye-arresting camerawork. A picture like, say, 'The Great
Waltz,' or 'The Chocolate Soldier,' would be ruined by that
treatment—they demand a highly pictorial, romanticized
touch."[50] The reverse is also true insofar as a tougher style
of camerawork demands a harder-hitting story.
   Tougher styles in camerawork were also economical,
even essential. Special war-time legislation banned the use
of Photofloods, except for military purposes. According to
William Stull, A.S.C., the Photoflood was already "open to
criticism because it was available only as an inside-frosted
bulb, which gives a somewhat diffused, soft-light."[51] Stull
pointed out that soft lighting in the cinematographer's
profession was always associated with "glamorizing
women." Conversely, undiffused lighting was always
associated with "photographing men for virile effects."[52]
   Other restrictions also seemed to point the industry—
reluctant to change—against its will in the direction of
greater realism. For example, Perry Ferguson for *American
Cinematographer* called the reduced $5,000 ceiling on expen-
ditures relating to set construction a godsend. In fact, "sets
are likely to have all too little connection with the reality of

what they represent." Ferguson illustrated his argument
by describing how "a movie night-club generally sprawls
over the whole of the studio's biggest sound stage, and has
plenty of room to dolly the camera everywhere between
the tables." Also, the "poor but honest steel-mill worker"
invariably lives in one of those "spacious apartments" with
"room enough . . . for a dozen people to move around in
without being crowded." Similarly, the heroine, a "poor
but honest stenographer," will more than likely reside in
even more luxurious surroundings—"the sort any actual
apartment-owner would figure at a rental of about $300 a
month!"[53] Ferguson went on to express his approval of the
way austerity measures were catalyzing the "tendency to
make use of real rooms, buildings and locations instead of
sets."[54]

Government regulations coincidentally blended in with
the parsimoniousness of *film noir* aesthetics. Figure #1, a
publicity still, gives some indication of the starkness of
Huston's sets and the frugality that characterized the sets
of many of the *films noirs* that followed. Second, it
emphasizes the importance of places in which characters
dwell. More than just backdrops, they are reflections of
internal character. Locations are even more important in
this respect since they are not just representations but the
actual places that people inhabit, and they tell a great deal
about the inhabitants. However, they are far more complex
and not easily broken down into discrete units of uncon-
testable knowledge. In the simplified setting of a studio, it
is possible to reach conclusions about the most casually
placed bits of paraphernalia. Everything in a studio serves
a distinct purpose. Everything can also be accounted for as
the handiwork of various departments and artistic personalities.

For example, in Spade's office, there is nothing of the
baroque. All the fancifulness of the arrangement can be
attributed to Brigid O'Shaughnessy, who is adorned in all
the flashy trappings of wealth. Spade's simplicity and
"squareness" is underscored by means of plain, rectangular office windows without curtains overlooking a painted
backdrop of buildings, billboards and sky. His desk is fairly

Figure 1. Spade's Office.

clean, not littered with paper. One sees an opened pouch of tobacco and a packet of rolling-paper for cigarettes, accouterments symbolic of Spade's independent mind and spirit.

Accordingly, Spade's attire is unexceptional, clean-cut (though not aseptic), dark, and conservative. A single plaque, displaying a certificate of some sort, hangs on the wall behind Spade and O'Shaughnessy. It attests to

Spade's professionalism. On top of a bulky file cabinet are a number of hefty volumes of the kind that one customarily finds in law offices and the like. It is noteworthy that Spade is a man who prefers spoken to written language. When he is confused about a certain question of legality, he telephones his lawyer. The only printed matter that he ever consults throughout the film is the shipping news inside a newspaper. Spade's craftiness is the product of intelligence that is analytical but not intellectual. Upon his desk is a stapler, a ledger, a tray containing miscellaneous papers, a penholder, and a blotter. Emanating logically if artificially from the direction of the window, the light illuminates Mary Astor's white, alabaster skin. This low-key lighting is harsh enough to produce a melange of shadows. J. A. Place and L. S. Peterson point out that at one time high-key lighting conferred on film "what was considered to be an impression of reality."[55] They further conjecture that the development of a cinematographic style predicated upon greater depth of field was a reaction against the use of diffuse, high-key lighting strategies.

The subject of Figure #2 is O'Shaughnessy's apartment, a deceptively pleasant contrast. Her surroundings are plush and ornate, in harmony with her sybaritic inclinations. While Spade works hard to conceal the underlying sentimentalism of his character, O'Shaughnessy must guard against exposing to view her own inner cruelty. In her case, pulchritude provides the necessary camouflage. She is herself unquestionably beautiful, and even her furniture is pleasing to the eye. But in the proliferation of striped patterns, one senses the secondary theme of imprisonment. Those who have seen the film or read the book know that this scene takes place shortly after the murder. She is deceiving Spade both to save her life and to get some use out of him.

The stripes on the upholstery in the room are reinforced by the striped shadows cast by the window blinds. It is significant that in Spade's office there are no blinds. Moreover, whereas the office is a geometrical configuration of verticals and horizontals, O'Shaughnessy's tempo-

Figure 2. Brigid's Apartment.

rary apartment is a cluster of curves and zigzags. Not surprisingly, her personality is more undulatory, more subtle than Spade's. Furthermore, although Spade visits her during the day, the natural light is too dim to obviate the necessity of using a lamp. With this modest, expressionistic device, one gets the idea of a nocturnal day. After all, O'Shaughnessy has all the makings of a classic vamp.

The subject of Figure #3 is Gutman's hotel suite, which is the most decorative of the three settings. Here there are few flat, rectangular surfaces. Instead, everything appears rounded and flamboyant. On a shelf above the fireplace there are two figurines and a vase. Above the latter is a classical-styled portrait with an oval frame. As with the spotlessly clean house of the decorous Mafioso in *The Big Heat* (Fritz Lang, 1953), appearances obscure the true nature of the occupants.

Each window is bordered on its sides by thick, heavy

curtains and veiled by a thin, dainty white fabric. Covering the floor is an exotic rug, upon which Spade tumbles unconscious. He did not perceive the drug mixed into his drink, served in tasteful glassware with an undoubtedly expensive brand of liquor. There is nothing plain about the furnishings in this room. The sofa has fringes and a table nearby supports an elaborate bouquet of flowers. A design has been carved into the fixture above the fireplace.

Just as O'Shaughnessy's glamorous outfit seemed out of place in Spade's office, Spade's nondescript dark suit with pinstripes seems disharmonious with the milieu. To be sure, his dangerous adversaries present an impressive array of male garb. Wilmer is enveloped by a voluminous coat, Cairo is impeccably attired in formal evening clothes, and Gutman is very dapper in what appears to be a silken smoking jacket. Proper habiliments divert attention away from the base, clandestine, and pecuniary motives of this anti-social group.

Into these and other settings, the camera enters unobtru-

Figure 3. Gutman's Suite.

sively, conspiring with the dialogue to imbue the film with
an aura of rapidly unfolding action—most of which
actually occurs off-screen. The static quality of the camerawork that ensues is counterpointed by editing that
achieves a sense of fluidity and rapidity. Well-timed
alternations among close-ups, medium shots, one- and
two-shots, over-the-shoulder shots and reaction shots
render a pace that is relentless throughout in terms of
momentum. As Karel Reisz and Gavin Millar remark,
dialogue sequences afford editors "a great deal of freedom
in cutting the scene in a variety of dramatically effective
ways. . . . By a variety of small tricks of presentation—by
the choice of the exact moment in a scene to cut to a
close-up, the timing of delayed reactions, the overlapping
of dialogue, and so on—the editor can accentuate and
control the drama of a given scene. Often, by a suitable
timing of words and images, he can produce dramatic
overtones, which the visuals alone did not have."[56]

The Maltese Falcon provides a useful verification of Reisz
and Millar's textbook analysis. The lengthy passages of
dialogue in The Maltese Falcon crackle with energy as a result
of virtuoso editing that perfectly complements Edeson's
superlative cinematography. Yet the editing of The Maltese
Falcon also intimates the way in which filmmakers brazenly
condescended to spectators. Filmmakers seemed to be
aware that they could spoon-feed spectators, who rarely
exercised their more critical faculties. There is no better
definition of studio-bound, Hollywood montage than Rousseau's description of the French theater: "A child would not
be able to eat his bread if it were not cut by his governess.
This is the image of what goes on in our new plays. The
maid is on the stage and the children in the audience."[57]

WRITING

The quick pacing of The Maltese Falcon is due in large part
to its retention of Hammett's sharply written dialogue.
Although the book was written in the late 1920s, the
acerbity of the language was still disturbing and offensive

to the movie kingdom's guardians of good taste. The head of the Production Code Administration, Joseph I. Breen, wrote to Jack L. Warner, advising caution and restraint. Getting Breen's opinion was part of the routine procedure of intra-industry censorship, designed to ward off governmental intervention. Breen found numerous allusions, implications, innuendoes and wordings objectionable.

For example, Spade and Iva were supposed to stay away from each other and not appear intimate. In the film, there is just enough contact to imply the sordid affair that worried Breen. Breen was also concerned about Joel Cairo's effeminacy. He disapproved of "the characterization of Cairo as a pansy, as indicated by the lavender perfume, high-pitched voice, and other accouterments." Also, the District Attorney was not to be referred to as a power-monger. When Spade finally rejects Brigid's romantic inveiglements, he was to tone down his explanation. After saying, "I won't because all of me wants to," he was not to add, "wants to say to hell with consequences and do it."

Furthermore, Spade was also not to say "damn her." Cairo was not to slap Brigid on-screen. Wilmer was not to be heard gutturally growling, "___ you." Even "Gutman's use of the interjection, 'by Gad', here [on page #84] and on Pages 92, 117, 121, 125, and 128, seems to be offensive if only by the number of times he uses it." Moreover, "there is a great deal of unnecessary drinking."[58] Hammett took these expressions, characterizations, and radical lifestyles from the street. But the street itself—in terms of location shooting—could not yet be brought into the picture.

Breen's scrutiny spoiled the attainment of modest, though essential, realist objectives. Thus subjected to the censor's microscope, the logistics of studio filmmaking discouraged experimentation and change. Even neutral observations were disallowed. Still, *The Maltese Falcon* was widely regarded as a realistic work. One reviewer raved about the fact that the film had a credible plot and "a sleuth who is human and doesn't have to wear a funny hat." Moreover, the dialogue "is genuine American talk of the

big city."[59] To Barnes, "Hammett wrote this yarn as it
might really have happened. The highest compliment to
the film is that it has followed the same procedure."[60] This
was indeed Huston's procedure, somewhat frustrated but
not defeated by Breen's interferences. Huston deferred to
Hammett's superior power as both storyteller and student
of human nature.

Hammett had at one time been a book reviewer for *The
Saturday Review of Literature* and *The New York Evening Post*.
In his reviews, he "stressed the importance of realism and
at the same time deplored the lack of it in the standard
mystery story."[61] To a large extent, Hammett practiced
precisely what he preached. Even if the situation in which
the characters find themselves in *The Maltese Falcon* is pure
malarkey, careful attention is paid to plotting their actions
and movements throughout San Francisco. According to
Julian Symons, the effectiveness of the book "rests in part
in the realization, fuller and richer than in the short stories,
of San Francisco's streets and scenes. Spade waits for Cairo
outside the Geary Theater on Sutter Street, sits with Effie
Perrine in Julius's Castle on Telegraph Hill, has an
apartment on Post Street."[62] Symons points out further
that the St. Mark Hotel in the novel was based on what was
once San Francisco's Hotel St. Francis. Similarly, the
Belvedere was modeled on the Hotel Bellevue.

Much of Hammett's work makes use of San Francisco.
After combing through this relatively small volume of
work and researching the life of Hammett, Don Herron
came up with a "Literary Walk in San Francisco." It guides
tourists on foot to landmarks taken from Hammett's novels
and stories. According to Herron, the Coronet—where
Brigid O'Shaughnessy resides throughout most of *The
Maltese Falcon*—was based on the Cathedral Apartments
on California Avenue and Jones Street.[63] Spade's apartment building is based on the one located at 891 Post
Street. Spade lived on the fourth floor in one of the
corners. Herron notes that this residency is very near to
Bush and Stockton, where Archer is murdered. Not
surprisingly, this intersection is "the most sought after
Hammett landmark in San Francisco."[64] Joe Gores—the

author of *Hammett* (1975), a suspense novel loosely based on its namesake's life and made into a film by Wim Wenders in 1983—placed the office of Spade and Archer in the Hunter-Dulin Building.[65] This is disputed by those who think it is the Hallidie Building. In either case, one has to acknowledge the importance of a geographical factor in Hammett's work.

Whereas the novel is undoubtedly more descriptive and penetrating than the film, the latter retains the same hard-boiled quality projected by the original source. The Spade of the novel is not exactly a blueprint for the Spade of the film. But this and other alterations do not filter out the tough-mindedness that is so essential to this kind of work. In fact, tough-mindedness is an essential tool for a realist enterprise striving to reveal rather than conceal the darker aspects of life. Throughout the book and film, things are said and done to destroy the simple-minded notions of morality that pervade classical Hollywood films. For instance, in delineating the character of Archer, Spade tells Brigid how his partner died "with ten thousand insurance, no children, and a wife that didn't like him." With the exception of Effie, no one is perfectly angelic or diabolic. Hammett provides the reader—and indirectly the spectator—with dirt on almost all the major characters.

Despite the expurgation of both action and dialogue, enough is preserved to make *The Maltese Falcon* one of the few novels that Hollywood did not seriously mar or mangle. Breen's warnings notwithstanding, the film manages to intimate an illicit affair between Iva and Spade, Cairo's effeminacy, O'Shaughnessy's promiscuity, and the cupidity of the whole merry lot of thieves. For the sake of expediency, Huston cut out the parable concerning Flitcraft and the character of Gutman's daughter. Otherwise, not only did he cull the great bulk of the film's dialogue from the novel, he even copied Hammett's adjectival phrases for the passages of description that are included in the screenplay. As a result, the actors and technicians who obediently followed the script were in effect faithfully abiding by Hammett's original vision.

The popular reception of the film as a work that was

ultimately a gradation more realistic than its predecessors can be attributed in large part to the development of the leading character. In its suit against CBS, Warner Bros. claimed that Sam Spade was a major part of the initial transaction that resulted in the acquisition of *The Maltese Falcon*. Simply put, Spade was considered a piece of artistic property purchased and possessed by Warner Bros. An attorney representing Warner Bros. prepared a literary analysis of this prototypical private-investigator. He pointed out that "one of the prime distinctions of Spade's characterization in *The Maltese Falcon* is its tridimensionality. He is not merely a *type*, but a personality endowed with individual characteristics, relatively complex attributes, and contradictory, conflicting emotional factors."[66] Spade was an exception to the rule stating that the best and longest acting careers were invested in types, not human beings with multifaceted personalities.

Others concurred with the opinion expressed by the attorney for Warner Bros. For instance, according to David T. Bazelon, Spade not only is more human than the usual private detective portrayed in mysteries, he is also more fully fleshed out than the Continental Op—the investigator in *Red Harvest*, the book written by Hammett which chronologically preceded *The Maltese Falcon*. To Bazelon, the Op is a nameless character in whom "*competence* replaces moral stature as the criterion of an individual's worth." Spade differs "primarily in the fact that he has a more active sexual motive of his own. This sexual susceptibility serves to heighten, by contrast, his basic job-doing orientation. So when Spade, in conflict, chooses to do his job instead of indulging in romantic sex, he takes on more dramatic meaning than does the hero of the Op stories." However, the Op and Spade are in complete accord over one vital issue: each proudly defines himself in terms of his job, "his real contact with life, his focus."[67] Spade entertains no illusions about business as the business of America.

Tracing the evolution of Sam Spade in *The Maltese Falcon*, one finds oneself ensconced inside a corridor without beginning or end. The character of Spade seems to have evolved from Hammett through the first two Warner Bros.

films to Huston, and then on to Bogart. Yet lurking behind
Hammett was the editorial leadership of Captain Joseph T.
Shaw. Before Shaw took over *Black Mask*, begun by H. L.
Mencken and George Jean Nathan, the journal emphasized plots over characters. Shaw used his influence to
reverse the order of importance, shifting the emphasis
from plot to character. When Hammett began to write, he
seems to have been acquainted with the Nick Carter,
Detective stories. In this popular, multi-authored pulp
series, situation always took precedence over character.[68]
As a protégé of Shaw, who juggled the Nick Carter
methodology to foreground character, Hammett was one
of many aspiring mystery writers. Under Shaw's editorial
supervision, Hammett devised the idea of a depraved
female manipulator in the person of Brigid O'Shaughnessy. At first, she seemed enigmatic. Symons describes
how "readers at the time were unsure. The tradition that
somebody loved by the hero must be a good woman was
strong."[69] As has already been mentioned, in this case, the
hero is himself not exactly heroic.

Shaw also demanded concise description that eschewed
hyperbole and exotic locales. According to Foster Hirsch,
Black Mask shared with Ernest Hemingway "a concern for
realistic description, and an interest in crackling dialogue
that depends on echo and repetition."[70] Hammett's style is
lean and muscular. Richard Layman calls his writing
"clean-cut, vivid and realistic."[71]

His most famous novel may have lent itself readily to
adaptation by the film medium, but Hammett himself was
not adept at screenwriting. In 1931, Darryl Zanuck fired him
for not doing "a good job of writing." In the aborted story
that displeased Zanuck, Spade was again to have been the
protagonist. According to Zanuck, the story "lacks a climax
and it lacks punch."[72] Jack L. Warner thought about hiring
Hammett to write a sequel to *The Maltese Falcon*, but
ultimately did nothing to acquire his services.

On the other hand, while by no means a novelist or a
writer of the same caliber as Hammett, Huston was
nonetheless a competent screenwriter. Not only was he
accustomed to the adaptation of ideas spun out by other

writers, but he also felt at home in the company of
collaborators. Novelists might insist on originality, but
Hollywood screenwriters were generally unburdened by
such millstones. Huston shared the screenwriting credits
for *Law and Order* (Edward L. Cahn, 1932) with Tom Reed;
The Amazing Dr. Clitterhouse (Anatole Litvak, 1938) with
John Wexley; *Jezebel* (William Wyler, 1938) with Clements
Ripley, Abem Finkel and Robert Buckner; *Juarez* (William
Dieterle, 1939) with Aeneas MacKenzie and Wolfgang
Reinhardt; *Dr. Ehrlich's Magic Bullet* (William Dieterle,
1940) with Norman Burnside and Heinz Herald; *High Sierra*
(Raoul Walsh, 1941) with W. R. Burnett; and *Sergeant York*
(Howard Hawks, 1941) with Howard Koch, Abem Finkel
and Harry E. Chandlee.[73]

The sibling rivalry of interacting Hollywood personnel
was detrimental to many writers of true genius—not just
Hammett, who managed to squeeze out just two screen-
writing credits. He created the story upon which *City
Streets* (Rouben Mamoulian, 1931) was based.[74] He also
wrote the screenplay for the adaptation of the play, *Watch
on the Rhine* (Herman Shumlin, 1943), written by his
companion, Lillian Hellman.[75]

Philip T. Hartung of *The Commonweal* divided the credit for
the dynamics of the dialogue in *The Maltese Falcon* equally
between Hammett and Huston. But as has already been
suggested, almost all of the spicy repartee that endows the
film with great vibrancy was lifted right out of the novel.
Critics have spoken with a hint of disparagement about this.
James Naremore, for instance, remarks that the "finished
screenplay is less an adaptation than a skillful editing of the
novel, which is mostly dialogue anyway."[76] Allen Eyles also
notes that "John Huston's approach was incredibly simple.
He stuck to the book."[77] In sum, one can say that what is
otherwise often a vice was in this case a virtue.

DIRECTION

To Huston, fidelity to the original source was a radical
departure from Hollywood methods. Such an adaptation

required a certain kind of self-effacement and achieved a certain transparency. In the final analysis, Huston provided a conduit for Hammett's novel to a public more massive than any single book can normally reach. Works such as *The Maltese Falcon* illustrate Bazin's defense of a cinema that borrows from the other arts. Such a "mixed cinema" restores the "dimension that the arts had gradually lost from the time of the Reformation on: namely a public."[78] Instead of denouncing the way Huston plundered Hammett's work, Bazin upheld and even advocated such piracy. He went on to say that a faithful, self-effacing adaptation of a story from a different medium was "compatible with complete independence from the original."

This is easy enough to see in the way Shakespeare raided other works for stories to use in his plays, but more difficult to discern in film. According to Bazin, to hew closely to the source material demands "all the more power of invention and imagination."[79] Huston did not just parrot Hammett's words and ideas. He preserved Hammett's artistic vision, just as "photography . . . embalms time, rescuing it simply from its proper corruption."[80] He re-structured and re-presented Hammett's unflattering opinion of contemporary society and the dark foreboding of the masterful novelist over its imminent future.

The one item that Huston lacked was freedom. Despite his severe limitations in terms of film art, Jack L. Warner was still the boss and the only figure at liberty to do as he pleased. His word could not easily be contravened. At one point, he capriciously changed the name of the film to "The Gent from Frisco."[81] Furthermore, Huston kept his cast pinned down to the script, effectively abolishing all spontaneity. According to Mary Astor, Huston's "shooting script was a precise map of what went on. Every shot, camera move, entrance, exit was down on paper, leaving nothing to chance, inspiration or invention."[82] Even casual movements were explicitly orchestrated.

For instance, the sequence during which Spade pulls Cairo aside in a hotel lobby took ten takes. It involved an elaborate shot that began in the middle of the lobby, went first to the reception desk and then to a secluded area away from the pedestrian traffic. Both Bogart and Lorre had trouble "staying within the camera angle and in on their marks."[83] Never drifting away from the shooting script, Huston for the most part shot speedily and efficiently, in fast takes with a minimum of retakes. The production records indicate that he maintained a steady pace of from one to three days ahead of schedule.

Indeed, precision, planning, and thrifty budgeting were the most vital matters of concern. Studio filmmakers strove to meet deadlines. It was only logical that they would also eliminate experimentation and the "fortuitous," which Kracauer regarded as "a characteristic of camera-reality."[84] Nothing could be left to chance; everything was controlled. Everything was exploited, too. Researchers in the Legal Department were instructed to find out if the bejeweled Maltese Falcon ever really existed. If it did, this choice piece of history could be exploited for the sake of publicity. Unfortunately, as one Joe Weston curtly reported, "no record can be found of a Maltese Falcon."

Researchers helped the filmmakers achieve an acceptable degree of verisimilitude. They went out and gathered photographs, slides and footage of various settings. But the actual places themselves were literally left out of the picture. Clips were submitted that showed the interiors of government offices, police stations, and contemporary hotel lobbies. Other clips dealt with miscellaneous San Francisco streets, offices and houses. A photostat revealed what the inside and outside of a Greek passport looked like.[85]

Certain legalities took precedence over art. The Publicity Department ascertained that Wilmer Cook and Brigid O'Shaughnessy were not among the names listed in the San Francisco telephone directory. The Los Angeles Chamber of Commerce Marine Department assented to the film's use of *La Paloma* as the name of the ship on which the falcon is brought to the United States. At the Los Angeles Public Library, a Warner Bros. employee studied up on the history of the Isle of Malta and how it was donated to the

Knights of St. John of Jerusalem in 1530. He found out that the knights did in fact pay tribute to their feudal benefactors by means of presenting "a falcon to the Viceroy, every year, on All Saints Day."[86] It had been a live falcon, not one made of stone, studded with jewels.

In sum, all the attention paid to details in preproduction helped to protect the film's legal backside later on. However, unless handled with finesse, this kind of fastidiousness could be stultifying. With censorship, commercial and legal concerns, the film seemed already in a straitjacket before the cameras started to roll. To worm through all these restraints and still present something akin to an accurate reflection of life as experienced in the San Francisco underworld was a tall order. The inevitable artificiality that resulted is in a way reminiscent of Courbet's *Reclining Nude* (1858), in which there is a picture, hanging on the wall, of a landscape with a frame around it. At first, one mistakes it for a window, looking out upon the world. But with a second look, one sees that it is a painting within the painting—another representation. In retrospect, almost all studio reproductions seem similarly conceived—distantly removed from the realities they attempt to mirror. But one must remember that this was not the perspective that prevailed among audiences in 1941.

To be sure, no accumulation of skillfully depicted petty details can guarantee an aura of unassailable realism. However, in combination with Huston's dark sensibility, *The Maltese Falcon* did in fact leave critics and spectators alike with an impression of realism. Lee Mortimer of *The New York Daily Mirror* called Huston's direction "at all times realistic, suspenseful and plausible."[87] Leo Mishkin of New York City's *Morning Telegraph* was struck by "the half-heard conversations" that occur during the sequences in which there are telephone calls.[88] In addition to the application of a wide-angle lens, Huston frequently alludes to off-screen space and sounds as extensions to the limits of the frame.

Often enough, off-screen space houses unseen peril. A good example of this has to do with the way in which the weapon used to murder Archer suddenly juts into the bottom of the corner of the frame. This composition clearly plays against the basic expectations of an eyeline match. Archer is smiling at the time, obviously unaware of the imminent danger. In such a situation, spectators are conditioned to expect a rhyming shot of the pleasant object he is looking at. Needless to add, it is not forthcoming. Throughout the film, Huston repeats this same technique. For instance, when Cairo aims a gun at Spade, the camera focuses only on his cane, shown in close-up. Spade is relaxed, as is the audience. But hidden behind the cane is the gun, uncovered in a delayed reverse shot.

These kinds of compositions did not just play games with the spectator's faculties of sight and hearing. They enhanced the theme of darkness. At the same time, they broadened the canvas of cinematic realism. So as not to alarm or make spectators uncomfortable, films rarely journeyed very far into the truer realms of evil and injustice. The continual threat of violence not only made films seem more realistic, they also charged the atmosphere with electricity. They intensified the element of suspense. Mishkin found "the accumulated tension . . . well nigh unbearable."[89] William Boehnel compared Huston's direction to that of Alfred Hitchcock, Carol Reed, and Fritz Lang, whose films are still paradigms of suspense. Mary Astor was also impressed by how the dialogue was "not just dull exposition."[90] For example, while Gutman drones on and on about the possible value of the falcon, Spade gradually loses consciousness.

Throughout production, Wallis urged Huston to sustain a sprightly tempo. One of the first scenes that Huston filmed entailed a sleep sequence in which Spade lethargically fields a telephone call that informs him of the murder of his partner. The clock on a small table reads exactly five minutes after two. Nearby is a copy of Duke's *Celebrated Criminal Cases of America*. After seeing the dailies, Wallis was alarmed, thinking that the film was going to lack the necessary pizzazz. In his view Bogart spoke too slowly and waited too long, staring into space, before calling his secretary. Wallis complained that "there is a long pause and this does not make for the punchy, driving kind of tempo that this picture requires." The extent to which aesthetics was dictated is clear in Wallis's statement that "wherever we have pieces of business, it must be fast." Wallis stressed that above all "there must be action in the picture."[91]

Huston was cooperative and replied that he was dutifully "shrinking all the pauses and speeding up all the action." He promised Wallis that the scenes involving Spade and the police detectives "will go so fast they will make sparks." Before the climactic scene inside Spade's apartment, the film "will be turning like a pinwheel."[92] Huston's success in this regard can be measured by a letter sent to Warner Bros. by someone from the Ohio Chamber of Commerce. The movie fan liked the film—but the only "criticism, as I see it is that the action is entirely too fast."[93]

The sequence which Wallis found objectionable was unusual because of its inordinate length. It consisted of a single shot, with some frame adjustment, that went on for approximately ninety seconds. According to Barry Salt, the average shot length in films during this period was less than ten seconds. Salt points out further that "in 1939 there was just beginning to emerge a movement towards the use of longer takes on the part of some directors."[94] Huston knew that he did not always have to cut to keep those "pinwheels" spinning. Like the use of wide-angle lenses, long takes serve the cause of cinematic realism. According to Bazin, long takes preserve the spatial and temporal integrity of reality. To Kracauer, they do not fracture the continuum of physical existence. In a variety of ways *The Maltese Falcon* looks forward to the greater visual and narrational realism of semi-documentaries.

The feeling of impending doom that is inherent in the film also registers as a stroke of realism. Perhaps this is because it is only in such states of mind that life seems real—all too real. This emotional component is partly achieved through lighting, which is predominantly low-key. According to Salt, except RKO and MGM, most studios routinely underexposed their shots. In the laboratory later on they doctored the resultant film with chemicals. The lighter quality that they were aiming for gave the audience the kind of lighting they were accustomed to seeing—full and evenly distributed. Low-key lighting undermined this brilliantly lit ebullience. MGM especially resisted it as an interference with the cultivation of a sense of good will, opulence, and well-being. While Wallis pressured Huston to accelerate the pace, Blanke pushed him to tighten up the story. It was Blanke who decided to truncate the final scene, causing the film to end prematurely just outside Spade's apartment. In the novel, Spade returns to his office, where the narrative begins. Effie is disgusted with Spade for turning Brigid in, even though he is able to prove that she murdered Archer. Spade shivers when Effie announces the arrival of Iva Archer. It was the announced arrival of Brigid that got the story going in the first place. In a wry comment on happy endings, Spade in effect gets "the girl." In the film's ending, Spade winds up with the worthless falcon. Borde and Chaumeton sum it all up as "Absurdité d'une destinée dérisoire."[95] Huston's direction is at its most painterly at this juncture. A patch of shadow cast by an elevator bar comes to rest over one of Astor's tearful eyes. Bogart is also caught in a kind of pose as he declaims that Shakespearean line about "the stuff dreams are made of." In general, all studio films were made of such stuff. But surely the cupidity and viciousness of the film are the stuff life is made of. To incorporate more of the stuff of life into films would require a few more years "on the quest." But the *rara avis* was out there, waiting to have its enamel chipped away and to be stripped bare.

NOTES

1. Hal Wallis, Inter-Office Memorandum to Steve Trilling, 22 May 1941, The Warner Bros. Collection, USC Cinema-Television Library and Archives of Performing Arts.
2. Rudy Behlmer, *America's Favorite Movies, Behind the Scenes* (New York: Frederick Ungar, 1982): 140.
3. William F. Nolan, *Hammett, A Life at the Edge* (New York: Congdon & Weed, 1983): 180.

4. Dashiell Hammett, Affidavit, circa 1948. Warner Bros. Archive. Princeton University Libraries.
5. Gordon L. Files, Affidavit: Dashiell Hammett vs. Warner Bros. Pictures, Inc., 18 October 1948. Warner Bros. Archive. Princeton University Libraries.
6. Hammett, Affidavit: 3.
7. J. C. Gilpin, budget breakdown, 20 January 1931, The Warner Bros. Collection, USC Cinema-Television Library and Archives of Performing Arts. The exact figure was $287,462.00.
8. John Baxter, *Hollywood in the Thirties* (New York: A. S. Barnes, 1980): 146.
9. Hammett, affidavit: 10.
10. Hal Wallis, Inter-Office Memorandum to Harry Joe Brown, 27 June 1934, The Warner Bros. Collection, USC Cinema-Television Library and Archives of Performing Arts.
11. Ibid.
12. Charles Belden, *Clock Struck Three,* 19 October 1939, The Warner Bros. Collection, USC Cinema-Television Library and Archives of Performing Arts.
13. John Howard Lawson, *Film: The Creative Process, The Search for an Audio-Visual Language and Structure* (New York: Hill and Wang, 1964): 139.
14. Dana Polan, *Power and Paranoia, History, Narrative, and the American Cinema, 1940–1950* (New York: Columbia University Press, 1986): 194.
15. Behlmer: 140.
16. Gerald Pratley, *The Cinema of John Huston* (New York: A. S. Barnes, 1977): 38.
17. Janet Staiger et al., *The Classical Hollywood Cinema, Film Style & Mode of Production to 1960* (New York: Columbia University Press, 1985): 326.
18. *The New York Tribune,* 3 October 1941: 17.
19. *The New York Sun,* 1 October 1941: 31.
20. *The New York Daily News,* 3 October 1941: 58.
21. Eileen Creelman, rev. of *The Maltese Falcon, The New York Sun,* 4 October 1941: 6.
22. Rev. of *The Maltese Falcon, Variety,* 1 October 1941: 9.
23. Howard Barnes, rev. of *The Maltese Falcon, The New York Herald Tribune,* 4 October 1941: 6.
24. Richard Dyer, *Stars* (London: British Film Institute, 1979): 123.
25. Hal Wallis, Inter-Office Memorandum to Henry Blanke, 24

June 1941, The Warner Bros. Collection, USC Cinema-Television Library and Archives of Performing Arts.

26. Janey Place, "Women in Film Noir" in *Women in Film Noir*, ed. E. Ann Kaplan (London: British Film Institute, 1980): 35.

27. Borde & Chaumeton: 10.

28. Richard Layman, *Shadow Man, The Life of Dashiell Hammett* (New York: Harcourt Brace Jovanovich, 1981): 110.

29. Louise Levitas, rev. of *The Maltese Falcon, PM's Weekly*, 5 October 1941: 19.

30. John Hobart, rev. of *The Maltese Falcon, The San Francisco Chronicle*, 12 December 1941: 9.

31. Barnes: 6.

32. Milton Meltzer, rev. of *The Maltese Falcon, The Daily Worker*, 6 October 1941: 7.

33. Borde and Chaumeton: 10.

34. W. E. H., rev. of *The Maltese Falcon, The Denver Post*, 31 December 1941: 19.

35. R. M. D., "Reviewing the Screen," *The Milwaukee Journal*, 18 January 1942, Section II: 4.

36. William Boehnel, "Cycle of Melodrama Seems Due in Movies: 'Maltese Falcon' Paves the Way," rev. of *The Maltese Falcon, The New York World Telegram*, 4 October 1941: 5.

37. Information pertaining to sets was obtained from a collection of photographs filed in The Warner Bros. Collection, USC Cinema-Television Library and Archives of Performing Arts.

38. Henry Blanke, Inter-Office Memorandum to Al Alleborn, 30 July 1941, The Warner Bros. Collection, USC Cinema-Television Library and Archives of Performing Arts.

39. "Inside Stuff—Pictures," *Variety*, 12 November 1941: 18.

40. Barry Salt, *Film Style and Technology: History and Analysis* (London: Starwood, 1983): 297.

41. Porfirio: 178.

42. Virginia Yates, " 'Rope' Sets a Precedent," *American Cinematographer*, July 1948: 230.

43. Bart Sheridan, "Three and a Half Minute Take," *American Cinematographer*, September 1948: 305.

44. Patrick L. Ogle, "Technological and Aesthetic Influences Upon the Development of Deep Focus Cinematography in the United States," *Screen Reader* (London: Society for Education in Film and Television, 1977): 82.

45. Ibid.: 85.

46. Jean Luc-Godard, review of *Swamp Water* in André Bazin,

Jean Renoir, trans. W. W. Halsey II and William H. Simon (New York: Simon & Schuster, 1973): 261.
47. "Technical Progress in 1941," *American Cinematographer*, January 1942: 6.
48. Ibid.: 45.
49. Charles G. Clarke, "How Desirable Is Extreme Focal Depth?" *American Cinematographer*, January 1942: 36.
50. Walter Blanchard, "Aces of the Camera—XXII: Arthur Edeson, A.S.C.," *American Cinematographer*, November 1942: 491.
51. William Stull, A.S.C., "Lighting Without Photofloods," *American Cinematographer*, December 1942: 520.
52. Ibid.: 534.
53. Perry Ferguson, "More Realism from 'Rationed' Sets?" *American Cinematographer*, September 1942: 390.
54. Ibid.: 391.
55. J. A. Place and L. S. Peterson, "Some Visual Motifs of Film Noir," *Film Comment*, January 1974: 31.
56. Karel Reisz and Gavin Millar, *The Technique of Film Editing* (London: Butterworth, 1981): 87.
57. Jean-Jacques Rousseau, *Politics and the Arts, Letter to M. D'Alembert on the Theatre*, trans. Allan Bloom (Ithaca, New York: Cornell University Press, 1977): 49.
58. Joseph I. Breen, Letter to Jack L. Warner, 27 May 1941, The Warner Bros. Collection, USC Cinema-Television Library and Archives of Performing Arts.
59. Joe Davidman, Review of *The Maltese Falcon*, *New Masses*, 21 October 1941: 28.
60. Barnes: 6.
61. Julian Symons, *Dashiell Hammett* (New York: Harcourt Brace Jovanovich, 1985): 59.
62. Ibid.: 69.
63. Don Herron, *Dashiell Hammett Tour* (San Francisco: Dawn Heron Press, 1982): 59.
64. Ibid.: 65.
65. Ibid.: 66–7.
66. Stephen Karnot, *Preliminary Draft of Analysis and Argument re: "Sam Spade" Character in The Maltese Falcon (Novel and Films) and in The Adventures of Sam Spade (Radio Series)*, July 1949: 13. The Warner Bros. Collection, USC Cinema-Television Library and Archives of Performing Arts.
67. David T. Bazelon, "Dashiell Hammett's Private Eye," *Commentary Magazine*, May 1949: 469–471.

68. John L. Fell, *Film and the Narrative Tradition* (Berkeley: University of California Press, 1986): 43.
69. Symons: 62.
70. Foster Hirsch, *Film Noir, The Dark Side of the Screen* (New York: Da Capo Press, 1981): 46.
71. Layman: 112.
72. Darryl Zanuck, Letter to Daniel Leonardson, 28 April 1931. Warner Bros. Archive. Princeton University Libraries.
73. Larry Langman, *A Guide to American Screenwriters, The Sound Era, 1929–1982; Vol. I: Screenwriters* (New York: Garland Publishing, 1984): 384.
74. *Film Noir: An Encyclopedic Reference to the American Style*, ed. Alain Silver and Elizabeth Ward (Woodstock, New York: The Overlook Press, 1979): 59. The film was scripted by Max Marcin.
75. Langman: 326.
76. James Naremore, "John Huston and *The Maltese Falcon*," *Literature/Film Quarterly*, July 1973: 241.
77. Allen Eyles, "The Maltese Falcon," *Films and Filming*, November 1964: 49.
78. Bazin, "In Defense of Mixed Cinema," *What Is Cinema? Volume I:* 75.
79. Ibid.: 67.
80. Bazin, "The Ontology of the Photographic Image," in *What Is Cinema? Volume I:* 14.
81. Hal Wallis to all Departments, Inter-Office Communication (29 August 1941), The Warner Bros. Collection, USC Cinema-Television Library and Archives of Performing Arts.
82. Mary Astor, *A Life on Film* (New York: Delacorte Press, 1971): 160.
83. Al Allehorn, Production Report to T. C. Wright, 17 July 1941, The Warner Bros. Collection, USC Cinema-Television Library and Archives of Performing Arts.
84. Siegfried Kracauer, *Theory of Film, The Redemption of Physical Reality* (London: Oxford University Press, 1979): 62.
85. General Research Record for *The Maltese Falcon*, undated, The Warner Bros. Collection, USC Cinema-Television Library and Archives of Performing Arts.
86. Herman Lissauer to Morris Goldberg, Inter-Office Communication, 3 October 1941, The Warner Bros. Collection, USC Cinema-Television Library and Archives of Performing Arts.
87. Lee Mortimer, rev. of *The Maltese Falcon, The New York Daily Mirror*, 4 October 1941: 17.

88. Leo Mishkin, rev. of *The Maltese Falcon*, *The New York Morning Telegraph*, 3 October 1941: 2.
89. Ibid.
90. Astor: 160.
91. Hal Wallis, Inter-Office Memorandum to Henry Blanke, 12 June 1941, The Warner Bros. Collection, USC Cinema-Television Library and Archives of Performing Arts.
92. John Huston, Inter-Office Communication to Hal Wallis, 13 June 1941, The Warner Bros. Collection, USC Cinema-Television Library and Archives of Performing Arts.
93. Clarence P. Woodbury, Letter to Warner Bros., 18 November 1941, The Warner Bros. Collection, USC Cinema-Television Archives of Performing Arts.
94. Salt: 291.
95. Borde and Chaumeton: 43.

III   FILM NOIR ON LOCATION:
        THE NAKED CITY

Two men murder a model named Jean Dexter. Then the stronger of the two men murders the weaker. The case is assigned to Lt. Dan Muldoon (Barry Fitzgerald), an aging police detective. A younger cop, Jimmy Halloran (Don Taylor), is hired to do most of the legwork. While gaining vital experience, he becomes more and more animated about his new role in upholding the law. But he is unprepared for the long hours of toil that bring no result. Through the Barry Fitzgerald character, one learns the plodding methodology of criminal detection. Through the Don Taylor character, one gets a sense of the dedication involved. More than once his picture-perfect home life is interrupted.

At first, the only suspect is Frank Niles (Howard Duff). He is engaged to Ruth Morrison (Dorothy Hart), a friend and colleague of the murder victim. He is a shady character. But as it turns out, he is only a link in a chain which, once known, finally uncovers the identity of the actual murderer. While he is not the murderer, his lies and subterfuge hold up the investigation, which seems to drag on endlessly without hope of solution.

A vial of sleeping pills leads the investigators to a Dr. Stoneman (House Jameson). On the outside, he is a pillar of the community. He is married, stable, and runs a respectable medical practice from a prestigious address. On the sly, however, he has been seeing Jean Dexter. He unethically supplies the beautiful blonde model with pills, so that her life can maintain a fast pace. Like Niles, Stoneman remains calm, insulated and safe, even under persistent scrutiny, until the body of the second killer surfaces in the East River. A police record shows that this man, Backalis, was a jewel thief. Halloran is able to establish that there was a connection between him and Niles. Finally, a list of stolen jewelry suggests the existence of a whole jewel-theft organization. It eventually comes out that Jean Dexter and Frank Niles headed the operation. They used Stoneman's social contacts to target victims and employed a muscle-man, Garza (Ted de Corsia), and his assistant, an alcoholic, to do the dirty work. Garza wanted a greater share of the cut. When Dexter refused, Garza made up his mind to kill her. The second murder was to cover up the first, but actually made possible Garza's capture. Having cracked the case, Halloran locates and chases Garza onto the Williamsburg Bridge, where he is shot dead.

PRELIMINARY COMMENTS

On Sunday, January 18, 1948, *The Naked City* was previewed by Mayor William O'Dwyer, the Police Commissioner, Arthur Wallander, and lesser officials. The producer, Mark Hellinger, whose courage made the film possible, had already met his untimely end a month before at the age of forty-four. He would have liked to hear how the mayor, with teary eyes, "spoke for fully ten minutes expressing his overwhelming approval of the picture, its authentic city background, its accuracy of detail in regard to the Police Department activities, and its great insight into the people and problems of New York." The Police Commissioner called the film "a magnificent job with no technical flaws whatsoever."[1] *The Naked City* was not the first *film noir* to exploit the possibilities of location work, but it made the most *emphatic* use of natural settings.

Variety noted with some astonishment how "a Manhattan police station scene was photographed in the police station; a lower eastside cops and robbers chase was actually filmed in the locale; the ghetto and its pushcarts were caught in all their realism."[2] Critics unanimously commended the film's keen sense of verisimilitude. But this startling series of backdrops was something more than that. It was the genuine article.

To *Parade*, *The Naked City* was "one of the most realistic crime dramas ever filmed."[3] To *Cue*, it was "a surprisingly realistic and candid portrait of New York at work and play."[4] *Look* was impressed by the appearance of "streets, people, subways, stores and homes."[5] Representing *The New York Times*, Bosley Crowther was moved by the "observation of life in New York's streets, police stations, apartments, tenements, playgrounds, docks, bridges and flashy resorts."[6] Some, but not all, took note of the darker message underlying the gloom-ridden vision projected by the film, which "begins in a plane over the city and ends in the gutter."[7] The larger implication of an urban society with only a thin layer of civilization to control a persistent will to savagery gets lost. Some even found this murder story faint-hearted. Yet, if nothing else, the locations themselves cut off the possibility of retreat to the comforts of old, Hollywood studio moralism. The pessimism of *film noir* had grown too large to be contained by studios. In the case of *The Naked City*, it was not something artificially grafted onto the urban landscape of film. It was already there in the buildings, streets and sidewalks, as tangible as the concrete. *Film noir* invented nothing, though it stylized everything.

It also cashed in on the public's impatience with Hollywood's pampering, its method of hiding from spectators the harshness of life with which they were well-acquainted. This systematic spoon-feeding clashed with what Paul Schrader described as "America's post-war mood." According to Schrader, "the public's desire for a more honest and harsh view of America would not be satisfied by the same studio streets they had been watching for a dozen years." Even in the aftermath of the late-1940s explosion of semi-documentary films, when plots grew more bizarre and contrived, "realistic exteriors remained a permanent fixture of *film noir*."[8] These exteriors were *film noir's* strongest ally. It was the environment that confirmed *film noir's* philosophical outlook. The environment's incessant production of crime and spiraling violence readily gave concrete form to *film noir's* idea that there is no hope, no savior, no future.

But if it ever seemed as though there were no turning
back, that just goes to show how Hollywood's appetite for
fantasy is not to be underestimated. *The Naked City* precipi-
tated such a barrage of take-offs and spin-offs that before
long New York City would appear on screen more as an
elaborate backlot than a real city. The success of *The Naked
City*, released in March 1948, was ironically the undoing of
the semi-documentary *film noir*. As David George explains:
"Film after film followed *Naked City* with the claim that
material came straight from the files of such-and-such a
police department. Chases round the sewers and up and
down tenement stairs; questioning of sleazy suspects by
hard-eyed detectives; spoken narratives introduced by a
date, a place, a time; the wail of police sirens and the thud of
running feet on pavements—these were fine while the
impulse stayed fresh, but the moment came when all that
remained was to turn the whole thing over to television and
the ultimate never-never world of *Dragnet*."[9]

A month into *The Naked City*'s run, David Sarnoff boldly
described the progress of television as "zooming like a V-2
rocket."[10] And television would disinter the old, studio
mentality with its own programming, providing more
comforts than the studios were ever able to provide.
Hollywood's own back-pedaling, together with television
networks' usurping of the power that once belonged to
studios, served to turn the orientation in media once more
away from the depressing realities of existence.

Yet, *The Naked City* does not hit the spectator over the
head with its pessimism. It is only suggested with the
unfolding of one out of a possible eight million scenarios.
As with the expressionistic undulation of the gauzy
curtains in Spade's apartment, there is an expectation of a
continued state of deceit and violent eruptions. Reviewers
of this film diverged widely over the interpretation of New
York City's nakedness. As John Tagg tells us, "the purely
visual image is nothing but an Edenic fiction." A photograph "needs to be anchored by a caption, if it is not to drift
in ambiguity."[11] *The Naked City*'s narrative—indeed, the
film noir narrative—serves as an illuminating caption,
reading, "bleak, anguished, and desperate."

Victor Hugo conceived of architecture as "man's first writing, his first fixing of cultural energy in a coherent, static form."[12] In *Journey to the End of the Night*, Céline's narrator, Bardamu, remarks about New York City's striking verticality. To Bardamu, there is nothing hospitable about this, nothing that would indicate the haven promised by the inscription on the Statue of Liberty. In Europe, "cities lie along the seacoast or on rivers, they recline on the landscape, awaiting the traveler, while this American city had nothing languid about her, she stood there as stiff as a board, not seductive at all, terrifyingly stiff."[13]

Céline could only view New York City from his own personal, albeit fresh and illuminating, perspective. Although the *caméra stylo* is also capable of personal observation, it can also resist the temptation to surround the cinematographic subject with a dominating interpretation. More so than the novel, it has the ability to approximate a window to the world. The partial execution of this function in *The Naked City* is confirmed by the multiplicity of ways in which different reviewers construed the intertexual meaning of its semi-documentary cinematography. Despite the contradictions between these views, they are all equally valid. As André Bazin has so elegantly pointed out in "The Evolution of the Language of Cinema," it is precisely "the unity of meaning of the dramatic event" that cuts cinema off from any integral connection with the real world.[14] Reality is ambiguous, a quality that good filmmaking reveals and preserves. And even if good *films noirs* are unambiguously bleak, their bleakness is nonetheless still open to interpretation.

PM Daily's reviewer found the New York City of *The Naked City* one that had been filtered through Hellinger's "rose-colored glasses." Peering through these spectacles, "we see a home town that belongs to us, our own home town, its irritations and hostilities transformed into darling eccentricities, the wrinkles in its face become lines of friendly beauty." To this critic, location footage was a whitewash: "[D]oesn't this town look good though, anywhere, any way you look at it, in any light, from any angle, no matter what it's up to, waking, sleeping, threatening, playing, working, hurrying, wondering." The reader was asked to "look at New York, only at New York, in Naked City. That's a fact, all right. How does that fact make you feel? Sentimental? That's what Hellinger thought."[15] Similarly, *The Daily Worker* thought "the film's reality is limited by a concern only for surface effects, never probing causes. . . ." *The Naked City*'s superficiality "was also a limitation of Mark Hellinger."[16]

But to *The Daily Mirror* there was "nothing maudlin about the film." One had to credit "Hellinger for having had the intelligence to eliminate the phony frills." He gave "a New York murder the simple and straightforward treatment the subject calls for." He "blue pencilled every temptation to get cute, eliminated the tricks, stuck sternly to life." *The Daily Mirror*'s perspicacious reviewer correctly ascertained that the story had been "lifted bodily from the newspaper morgue slips on the late Dot King."[17] Headlines from the 1930s frequently allude to bathtub-style murders, such as the one upon which *The Naked City* was based. To another critic, the film's murder victim "might well have been Sheila Mannering, so closely does the picture cleave to actuality."[18] Most critics reviewed the film favorably and regarded it as uniquely free of excessive Hollywood slickness.

To *The Commonweal*, *The Naked City* was "a fascinating portrayal of life in the big city when its glamor has been stripped away."[19] *The New York World Telegram* called the film "about the most faithful version of actual police methods that the screen has offered." Rather than tedious, it was enthralling to see "the incredibly laborious drudgery that lies beneath the veneer of intuition and gunplay in which most movie mysteries deal."[20] *The New York Post* concurred, saying that the film was "the best, most authentic view of a murder investigation the screen has offered."[21] To *The Denver Post*, *The Naked City* boldly showed the city's "ratty rooms, dark streets, smelly wharves . . . and cold mortuaries." Moreover, the villains in the film were "as realistic as the film itself."[22]

The story begins lodged within an eclectic array of early morning shots while it is still dark. Various people throughout the city are seen either at work or at play. Like the actualities of les frères Lumière, Dassin selected very mundane compositions for subject matter. Dassin's preoccupation with such banal imagery was not an isolated case. *The Naked City* shared a pre-television passion for documentary images with other contemporary works, as is evident from an article published the same week the film was released. Writing for *The New Republic*, Robert Hatch stated that documentaries are returning "movies to the days when the only tool the picture makers had was a box set on a tripod; before there was a gadget to compensate for every shortcoming of craftsmanship."[23] The prologue of *The Naked City* reawakens the exploratory spirit of cinema formed in such pioneering efforts as *L'arrivé d'un train en gare* and *La Sortie des ouvriers de l'usine Lumière* (both les frères Lumière, 1895).

The prologue begins with an assemblage of semi-documentary footage showing men, women and machines at work during a graveyard shift. The diegesis starts within this "city symphony" hodgepodge. Figure #4, another publicity still, is very close in graphic design to a shot that occurs within the prologue. With this shot, the fiction blends into the documentary imagery. One can discern the beaming face of Dr. Stoneman, a key character in the story, looking over the shoulder of a woman playing cards. Dr. Stoneman operates a respectable medical practice, but secretively carries on an affair with a young model named Jean Dexter. He provides her with strategic contacts in high society which she uses to steal fashionable jewelry. A friend, Frank Niles (Howard Duff), is in cahoots with her. An alcoholic and an ex-professional wrestler perform the actual thefts. Things go wrong when the two "workers" demand a larger portion of the take. Figure 4's composition enables Peter Biskind to remark that in *The Naked City*, "the class criticism is biting. Rich folk are all neurotic or grasping. . . ."[24] In this shot, following a spate of shots showing the less privileged at work, the well-to-do appear in a frivolous light.

In *The Naked City*, the average New Yorker leads a more serious and structured life. *The Sun* noted how the film

Figure 4. The rich at play.

began "with a series of impressions of New York late at night, of New York early in the morning, of New York as millions set off for work."[25] *Parade Magazine* observed how "hundreds of New Yorkers appear as extras."[26] Another reviewer deemed *The Naked City* "no ordinary movie" because of the role played by "the city itself and its people (and I mean real people, not actors)."[27] Many of the workers who appear in the opening sequence were indeed professional actors and actresses. But they did little else besides pose for the camera. However, during the final chase across the Williamsburg Bridge, ordinary mothers with their strollers are clearly visible along the edges of the frame. They seem fascinated by the way Don Taylor is sprinting by them. According to *The Daily Worker*, "There are a lot of faces in it [*The Naked City*] that are not Hollywood's."[28] All this occurred more than ten years before Jean-Luc Godard dramatized the sharp division between film and reality in the Paris streets of *Breathless* (1959).

American Cinematographer noted how of the twenty-four major roles in the film, "twenty parts were filled by New York radio and stage actors, most of whom were making their first screen appearances."[29] In *The Naked City* there were only four actors who had substantial experience acting in films. Among these, Barry Fitzgerald had considerable box-office appeal. He was paid $100,000 for both his performance and his mere presence, which gave the film a competitive edge in the fickle marketplace.[30] Hellinger wanted to advertise the fact that Howard Duff was the voice of Sam Spade on the radio. Referring to Duff as Spade, he planned to "personally introduce Sam Spade to every syndicated columnist in New York."[31] *Movie Life* presented a spread of photographs depicting Duff and Dorothy Hart gallivanting about inside a magic shop on Hollywood Boulevard. Captions referred to Duff as "Detective Sam Spade" and identified the beautiful Dorothy Hart as a "former cover girl."[32] *Motion Picture Magazine* told how Duff showed "promise of becoming a real screen personality." The same fan magazine predicted that Don Taylor, as Inspector Halloran, might "well be the next idol of the teen-agers and the bobby-sox crowd."[33] A sneak preview was held on December 16, 1947 at the West Coast's Loyola Theatre. In a popularity poll, Don Taylor finished second to Barry Fitzgerald. *Screen Romances* planned to write an editorial on Taylor in light of the possibility that he would become a new national heartthrob.

Hellinger wanted Mayor William O'Dwyer and Police Commissioner, Arthur Wallander, to appear in the film talking with "actual City hall reporters." But he failed to convince them that their presence could have provided a much needed sense of reality. This sense of reality, in turn, "humanizes . . . and supplies a warmth that no actor in make-up could ever achieve."[34] Foster Hirsch notes how, "following the war, *noir* absorbed some of the concerns of Italian Neo-Realism."[35] Similarly, Paul Jensen states that, like neorealism, "American films also felt an impulse toward a greater sense of reality."[36] According to Garbicz and Klinowski, "the trend that was inspired by the producer, de Rochemont, found especially in *The Naked City* many points of contact with the imagery of the Italian Neorealists."[37] The employment of non-actors and actors without professional film-acting experience is one of several parallel traits shared by Neorealism and semi-documentaries like *The Naked City*. But the use of at least one major star, a photogenic model, and publicity is something that semi-documentaries had in common with the most commercial Hollywood ventures. Thus, *The Naked City* had new ideas, even revolutionary ones, but never a full commitment to them. That sort of radical, no-holds-barred commitment was no doubt impossible. According to Borde and Chaumeton, "le documentaire américain est en réalité un documentaire à la gloire de la police."[38] In addition to *The Naked City*, Borde and Chaumeton identify a number of semi-documentaries involving the police in key and heroic roles. Among them are *Kiss of Death* (Henry Hathaway, 1947), *Crossfire* (Edward Dmytryk, 1947), *He Walked By Night* (Alfred Werker, 1948), *Street With No Name* (William Keighley, 1948), *Port of New York* (Laslo Benedek, 1949), *Where the Sidewalk Ends* (Otto Preminger, 1950), *Panic in the Streets* (Elia Kazan, 1950), *The Enforcer* (Bretaigne Windust, 1950), and *The Big Heat* (Fritz Lang, 1952).[39] All are tributes to the authorities as well as to the system they uphold. Also, like the gangster film, the semi-documentary *film noir* is itself a short-lived cycle stretching only from the late-1940s to the early 1950s. Just as gangster films never achieved an accurate depiction of crime, semi-documentaries never departed from gilded portrayals of police departments in major cities.

The conservative outlook these films brandished was nourished by a certain mythologizing. For example, the police never solved the Dot King Case, upon which *The Naked City* was based. As Wald found out from his research, police detectives stopped the investigation prematurely because it involved a wealthy "Sugar-Daddy," whose name was not disclosed. This real-life Dr. Stoneman wanted his name kept out of the newspapers. Wald used the police as well as "the system" as a sort of *deus ex machina.* To bring about a plausible resolution, Wald grafted onto his use of the Dot King Case the mitigated circumstances of another case having to do with a bisexual man, who became the model upon which the Frank Niles character was based.[40]

The bottom line throughout the ordeal of bringing *The Naked City* to the screen was commercial. No one entertained lofty notions about the medium's ability to edify. Everyone involved in this project wanted to create a moneymaker. But the commercialism that informed the creators of *The Naked City* was not the crass variety. In fact, within the broad category of commerce in moviemaking there is a great deal of leeway. The genius of this film has to do with the way in which it satisfies the requirements of general, run-of-the-mill escapism while providing a document of the past, a glimpse of its way of living and thinking. *The Naked City* is not a great film, but it is a film that is more *responsible* than most. It is more honest, more true-to-life, more contemporary, if only because it is less false, less sensational, and less of a time-machine to the past or the future—another form of escapism. Its worthiness for the purpose of study has to do with the way that it set high standards of realism for itself. As Bazin puts it, what is important is "the representation of reality at the expense of dramatic structures"—not the other way around.[41]

The exhibition of the film began with fanfare that was typical for its day. In a preview at the Capitol Theatre, it was preceded by a two-hour-long stage show emceed by Milton Berle.[42] The following day, the film's first run on the East Coast officially commenced at nine o'clock in the morning with a number of musical entertainers: Tex Beneke and his orchestra, Garry Stevens, the Moonlight Serenaders, Pete Candoli, and Jack Sperling. An advertisement in *The New York Herald Tribune* billed the film as "The Biggest Combination Show in the History of the Capitol."[43] *The New York World Telegram* looked forward to a visit on stage before the screening by "Dean Martin and Jerry Lewis, Broadway's Newest Comedy Sensations."[44]

The film or "Combination Show" grossed a good $145,000 during its first weekend in New York City.[45]

As it turned out, *The Naked City* was more than a local phenomenon with limited appeal. It was also successful in every major city across the United States. The five cities with the most movie theaters were: New York City (598), Chicago (302), Los Angeles (217), Philadelphia (201), and Detroit (167).[46] Other cities had far fewer theaters and were also unable to charge as much. Nevertheless, the film did relatively good business wherever it played—in terms of 1948 dollars. In a single week, the film grossed $64,000 in Los Angeles,[47] $33,000 in San Francisco,[48] $40,000 in Philadelphia, $19,000 in Pittsburgh,[49] $17,000 in Louisville,[50] $22,500 in Buffalo,[51] $41,000 in Boston, and $15,000 in Seattle.[52] In March of 1948 *Variety's* National Box Office Survey rated *The Naked City* second only to *Gentleman's Agreement* (Elia Kazan, 1947), which had just won the Academy Award for Best Picture.[53] In its April survey, *Variety* designated *The Naked City* the most popular film. Toward the end of the month, it still commanded a lead, finally falling behind *I Remember Mama* (George Stevens, 1948) in popularity. Universal-International bought two full pages of space in *Variety* to circulate a note of gratitude to the manager of the Capitol Theatre "and his efficient staff whose fine theatre operation made the huge crowds comfortable." The same advertisement correctly predicted that "every city will love the great picture about the world's greatest city!"[54]

But a sour epilogue appends this whole story of artistic struggle or creative valor. Universal very nearly shelved the film. At first the front office executives were emphatic, insisting "that there could be no question of the film being released." The film was summarily dismissed as a "travelogue."[55] It was sent into distribution only after it had been savagely mutilated so as to suppress Dassin's use of the camera to express social commentary. All the same, enough was salvaged to make the film an Academy Award winner for both cinematography and editing. Although *The Naked City* has not dated well and is rarely shown, the idea of using cinema not just to entertain but to heighten awareness remains vibrant.

CAMERA

Whereas Edeson employed a wide-angle lens to make the best possible use of sets built in cramped spaces, Daniels did not have to resort to any such trickery. With five boroughs and an infinite variety of camera set-ups to choose from, there was no point in trying to stretch space. Because of the inclusion of some one hundred and seven locations, *The Naked City* has been called "the crowning work of the American police documentary school."[56] Daniels' cinematography, which won an Academy Award, made an honest man out of Hellinger, who remarks, "This is the city as it is." In *The Maltese Falcon*, night scenes were shot during banking hours. In *The Naked City*, night scenes were shot night for night. Moreover, when the filmmakers went somewhere to shoot, they resisted the temptation to distort, camouflage, or manipulate. As Hellinger phrases it, they shot "the buildings in their naked stone, the people without makeup."

The film commences with a moving camera, night-for-night, aerial shot of Battery Park. The remainder of Manhattan is stretched out in the hazy distance, not unlike "a patient etherised on a table."[57] The prologue continues with a succession of additional, complementary shots of rooftops, a General Motors billboard, a Chevrolet poster, and an American Airlines airplane in flight. Exploratory shots such as these comprise a leitmotif, insofar as they crop up again and again throughout the film. Furthermore, they are not haphazardly strewn together. One reviewer observed how "wherever the script gives the scenic men a chance they have chosen backdrops which mean a great deal to New Yorkers who know and love their city. The East River bridges, the lower East Side, the Roosevelt ambulance, the squares and the circles, the subway and the El, the streets and the people on them, the mean buildings and the great ranges of skyscrapers, the buildings at night with a million lights and the buildings solid in daytime."[58]

Speaking of *The Image of the City in Modern Literature,* Burton Pike mentions that "when a writer looks at the city from above, he is placing himself (or his narrator) and the reader in an attitude of contemplation rather than involvement."[59] Similarly, the same state of release is achieved cinematically with panoramic, high-angle shooting. Periodically, scenic master shots momentarily distract attention away from the narrative and at the same time cement it to the real setting onto which it is projected. The concrete jungle functions as a movie set, but also "plays itself," retaining its own spatial integrity, intricate physical characteristics, and impersonal indifference. When the angle of vision is lowered, the spectator is invited to lose his or her meditative detachment. To look at the city "from street level is to experience it actively. Here one finds oneself in a labyrinth."[60] By means of camera positioning, *The Naked City* fluctuates in terms of angles of perception from high to low, reflection to absorption.

Although there was not much difficulty—barring inclement weather—shooting passive things of stone and mortar, the use of non-actors created serious problems. Since people tend to pose for the camera, the capture on film of everyday existence can be deceptively cumbersome. Some shooting had to be done surreptitiously. The camera crew was therefore equipped with "a panel truck whose sides were actually two-way transparent mirrors."[61]

The buildings and streets may have been there for the taking, but the people and their lives were not. Cat and mouse games began, with filmmakers and people alternating roles. The lack of mutuality became glaringly apparent as either the people interfered with the shooting or the filmmakers became a nuisance to the community. At the Center Street Police Station, the camera crew was told "to stop and come back." Before departing, they managed to secure exteriors. Later, at the Rialto Dance Hall on 43rd Street and 7th Avenue, crowds of curious onlookers prevented the crew from getting anything on film. They

90 Autopsy

had waited in vain until after midnight. Then, after two more frustrating hours, they "called it off due to people standing around on sidewalk staring."[62] The crew was forced under the circumstances to negotiate with the environment. They could not dominate it. But, on the other hand, it could not totally discourage them. The end result is full of inadvertent gains and mitigated losses. *American Cinematographer* noted that "several buildings of the city were photographed for the last time, having since been demolished to make room for the United Nations Buildings."[63] Interiors were shot in the Roxy Theatre,[64] in the offices of the Mirror Newspapers (replete with a row of linotype operators)[65] and Stillman's Gym,[66] none of which any longer exists. Similarly, the elevated Third Avenue El—now a subterranean subway line— formed the backdrop to an important chase sequence, prefiguring the final one on the Williamsburg Bridge.[67] This scene, during which the killer, Garza, demonstrates his superior physical agility, took place night-for-night at the 59th Street and 3rd Avenue Station. An earlier scene, introducing Dorothy Hart as Jean Dexter's friend Ruth Morrison, took place on 57th Street inside the Livingstons's Dress Shop, which also no longer exists.[68]

In an attempt to be as comprehensive as possible about a sprawling city with widely divergent characteristics, the filmmakers achieved a certain ubiquity. Ruth Morrison's giggly mother, Mrs. Hylton, is shown inside what was Toots Shor's apartment on Park Avenue.[69] Dr. Stoneman's office was situated in the Squibb Building on 5th Avenue. Despite a number of interiors shot at Universal Studios, production notes stress the fact that the crew filmed in an "actual office suite."[70] At a pier off 18th Street near Avenue C, local boys diving into the East River discover the corpse of Garza's partner, Backalis. Frank Niles is found unconscious in his apartment on 46th Street and East River Drive.[71] At the end of Jay Street, a dead end in Brooklyn, Lt. Muldoon talks heart-to-heart with Jean Dexter's parents.[72] Lt. Muldoon lives in an apartment located on West 15th Street[73] and Garza hides in his apartment on Houston Street.[74] There are numerous other sites, most of which appear just once. One can readily imagine the trouble the location crew encountered in having to travel, get things set up, and haul everything away time after time. Among the locations that were filmed but later discarded were the house of the murder victim's parents on 9th Avenue in Astoria[75] and the Stoneman residence on Central Park West.[76]

Location work made filmmakers aware that they were part of the world, subject to its unpredictability, and not an elite corp of sacristans ensconced within the sanctuaries of Hollywood studios. They were compelled to assume some of the hardships and burdens of everyday life. For example, the crew lost two full hours of precious daylight one afternoon. An assistant director mistakenly led them to the top of the Rockefeller Building while their heavy equipment was delivered to Radio City Musical Hall.[77] Lighting concerns kept the crew moving from one site to another before they succeeded in getting the exterior of a church.[78] Another time, they went to a hospital but failed to obtain the shot they wanted because an ambulance was not available.[79] Trying to get a falling camera shot during the final chase scene at the Williamsburg Bridge, the camera smashed against the side of the bridge.[80] Wind, haze, and rain foiled numerous attempts to shoot an exterior of a newsstand on 23rd Street and Broadway.[81]

The weather was so recalcitrant that Dassin could not get the final sequence in the can before leaving New York City. His assistants, Jack Hively (direction) and William Miller (camera), remained behind to await a break in the stubborn haziness. Before going to Los Angeles to shoot interiors, Dassin managed to get a down-angle shot of Lt. Muldoon at the bridge. This particular angle of vision allowed the crew to employ booster lights.[82] The next day, overcast skies prevented any work from getting done even with the aid of powerful lights such as these.[83]

Actors and actresses who were still needed went to Universal Studios in California. Among the cast, only Ted de Corsia, as Garza, and Kermit Kegley, as Lt. Qualen, remained in the East. Both accepted cuts in wages of fifty percent. De Corsia's weekly salary of $1,250 was reduced to $625[84] and Kegley's salary of $500 per week was halved to $250.[85] The shooting continued into September. Not only did the filmmakers have to contend with the urban whirlpool of humanity, they also had to deal with nature. In both areas, studio filmmakers had little or no experience.

Despite the delays, the end seems to have justified the means, including the additional expense. Of all the locations, exceeding one hundred in number, the Williamsburg Bridge is the most memorable. The reviewer for *The Denver Post* referred to "a terrific climax on the Washington Bridge."[86] He simply was not familiar with the names of several bridges linking Manhattan to New Jersey and the other boroughs. The spectators who attended the Los Angeles preview, held just three days before Hellinger's death on December 21, also took special notice of this scene.[87]

While waiting for enough sun to film this awesome sequence, the crew went about town collecting an eclectic assortment of exteriors. These included The Daily News Building, then located on East 18th Street and 4th Avenue; the Empire State Building; a fire escape on Avenue B; the U.S.S. America, docked at Pier 62, North River; various parts of the Lower East Side; and the sun setting over New Jersey, shot from across the Hudson River on Riverside Drive.[88]

Kegley, portraying one of the cops in pursuit of Garza on the Williamsburg Bridge, left after the first week in September. De Corsia remained until the end of the month, at which time Dassin and Daniels returned to New York City. In October, the crew took exteriors of the Elizabeth Police Station for *A Double Life* (George Cukor, 1947).[89] Daniels supervised his crew in getting skyline shots taken from the air.[90]

Dassin was doggedly determined to film Garza trapped on top of the bridge despite the fact that according to the Continuity Breakdown with which he was working, Garza "falls on the third rail."[91] The change indicates that Dassin allowed a location to sway his artistic vision in favor of an element that was not established in the script. There was a

whole new world outside the studio, which exerted its
presence in unpredictable manners. Essentially, the environment became a co-author. The depiction of Garza's
mortal predicament on top of the Williamsburg Bridge is a
kind of visual coup. It is also as existential as it is
sensational. A sweeping panoramic shot of the city shows
in an instant its vast indifference and distance from human
concerns, even from those that are urgent matters of life
and death. Technically, this sequence made conspicuous
the kind of resonance and depth of location cinematography unavailable in the studio. There are countless other
examples of *film noir* characters lost in the general swirl of
city life. They are threatened not so much by internal
flaws, complemented by an unjust society, as by an
impending sense of doom that is an integral part of the
cold environment. There are eight million dark corners in
The Naked City.

The cinematography makes ample use of wide-angle
strategies to give the frame a proportional, straightforward
look without distortions or effects. Despite a myriad of
settings in *The Naked City*, Barry Salt has made the
observation that "the approach is the same as regards the
types of lights used and the angles from which they were
applied."[92] *American Cinematographer* was surprised by
Daniels' "complete about-face from the softly-lighted,
glossily diffused type of approach he used to employ as
Garbo's special cameraman."[93] Daniels was known for his
accentuation of glamor in such Garbo vehicles as *Flesh and
the Devil* (Clarence Brown, 1927), *Anna Christie* (Clarence
Brown, 1930), *Grand Hotel* (Edmund Goulding, 1932),
Queen Christina (Rouben Mamoulian, 1933), *Anna Karenina*
(Clarence Brown, 1935), *Camille* (George Cukor, 1936), and
Ninotchka (Ernst Lubitsch, 1939).

This gauzy, feminine cinematography amounted to a
complete reversal from the masculine orientation received
in his earlier association with Erich von Stroheim. Daniels
never forgot the lessons he learned from his acquaintance
with the eccentric master of the silent era. Once he had to
descend thousands of feet into a Northern California
goldmine to get shots for Stroheim's masterpiece, *Greed*

(1925). A few feet would have sufficed to achieve the same effect, but Stroheim strove to avoid "weak," if logical, compromises. Although Stroheim's determination to deal with nature beyond the necessities of filmmaking practice was unbusinesslike, it was bold and creative. According to André Bazin, Stroheim played a major role in the evolution of cinematic realism. Bazin liked his rejection of "photographic expressionism and the tricks of montage." In his films, "reality lays itself bare like a suspect confessing under the relentless examination of the commissioner of police."[94] The Naked City production was fortunate to have Daniels behind the camera. He was no stranger to productions that aspired to levels of realism in excess of the industry's minimal standards. For Stroheim, he shot Blind Husbands (1919), The Devil's Passkey (1920), Foolish Wives (1922), and Merry-Go-Round (1923). Furthermore, according to Daniels, for Rasputin and the Empress (Richard Boleslawski, 1933) he "had to reconstruct the time as though it were a newsreel."[95]

The Academy conferred on Daniels its award for Best Cinematography, confirming the mainstream's recognition of a trend in filmmaking that favored "down-beat subject matter" and "an increase in the amount of location filming."[96] But the semi-documentary, even in its most ascendent years, never overshadowed rival trends that relied on cinematic instruments of deception. This is reflected in the Scientific or Technical Academy Awards of 1948. Paramount was awarded for its development of light-weight plaster process for set construction. RKO was similarly honored for the perfection of a method to simulate snowfalls on sets.[97]

According to Bazin, cinema "owes virtually nothing to the scientific spirit." Instead, "cinema is an idealistic phenomenon."[98] Aesthetics predominate in the invention and improvement of technique. True enough, technological advances enabled Daniels to film outside the studio, but considered alone, these advances are insufficient to motivate a project as complex and innovative as The Naked City. Nevertheless, Bazin overestimated the willingness of either Hollywood or its massive audience to relinquish an attachment to "tinsel." Cinema has yet to prove itself "the asymptote of reality."[99]

WRITING

The story used in *The Naked City* was conceived by Malvin Wald. It is a fictional account of a homicide written for Mark Hellinger, gauged to gain his approval, without which the film would not have been possible. Neither Wald nor Hellinger was as focused ideologically as were Jules Dassin and Albert Maltz. All the same, they were men of the times, and creative men and women, especially of the 1930s and 1940s, were repeatedly exposed to idealistic left wing rhetoric. The use of documentaries as an alternative filmmaking practice was, essentially, a key product of the Left. While Hellinger and Wald were fortunate enough to escape the troubles that effectively terminated the Hollywood careers of both Dassin and Maltz, they could not escape the times. In some sense, even if they did not involve themselves directly in left wing activity, they were nonetheless aware of the issues that were being espoused. Also, their partnership with Dassin and Maltz suggests a neutrality that was tolerant rather than hostile to the opposition.

According to Patrick Ogle, the "1930's saw the rise of the documentary film as an international movement." Distant rumblings of conflict in Europe and Asia, followed by mobilization, kept the movement alive. Not infrequently, documentary passages appeared in feature films during the 1940s and 1950s. Not surprisingly, many of these were combat films; many filmmakers served in the armed forces. Ogle points out that a sizable number of Hollywood "cinematographers spent the duration in military service filming real events with sixteen millimeter equipment."[100] It was in the First Motion Picture Unit of the Army Air Force that Malvin Wald learned the art of writing scripts for the creation of documentaries.

Documentaries were essential to the war effort. They

aided soldiers in the operation of sophisticated weaponry needed to fight the enemy. It was Wald's task to break the essential information down so that it could be grasped by ordinary, non-scientific minds. As screenwriter for *The Naked City*, Wald undertook the same role as middle-man, absorbing highly-classified data and disseminating it to a predominantly non-professional public. His purpose may have changed radically, from winning a war to entertaining, but the same methodology adequately served the needs of both. Moreover, both endeavors entailed a split-page format, allocating one side to visuals, the other to narration. Instead of intermingling plastic compositions and dialogue, parallel columns neatly matched words to the appropriate image.

Wald's original story was entitled "Homicide Squad Story." It was dated November 2, 1946, a couple of weeks after he went to New York City to research his novel idea. Unlike the film's final version, Wald originally situated Halloran in the night shift, noting that "most murders occur at night."[101] The murdered woman's body is found in a building on West 69th Street instead of West 83rd Street, her name is Jean Harmon instead of Jean Dexter, and her folks are from the Bronx, rather than elsewhere. But a far greater number of the film's details are already present in this embryonic treatment. These include the name of Dr. Stoneman found on a vial of sleeping pills at the scene of the crime, and the mysterious identity of the man (who turns out to be none other than the same Dr. Stoneman) whose expensive pajamas are found in a closet.

Although a fictitious creation, the story was based on facts derived from actual cases. They were fresh in Wald's mind when he devised a plot that would provide the basic structure for the film. Only a few days earlier he had been combing through files at the New York Police Department's Statistical and Criminal Identification Bureau. The story he came up with is plausible, incorporating a fair sampling of the data he collected from reading reports, visiting crime labs, and interviewing detectives. Ultimately, except for a majority of scenes set in daylight, to take advantage of the sun, the film makes few concessions to Hollywood expediency. The propensity to dramatize or sensationalize is greatly curtailed. Much of *The Naked City* is a painstaking exposition of crime detection, a narrative recitation of the findings of Wald's investigation.

Furthermore, Wald knew that Hellinger was critical of the minor inaccuracies of such 20th Century-Fox Productions as *The House on 92nd Street* and *The Dark Corner*, forerunners of *The Naked City*. *The Dark Corner* resolves on the discovery of a jacket that is sent to the cleaners. The jacket is finally retrieved after a furious single day's search. From New York City, where he was conducting his research, Wald explained to Hellinger: "You were certainly right when you said that the laundry episode in the *Dark Corner* was phoney because Lucille Ball and Mark Stevens tracked down an ink-stained jacket in one day." In a similar case "It took over 100 detectives in every precinct in all five boroughs days to track down the right store and even then the storekeepers weren't sure of the identity of the guilty men."[102] Later, Wald added that an officer working in the Technical Research Laboratory found Hellinger's production of *The Killers* (Robert Siodmak, 1946) "one hundred percent technically accurate."[103]

Among Wald's literary influences were Walt Whitman and Thomas Wolfe. Both were writers who felt a mystical bond with New York City. Both were well-acquainted with the city. And both seem also to have been intrigued by the juxtaposition of Manhattan and Brooklyn. Whitman poeticized "Crossing Brooklyn Ferry" and Wolfe commemorated his own nocturnal crossings between Brooklyn Heights and Manhattan in *You Can't Go Home Again* (1934). Other influences, such as John Steinbeck's *The Grapes of Wrath* (1939) and John Dos Passos's trilogy, *U.S.A.* (1937), both contained extensive journalistic interludes. Films like Roberto Rossellini's *Open City* (1945) and *The City* (Ralph Steiner and Willard Van Dyke, 1939), a silent documentary with voice-over narration, were also influential. *Open City* is still a highly regarded film. Less known today, *The City* dealt with overcrowding, slums, and the general state of unhealthiness in urban areas. It was shown at the 1939 New York World's Fair, and has been summarized by Erik Barnouw as "an exposition of the urban crisis."[104] Hellinger liked Wald's idea from the start but was not sold on it. Dassin's enthusiasm for the project and the promise of bringing Albert Maltz's talents to it sweetened the pot. Using his own private assets as collateral, Hellinger took out a risky loan from the "movie bank," The Bank of America. The budget of approximately one and a quarter million dollars was a hefty sum for 1947, negating the notion that location shooting in The Naked City was the outcome of the rising costs of set construction.[105] Despite the success of other semi-documentaries, the idea of the film was still revolutionary in concept and still precarious in terms of box-office draw. It took a great deal of courage for Hellinger to make the decision to go ahead with it. Furthermore, after he registered the working title, "Homicide," with the Johnston Office, Hellinger learned that Jack L. Warner was fishing around for a comparable and competitive story to be filmed on location in New York City. He nonetheless remained firm and his pugnacity intimidated Warner, who backed down and switched the location of the film he envisioned to Los Angeles.[106]

Ordinarily, Hellinger contributed to the writing phase of production even though he always hired competent, trustworthy writers. At the time, he was very ill, having never in his lifetime been considered either young or healthy. He was also reluctant to tamper with a script with a documentary slant. Conscious of his own lack of expertise, he did not want to burden Wald with an unenlightened collaboration. Maltz's rewrite also proceeded without interference. In fact, for the film, Hellinger spoke most of Maltz's narration verbatim. He was able to grant both his writers artistic license because he shared with them a certain aesthetic bond. Like Wald, Hellinger served in World War II as a writer. He had been a war correspondent in the South Pacific and India. Earlier, one of his stories was used as the basis for a post-World War I subject, The Roaring Twenties (Raoul Walsh, 1939). It contained documentary-like passages at key intervals to illustrate relevent events in American history. Earlier still, he had taken a fancy to *Black Legion* (Archie Mayo, 1936), a film that was taken from a series of newspaper articles. These exposed the uprising of a neo-fascist organization used to infiltrate a working class section of Michigan. This was also the theme of Albert Maltz's novel, *The Underground Stream* (1940). Hellinger called *Black Legion* "a great film" and noted especially how "there are no stars," despite the presence of Humphrey Bogart and Ann Sheridan.[107]

According to Wald, the screenwriter builds a film's foundation and the director then decorates it. *The Naked City* was almost certainly designed as a house for Hellinger to dwell in. For this reason, Bosley Crowther called *The Naked City* "a virtual Hellinger column on film."[108] In his column, Hellinger wrote compassionately about a motley collection of New Yorkers including mobsters, tailors, bus boys, and mailmen. Like Damon Runyon's stories, Hellinger's were not wholly fictional. Like O. Henry, he liked them to end with an unexpected twist.

The character of Garza seems most to reflect Hellinger's literary influence. He is the non-drinking, non-smoking epitome of self-control and self-discipline—until his final few moments. Once he is discovered he becomes frantic. In a frenetic attempt to escape, he races through a graveyard, scales backyard walls, sprints down alleys, and rushes headlong through crowds. In a panic, he shoots a seeing-eye dog that catches his sleeve. This sudden lack of the mental acumen he had previously displayed reveals his whereabouts. Bleeding profusely, he appears totally helpless and confused seconds before his death. He is not only the culprit, but also a victim—if only of circumstances. According to one reviewer, "In *Naked City* even a cold blooded killer has an extenuating story to him when you consider: he once used to be an acrobat, and they killed vaudeville, and wrestling's uncertain. And yet, always hoping, he keeps in condition, doing an odd job of murder now and then only to spell it out while waiting for the work he enjoys, poor chap."[109]

Garza was a major part of Wald's invention of a solution

needed to account for the mystery of the Dot King slaying, upon which—as has already been mentioned—the film is based. The idea of a jewel-theft ring that deteriorates into a pair of murders jells with what Wald already knew about life in the big city and learned from his research. It is designed not to evoke wonder, like the story of *The Maltese Falcon*, but to show the way crooks operate and cops track them down. For instance, Garza lives on the Lower East Side because it had a reputation—still applicable—for hostility to the authorities. In Wald's original story and subsequent screenplays, Garza lives close to the Williamsburg Bridge in order to facilitate his attempted flight. He lives in the Lower East Side because his neighbors are the least likely in the city to cooperate with the police. Police detectives had told Wald that the Lower East Side looked unfavorably upon cops.

Maltz could not have known it at the time, but he was about to be pursued across the political landscape and sentenced to prison as though a criminal, not unlike Garza. When hired to put the finishing touches on Wald's screenplay, he was already fast approaching the crossroads of his career and life. For years he had been second only to Clifford Odets as America's foremost political writer. Now both the unraveled Left and the constricted Right attacked him for separate reasons. Communist Party affiliates questioned his loyalty. Right–wingers questioned his membership in a radical organization.

Maltz joined the Party in the mid-1930s. His writing reflects a sincere interest in the plight of minorities and others excluded from privilege whom he thought the capitalist system ignored. He himself came from a much higher economic stratum. But he was always willing to lend a helping hand to those less fortunate. Driving along the highways of California not long before starting work on *The Naked City*, Maltz stopped for an old, forlorn hitchhiker. The arthritic itinerant worker he happened to pick up served as a model character for *The Journey of Simon McKeever* (1949). Like Wald, Maltz liked to cut his fiction out of the cloth of reality. When he took on the assignment of rewriting the script for *The Naked City*, he warned against the use of a prologue that would involve "gunfire, racing autos, sirens and Barry Fitzgerald in the clutches of a gang." He urged that the "authenticity of the commentary" should not be negated by the "trickiness of the plot." To Maltz, "absolute reality is the slide rule." His chief personal objective in working on *The Naked City* was to make a "real drama" with "real people and real effects." He stressed the need to find places within the film for the "utterly real faces—of working women who look like working women, of men awakening in the morning who look as men do."[110]

Maltz's alignment with the downtrodden is also expressed in a short film he scripted called *The House I Live In* (Mervyn LeRoy, 1945). In his own words, this winner of a Special Academy Award was "a cooperative, non-profit effort to further racial tolerance in the U.S."[111] Made in a patriotic spirit at RKO Studios in conjunction with the United States Government, it starred Frank Sinatra. Sinatra sings the title song and lectures a group of children on the subject of tolerance. Throughout his life and career, Maltz sought to reach out to oppressed peoples and build a bridge of sympathy in both words and endeavor.

About ten years before, he co-edited a short-lived journal entitled *Equality*. Its purpose was "to counteract the anti-Semitic sermonizing of Father Coughlin" and all other forms of bigotry.[112] In this conflict, Maltz appealed to the reader's sense of reality. To be effective, racism needed to contravene even common sense. To Maltz, realism and moralism are almost interchangeable. In an editorial review of *Gone With the Wind* (Victor Fleming, 1939), Maltz called the glorification of racist Southerners "vicious reactionary nonsense." He decried Hollywood's ability to replicate trivial period minutiae while undermining the historical issues which are most crucial to the present. To Maltz, *Gone With the Wind* was pettiness on a grand scale. He hated the film, especially its depiction of the burning of Atlanta as "a locust plague of brutes trampling on the fair South." He disliked the way it totally ignored the arrogant social matrix that gave birth to the institution of slavery. Urging his readers to "boycott" the film, he wrote: "We may be sure that every last detail of the costumes of the period was investigated, checked and re-checked. There are no errors there. It is merely history that Hollywood has not bothered to verify."[113] Maltz opposed Hollywood's flagrantly self-serving use of history. He knew that the film industry denatured current events, too.

For some time, Maltz had wanted to see the film industry usher in some healthy changes. He was familiar with the oppressiveness of the creative climate in which films were conceived. No matter what the level of artistry, "the final product of any studio, the good and the bad war films, musicals, mysteries, reflect in considerable measure the social responsibility (or lack of it), the understanding, intelligence and aesthetic taste of the top executives in production control."[114] Maltz hoped that at least some of Hollywood's films would become as sophisticated as foreign films. He seems to have had some familiarity with foreign cinemas. For example, he revered a film from the Soviet Union called *The Great Turning Point* (Friedrich Ermler, 1946). According to Jay Leyda, this war film strove for a superior level of accuracy. Ermler and his co-scenarist, Boris Chirskov, went to the front as part of their preparation for production. While they were there, they decided to scrap their original script in order to write one that took greater account of their first-hand observations. As a result, "of all films to make drama out of military strategy, including its successors, Ermler's film has the most validity as cinema and, perhaps, as life, too."[115]

In a speech delivered to a symposium in Los Angeles in January 1947, a few months before beginning work on *The Naked City*, Maltz spoke about cinema's "aesthetic responsibility." Citing *The Confessions of a Nazi Spy* and *The House on 92nd Street*, Maltz declared that it was wrong "to maintain that the American film industry has produced no films that dramatize aspects of national crises rather than individual emotional crises."[116] *The House on 92nd Street* was influential to others as well. According to Leo Rosten, who had this film in mind as a model when he wrote the script for *Walk East on Beacon Street* (Alfred L. Werker, 1952), it "was one of the pictures that made quite a dent. It was done in documentary form. It was filmed with the F.B.I. people in many cases, and it carried the ring of great authenticity."[117]

DIRECTION

Some reviewers compared *The Naked City* to Hitchcock films. Dassin may even have unconsciously striven to emulate the master of suspense. While apprenticed to RKO as an assistant director, Dassin observed Hitchcock direct *Mr. and Mrs. Smith* (1941). But Dassin could never have sought seriously to rival Hitchcock's perfection and rigid lack of departure from a carefully wrought storyboard. Quite the contrary; Dassin encouraged bursts of spontaneity. In an interview with *Films and Filming*, he maintained that there was "very little pre-planning in my films. There's a lot of improvisation. If I pre-plan, it's just in terms of the general ambiance. I'm one of those unfortunates who can't really decide until I have the actors there before me."[118] Only on rainy days, or days during which the equipment broke down, did rehearsals take place.

Hitchcock experimented with locations very early in terms of the history of American cinema when he decided to set *A Shadow of a Doubt* (1943) in Santa Rosa, California. His most formidable contribution to the semi-documentary craze did not occur until *The Wrong Man* (1957). Even Hitchcock could not have provided Dassin with a precedent for the use of such a superabundance of locations as are evident in *The Naked City*. Dassin was one of the first American directors to have the courage to experiment with locations on a full scale. His tendency to improvise must have proved useful enough in adapting to filmmaking situations that were not nearly as predictable as those obtaining in a studio. The interviewer for *Films and Filming* explained that Dassin's heightened realism "was modified by the locations themselves, and the concomitant naturalism of the photography."[119] Instead of confining himself to fewer locations, Dassin never stopped scouting on Sundays and during rainfalls for additional backdrops. Whereas inside a studio, various street settings can take on a similar look and feel, real streets tend to be more distinctive. The selection of a certain alley or intersection in preference to another could make a tangible difference. The change to locations from studio facsimiles entailed an ancillary change in the fundamental material of filmmaking. The raw substance put before the camera lens went from artificial to natural. This shift resulted in less directorial control, which irked Dassin. Years later, after his youthful intoxication wore off, he complained about feeling that he had "to shoot inside real cafes or real skyscrapers. All that did was to limit the movements of the camera and, consequently, the staging of the scene." What initially motivated involvement in the film later proved to be a millstone. Locations also hampered actors, who "were uncomfortable through lack of space."[120] There is indeed a perfunctory quality to the *mise-en-scène* of many sequences. Their *raisons d'être* seem all too obvious in the way they highlight this or that particular view of the city.

On the other hand, some shots are rather elaborately staged, photographed and choreographed. Figure #5 shows an exterior from the film of the Chelsea Police Station on West 20th Street. Frank Niles exits the building after fielding Lt. Muldoon's questions. The camera is positioned across the street and off to one side of the entrance. A squad car is parked on the street in front. In the background, adjacent to the right of the station, one sees a number of residential buildings, their windows, and fire escapes. Two uniformed policemen linger in the gaping shadow of a doorway while passersby head either east or west along the sidewalks. Appearing in the foreground is an ice-cream vendor surrounded by four young customers. There is a documentary element to this arrangement despite the fact that all five of the aforementioned participants were hired and directed by Dassin.

The broad-shouldered man standing next to a fire hydrant with his back turned to the camera is Garza. He is nonchalantly munching on an ice-cream bar while monitoring Niles's movements. A transcription of continuity and dialogue explains: "Frank exits past camera as two cops in plainclothes come out of station and follow Frank—two cops exit past camera—Garza turns and looks after them—comes toward camera—exits at opposite side—."[121]

Dassin makes use of the entire canvas. His direction indicates attention to details and to the incorporation of both the right and left sides of the frame. Comparable studio compositions could only have approached this complexity with their manicured versions of the same. The depth and plasticity resulting from the raw material of actual places and the daily activity of the people who live there are complemented by Hellinger's commentary: "It's been a long day, Niles, but now you can go wherever you

Figure 5. The Chelsea Police Station.

like. Except that two men will follow you day and
night—two men in three shifts. That makes six altogether—or is it seven?"

It took several months of uncertainty, accidents, confusion, frustration and tensions before Dassin arrived at a
final cut. What he found most satisfying about directing
The Naked City was the opportunity it afforded him to
weave social commentary into the film. Cinematographic
comments on inequality, impoverishment and injustice
were there virtually for the taking in such an economically
and demographically diverse city. Unfortunately, if Dassin's account of the film's genesis is to be believed, *The
Naked City* is but a hackneyed fraction of the original final
cut. To appease a critical front office, significant changes
were made before the film was released. The executives
who approved the butchery of Dassin's film remain
anonymous, but they were typical of their breed. After a
closed screening at Universal, Dassin was told "that there
could be no question of the film being released."[122] It was
denounced and thought better-off destroyed, with the
location work salvaged solely for the sake of stock footage.

According to John Francis Lane, who interviewed Dassin in the late 1950s, "things that weren't in the script
when it was approved in Hollywood got into the film as he
[Dassin] shot it in New York."[123] Dassin's *caméra-stylo*
failed to survive the gauntlet of Universal executives. The
latter were determined not to allow a film with its
imprimatur to emphasize disparities in wealth and privilege. Conservative-liberal relations here as well as in the
film industry at large reached an impasse. And conservatives were in no frame of mind to make a progressive leap
of faith.

According to Gordon Gow, *Brute Force,* Dassin's production immediately preceding *The Naked City,* "epito-
mized the liberal climate that prevailed in Hollywood."[124]
Other liberal-minded films included *The Treasure of the
Sierra Madre* (John Huston, 1948), which treated the subject
of greed; *Boomerang* (Elia Kazan, 1947), another semi-
documentary that dealt with the depiction of corruption in
local politics; *Crossfire* (Edward Dmytryk, 1947), which had

to do with anti-Semitism; and *The Snake Pit* (Anatole Litvak, 1948), which portrayed mental illness.

This permissiveness was not uniform throughout the industry and lacked the power to oppose a more effective and polished machinery of repression. *The Naked City* was ultimately crushed by those who feared HUAC, Mc-Carthy, and Louella Parsons. Internal dissension among those who were targets only made matters worse. Dassin was no longer a member of the American Communist Party, but his departure from that organization did not help mitigate the circumstances any. The Right was determined to purge the entertainment industry and Dassin's partnership with Maltz, who was still a member, only made matters worse. Dassin eventually became a friendly witness, a stance that infuriated Maltz, who defiantly pleaded the Fifth Amendment and as a result went to jail as one of the Hollywood Ten.

Although Maltz co-wrote rather than co-directed *The Naked City*, his writing best articulates the scope of direction that Dassin tried to give his penultimate American film. In his production notes, written to establish guidelines for filmmaking above and beyond the parameters of the screenplay, Maltz urged that "the CAMERA EYE, whenever possible, reflect the rich and infinite detail of the daily life in New York." A socially conscious perspective should be deployed to emphasize "the architectural beauty and squalor that exist side by side."[125] Maltz wanted the film's honesty to have a rawness about it, but without the kind of callousness that would shock censors, studio executives and ticket-buyers. The prologue should be smoothily crafted to blend in with the film's narrative rather than appear quaint, in the manner of some contrivance.

Also, the voice-overs should not have that gong-like quality of most voice-of-God narration. Maltz is responsible for humanizing Hellinger's comments. For instance, in the prologue, during a sequence showing downtown New York, Wald wrote: "This is New York—a city of steel and stone—of building and pavements."[126] Maltz underscored the desolation of a deserted Wall Street by having Hellin-

ger say that there were "no bulls" and "no bears." Maltz
also humanized Hellinger's representation of the voices of
the people. For instance, Wald's screenplay pictures a disc
jockey playing "a hot jive recording," sans narration.
Maltz added a voice for the jockey, who says, "You put on
a record . . . You take it off . . . you put on another . . . Does
anyone beside my wife listen to this program?" Wald's
linotypist slaves silently amid "the click of the linotype
keys." Maltz's linotypist, who works alone, absorbed by
an exhausting interaction with machinery, muses: "It's
wonderful working on a newspaper . . . you meet such
interesting people." A woman cleaning floors is presented
along with "the whir of the vacuum cleaner." Maltz
penetrates her mind; she is plaintively thinking: "Sometimes I think this world is made up of nothing but dirty
feet."[127] In general, Maltz lightened Wald's script, some of
the passages of which were imbued with an intellectual
bias. For example, when a detective conducts a search of
Niles's office, according to Wald's original screenplay, he
finds a book entitled "The Philosophy of Nietzsche."[128]

Everything should be simple and straightforward, including the story. Maltz tried to blend in a lot of the cynical
repartee and homespun sarcasm that are an integral part of
New York. Like Wald, Maltz thought nothing should be
invented that is blatantly at odds with the way the city
really is or how its police department functions. His model
was *Brief Encounter* (David Lean, 1945), which exhibited the
sort of balance, intelligence and "dramatic handling"[129]
that *The Naked City* was to emulate.

Brief Encounter, a romantic story, was saturated with
Rachmaninoff's 2nd piano concerto. Maltz advocated a
different aural approach that would not obliterate the
sound of real noises with sentimental movie music. He
wanted the spectator to hear "the lapping of water when
Backalis is pushed off the dock by Garza." The film
indicates that Dassin accepted Maltz's advice, as he also
did by allocating space on the soundtrack to "the pound-
ing of feet on a fire-escape when Halloran chases Garza
from Niles' apartment." Dassin probably would not have
interfered with the idea of the soundtrack making conspic-

uous "the breathing of Stoneman before he commits suicide,"[130] had this act of self-destruction not been censored as an undesirable evasion of justice. Hellinger liked Maltz's way of phrasing his lines. He refers to the Jean Dexter murder case as "the marmalade on ten thousand pieces of toast." As Halloran rides a subway in Queens, Hellinger remarks, "In the newspapers there's a new murder story. It's hit the headlines—full lay-out of pictures on page three . . . Don't bite your nails, honey. Very few stenographers are murdered." Wald's version is more impersonal: "In the evening rush hour, the latest news sharpens the city's appetite . . . The people now know about Jean Dexter's jewelry . . . And call her the Diamond Girl . . . And they also know about Lt. Mulvey [changed to Muldoon] . . . News stories have announced that he is in charge of the case."[131]

Similarly, in Wald's screenplay, Detective Constentino sips beer in a tavern while trying to overhear conversation that might yield a clue. According to the narrator, Constentino is one of several Homicide detectives "methodically working towards that break in the case."[132] Maltz's version, adopted by Dassin for the film, shows the detective bashfully entering a beauty parlor while Hellinger says: "How about a permanent? Or those eyebrows? Ever have them plucked?"

Dassin tried to execute Maltz's idea that *The Naked City* should be dedicated to making as much as possible a fair and accurate representation of New York City life. The film's denuded state of existence is due in part to the fact that Maltz "was under suspicion of being a communist." As has already been pointed out, "executives at Universal made substantial cuts which deemphasized the strong contrasts between wealth and poverty."[133] The shooting script called for a shot of a derelict "sleeping in a doorway," a slice of life that Dassin filmed on the Bowery in front of the Hotel Progress.[134] But Universal's Legal Department failed to obtain a release sanctioning the use of this verbally ironic marquee. Dassin also claims to have shot a pair of homeless men who exchanged pieces of tattered clothing in front of an opulent jewelry store. The

Figure 6. The Williamsburg Bridge. Reality reflected or displaced?

final screenplay contained several characters of wealth without merit who never materialized on screen. For instance, as Garza goes to a street corner to buy a newspaper, "a well-dressed man takes a paper. As he is fishing for change, he observes a newsboy with back turned. He walks off quickly without paying, a pleased smirk on his face."[135] In the opening montage sequence, a rich man with a poor stomach bends his butler's ear, saying: "Milk! Isn't there anything else for ulcers except milk?"[136]

NOTES

1. Gilbert Kurland, Telegram to James Pratt, Production Manager, 18 January 1948, Mark Hellinger Collection, USC Cinema-Television Library and Archives of Performing Arts.
2. *Variety*, 21 January 1948: 8.
3. Kay Sullivan, rev. of *The Naked City*, *Parade*, 7 March 1948: 22.
4. "Mark Hellinger's Last Picture Opens at the Capitol Theatre." Rev. of *The Naked City*, *Cue*, 6 March 1948: 16.
5. Rev. of *The Naked City*, *Look*, 16 March 1948: 96.
6. Bosley Crowther, *The New York Times Film Reviews, A One-Volume Selection, 1913–1970*, ed. George Amberg (New York: Arno Press, 1971): 238.
7. "New York Is the Star of 'Naked City,' " *Cue*, 14 February 1948: 15.
8. Paul Schrader, "Notes on Film Noir," *Film Comment*, Spring 1972: 10.
9. David George, "Film as Literature," *The Jerusalem Post Magazine*, 8 August 1980: 15.
10. David Sarnoff, "Every Chance in the World," *American Magazine*, April 1948: 135.
11. John Tagg, *The Burden of Representation, Essays on Photographies and Histories* (Amherst: University of Massachusetts Press, 1988): 188.
12. Burton Pike, *The Image of the City in Modern Literature* (Princeton, N.J.: Princeton University Press, 1981): 52.
13. Louis-Ferdinand Céline, *Journey to the End of the Night*, trans. Ralph Manheim (New York: New Directions, 1983): 159.
14. Bazin, "The Evolution of the Language of Cinema" in *What Is Cinema?* Volume I: 36.

15. Cecelia Ager, "Hellinger Film is a Love Song to NYC," *PM Daily*, 5 March 1948: 15.
16. Herb Tank, " 'The Naked City,' Good Job, Well Done," *The Daily Worker*, 5 March 1948: 12.
17. Lee Mortimer, " 'Naked City' Is Top Mystery Thriller," *The New York Daily Mirror*, 5 March 1948: 32.
18. Leo Mishkin, "'Powerful 'Naked City' Will Stand as Lasting Memorial to Hellinger," *The New York Morning Telegraph*, 5 March 1948: 2.
19. Philip T. Hartung, rev. of *The Naked City*, *The Commonweal*, 12 March 1948: 546.
20. Alton Cook, "Intense 'Naked City' Bares Real New York," *The New York World Telegram*, 4 March 1948: 30.
21. Archer Winsten, " 'The Naked City,' Hellinger's Best," *The New York Post*, 5 March 1948: 24.
22. Harry Lowery, rev. of *The Naked City*, *The Denver Post*, 14 April 1948: 19.
23. Robert Hatch, "The New Realism," *The New Republic*, 8 March 1948: 27.
24. Peter Biskind, *Seeing Is Believing, How Hollywood Taught Us to Stop Worrying and Love the Fifties* (New York: Pantheon Books, 1983): 194.
25. Eileen Creelman, rev. of *The Naked City*, *The New York Sun*, 5 March 1948: 23.
26. Sullivan: 22.
27. Hartung: 546.
28. Tank: 12.
29. Herb A. Lightman, "*The Naked City:* Tribute in Celluloid," *American Cinematographer*, May 1948: 178.
30. Cast, "The Naked City," 3 October 1947, Mark Hellinger Collection, USC Cinema-Television Library and Archives of Performing Arts.
31. Mark Hellinger, Letter to Wyck Cryder (undated), Mark Hellinger Collection, USC Cinema-Television Library and Archives of Performing Arts.
32. *Movie Life*, June 1948: 50.
33. "The Naked City Is *The Movie of the Month*," *Motion Picture Magazine*, May 1948: 64.
34. Mark Hellinger, Letter to Hon. William O'Dwyer, 16 June 1947, Mark Hellinger Collection, USC Cinema-Television Library and Archives of Performing Arts.
35. Hirsch: 53.

36. Paul Jensen, " 'The Return of Dr. Caligari': Paranoia in Hollywood," *Film Comment*, Winter 1971–2: 36.
37. Adam Garbicz and Jacek Klinowski, *Cinema, The Magic Vehicle: A Guide to its Achievement, Journey One: The Cinema Through 1949* (Metuchen, N.J.: Scarecrow Press, 1975): 470.
38. Borde and Chaumeton: 8.
39. Ibid.: 208.
40. Malvin Wald, Interview with Author, 30 April 1987.
41. Bazin, "*Cabiria*: The Voyage to the End of Neorealism," in *What Is Cinema?* Volume II: 87.
42. *Variety*, 10 March 1948: 6.
43. *The New York Herald Tribune*, 3 March 1948: 16.
44. *The New York World Telegram*, 3 March 1948: 26.
45. *Variety*, 10 March 1948: 15.
46. *Variety*, 28 April 1948: 9.
47. *Variety*, 31 March 1948: 13
48. *Variety*, 24 March 1948: 12.
49. *Variety*, 31 March 1948: 13.
50. *Variety*, 7 April 1948: 13.
51. *Variety*, 14 April 1948: 13.
52. Ibid.: 15.
53. *Variety*, 7 April 1948: 6.
54. *Variety*, 10 March 1948: 4–5.
55. Jules Dassin, Letter to Author, 3 July 1987: 1.
56. Garbicz and Klinowski: 471.
57. T.S. Eliot, "The Love Song of J. Alfred Prufrock" in *T.S. Eliot, The Waste Land & Other Poems* (New York: Harcourt Brace Jovanovich, 1962): 3.
58. Mishkin.
59. Pike: 34.
60. Ibid.
61. Lightman: 179.
62. *Homicide*, Daily Production Report, 10 June 1947, Mark Hellinger Collection, USC Cinema-Television Library and Archives of Performing Arts.
63. Lightman: 179.
64. *Homicide*, Daily Production Report, 9 June 1947, Mark Hellinger Collection, USC Cinema-Television Library and Archives of Performing Arts.
65. Ibid.: 11 June 1947.
66. Ibid.: 27 June 1947.
67. Ibid.: 4 August 1947.

68. Ibid.: 29 June 1947.
69. Ibid.: 21–24 July 1947.
70. Ibid.: 5 July 1947.
71. Ibid.: 14 July 1947.
72. Ibid.: 18 July 1947.
73. Ibid.: 7 August 1947. The apartment was located at 7 West 15 Street, No. L-31.
74. Ibid.: 29 July 1947.
75. Ibid.: 22 July 1947. The house was located at 2620 9th Avenue in Astoria, New York.
76. Ibid.: 8 July 1947.
77. Ibid.: 31 May 1947.
78. Ibid.: 4 June 1947.
79. Ibid.: 4 June 1947.
80. Ibid.: 7 October 1947.
81. Ibid.: 9 July 1947.
82. Ibid.: 17 August 1947.
83. Ibid.: 18 August 1947.
84. Mark Productions, Inc., Letter to Ted de Corsia, 18 September 1947, Mark Hellinger Collection, USC Cinema-Television Library and Archives of Performing Arts.
85. Gilbert Kurland, Letter to Kenneth B. Rossall, accountant for Hellinger Productions, Inc., 9 September 1947, Mark Hellinger Collection, USC Cinema-Television Library and Archives of Performing Arts.
86. Lowery.
87. Summary of Preview Cards, 18 December 1947, Mark Hellinger Collection, USC Cinema-Television Library and Archives of Performing Arts.
88. *Homicide*, Daily Production Reports, 29–30 September and 1–11 October 1947, Mark Hellinger Collection, USC Cinema-Television Library and Archives of Performing Arts.
89. Ibid.: 14 October 1947.
90. Ibid.: 20 October 1947.
91. Continuity Breakdown, Mark Hellinger Collection, USC Cinema-Television Library and Archives of Performing Arts.
92. Salt: 287.
93. Lightman: 178.
94. Bazin, "The Evolution of the Language of Cinema," *What Is Cinema?* Volume I: 27.
95. Charles Higham, *Hollywood Cameramen: Sources of Light* (Bloomington: Indiana University Press, 1970): 66.
96. Salt: 289.

97. Cobbett Steinberg, *Reel Facts, The Movie Book of Records* (New York: Vintage Books, 1982): 217.
98. Bazin, "The Myth of Total Cinema," *What Is Cinema?* Volume I: 17.
99. Bazin, "*Umberto D: A* Great Work," in *What Is Cinema?* Volume II: 82.
100. Ogle: 83.
101. Malvin Wald, *Homicide Squad Story*, 2 November 1946, Mark Hellinger Collection, USC Cinema-Television Library and Archives of Performing Arts.
102. *Idem,* Letter to Mark Hellinger, undated, Mark Hellinger Collection, USC Cinema-Television Library and Archives of Performing Arts: 2.
103. *Idem,* Letter to Mark Hellinger, 11 October 1946, Mark Hellinger Collection, USC Cinema-Television Library and Archives of Performing Arts: 5.
104. Erik Barnouw, *Documentary, A History of the Non-Fiction Film* (London: Oxford University Press, 1979): 123.
105. F. D. Thompson, Chief Estimator, Summary of Production Budget, 6 June 1947, Mark Hellinger Collection, USC Cinema-Television Library and Archives of Performing Arts.
106. Mark Hellinger, Inter-Office Communication to E. P. Ward, 26 November 1946, Mark Hellinger Collection, USC Cinema-Television Library and Archives of Performing Arts.
107. Mark Hellinger, *The New York Daily Mirror,* 22 January 1937: 24.
108. Crowther, *The New York Times Film Reviews, A One-Volume Selection, 1913–1970:* 238.
109. Ager: 15.
110. Albert Maltz, Production Notes for Mark Hellinger, 7 April 1947, The Mark Hellinger Collection, USC Cinema-Television Library and Archives of Performing Arts: "B".
111. Albert Maltz, Special Collections, Mugar Memorial Library, Boston University.
112. David Talbot and Barbara Zheutlin, *Creative Differences, Profiles of Hollywood Dissidents* (Boston: South End Press, 1978): 16.
113. Maltz, Special Collections, Mugar Memorial Library, Boston University.
114. Ibid.
115. Jay Leyda, *Kino, A History of the Russian and Soviet Film* (New York: Collier Books, 1960): 392.

116. Maltz, Special Collections, Mugar Memorial Library, Boston University.
117. Leo Rosten, Popular Arts Project, Volume VII (1960), Oral History Research, Columbia University: 2201–2202.
118. Gordon Gow, "Style and Instinct," *Films and Filming*, February 1970: 23.
119. Ibid.: 26.
120. Jules Dassin, "I See Dassin Make 'The Law'," Interview by John Francis Lane, *Films and Filming*, 4 September 1958: 28.
121. Malvin Wald and Albert Maltz, *The Naked City*, Continuity and Dialogue (15 January 1948). Deposited with the New York State Censorship Board. New York State Archives, Albany, New York.
122. Jules Dassin, Letter to Author, 3 July 1987: 1.
123. Lane: 28.
124. Gow: 25.
125. Albert Maltz, *HOMICIDE, Production notes for Mark Hellinger*, 7 April 1947, Mark Hellinger Collection, USC Cinema-Television Library and Archives of Performing Arts: A.
126. Malvin Wald, *Homicide*, 17 March 1947, The Mark Hellinger Collection, USC Cinema-Television Library and Archives of Performing Arts: 1.
127. Albert Maltz, Albert Maltz file, Mark Hellinger Collection, USC Cinema-Television Library and Archives of Performing Arts.
128. Malvin Wald, *Homicide*, 17 March 1947, Mark Hellinger Collection, USC Cinema-Television Library and Archives of Performing Arts: 39.
129. Albert Maltz, Albert Maltz file, Mark Hellinger Collection, USC Cinema-Television Library and Archives of Performing Arts: 39.
130. Ibid.
131. Malvin Wald, *Homicide*, 17 March 1947, Mark Hellinger Collection, USC Cinema-Television Library and Archives of Performing Arts: 56.
132. Ibid.: 96.
133. Horton: 24.
134. Shooting Script, Mark Hellinger Collection, USC Cinema-Television Library and Archives of Performing Arts.
135. Malvin Wald and Albert Maltz, *The Naked City, A Screenplay* (Carbondale: Southern Illinois University Press, 1979): 60.
136. Ibid.: 10.

IV FILM NOIR IN LIMBO: TOUCH OF EVIL

Just on the American side of the Texas-Mexico border, Rudy Linnekar, big man around town, is killed in an explosion by a homemade time-bomb in his convertible. Legendary redneck cop, Hank Quinlan (Orson Welles), is summoned to the scene. He is a grotesquely fat alcoholic who happens at the moment to be on the wagon. As he is venomously prejudiced against Mexicans, he does not take kindly to the appearance of Mike Vargas (Charlton Heston), a Mexican police detective specializing in narcotics. The recent arrest and conviction of a drug lord named Grandi from Mexico City has won Vargas a great deal of recognition among law enforcers. Vargas's presence on the border at the time of this incident, however, is purely coincidental. Accompanied by his newlywed bride, Susan (Janet Leigh), an American, he is on his way to a honeymoon in the United States.

To crack open the case, Quinlan relies—as is his custom—on intuition. The source of his intuition is a bum leg. It "tells" him that Sanchez, a Mexican involved with Linnekar's daughter, is the culprit. In order to arrest him, he plants incriminating evidence in Sanchez's house. The evidence consists of two sticks of dynamite. These were acquired but not used in the manufacture of the bomb that killed Linnekar. Vargas, sensitive to his country's image, accidentally catches Quinlan in this desperate act of deception.

The two cops lock horns. While Vargas seeks to impugn Quinlan's integrity as a sworn officer of the law— Quinlan's whole *raison d'être*—Quinlan tries to frame Vargas as a drug addict. To do so, he permits a gang of seedy youths to abduct and drug Vargas's wife, Susan. Quinlan's nefarious scheme also entails the strangulation-

murder of Uncle Joe Grandi (Akim Tamiroff), a local
hoodlum and brother of the man Vargas jailed in Mexico
City. Pete Menzies (Joseph Calleia), Quinlan's faithful
sidekick, finds Quinlan's cane at the scene of the crime. He
tells Vargas and reluctantly agrees to approach Quinlan
with a microphone concealed underneath his jacket.
While Vargas monitors a recording device close by but
out of sight, Menzies draws Quinlan away from an old
brothel where, in seclusion, he drinks himself into a
stupor. Following Menzies' lead, they talk candidly about
their partnership in the past. Finally, Quinlan openly
admits to a series of abuses in the corrupt execution of
justice. His famous intuition appears to be a fraudulent
invention, but suddenly Quinlan's "leg" indicates that
Menzies is betraying him to his foe, Vargas.

After mortally wounding the "walking microphone that
used to work for me," Quinlan is about to shoot Vargas
"for resisting arrest," when Menzies, dying, fires and kills
his boss. As Menzies and Quinlan both die, Vargas is
reunited with his wife. At the same time, it is learned that
Sanchez, Quinlan's suspect, has confessed.

PRELIMINARY COMMENTS

Unlike *The Maltese Falcon* and *The Naked City*, *Touch of Evil*
had only a brief, lackluster run in neighborhood theatres
and drive-ins. The film's weak box-office was also a
reflection of the poor reception of *films noirs* toward the end
of the cycle. More popular films in 1958 included Hitchcock's *Vertigo*, Joshua Logan's *South Pacific*, and Vincente
Minnelli's *Gigi*. *Touch of Evil's* thematic concern over tense
American-Mexican relations made little impact upon audiences despite the film's coincidental release in the midst of
Vice President Richard M. Nixon's stormy tour of Latin
America.

In 1941, Welles's *Citizen Kane* emerged as a melancholic
meditation on the American Dream that went against the
grain of 1930s utopianism. Gregg Toland's cinematographic elasticity, under Welles's direction, undermined in-

grained visual strategies that had come to dominate the American cinema. *Touch of Evil* went even further than *Kane* in terms of revolutionary, wide-angle cinematography and twisted, narrative convolutions. Its temporal structure is at least as intense as *Kane's* is complicated, simply by virtue of the fact that *Touch of Evil* transpires in such a short period of time.

But few guardians of the status quo were piqued by the continuing audacity of the aging *enfant terrible*. By 1958, Hollywood was no longer *the* Goliath of the entertainment industry or even on the cutting edge of American artistic endeavor. There was no level of authority commensurate with studio hegemony against which either Welles or *film noir* could pitch an alternative, subversive cinematic practice. In *Touch of Evil*, several characters are obsessed with drug culture and Hank Quinlan, out of desperation, accuses Miguel Vargas of being a dealer. The agonizing story that ensues, and the way in which it is told, metaphorically alludes to the frantic search of a junkie for a vein. Hollywood, the Dream Factory, collapsing as the main artery for the dissemination of American Dreams, forced filmmakers to move away and seek other points of entry into the entertainment-craving psyche of the spectator.

By then, several types of commercialized art were vying for supremacy. From the moment *Touch of Evil* begins, Henry Mancini's up-tempo Latin jazz score competes against its visual counterpart as a dominant—rather than subsidiary—component of the film. Later, the blare of loudspeakers in the Mirador Motel sequences serves to affirm the inundation of popular culture with the louder, dissonant, and insistent music of rock 'n' roll. With this mixed together with busty shots of Janet Leigh's Susan Vargas in lingerie, the once subtle suggestion of sexuality is effectively banished from the screen. The romantic portion of most *films noirs* subsisted on an undercurrent of erotic tension. *Film noir* music most often wavered between sultry standards like "I Can't Believe That You're in Love with Me" in *Detour* and "Laura" in Preminger's film of the same title, and cool jazz scores like those that prevail in *The Big Combo* or *The Sweet Smell of Success*. As Robert Porfirio points out, the soundtracks of earlier *films noirs* present a compendium of popular tunes: "Melancholy Baby" in *Scarlet Street*, "Don't Fence Me In" in *Night and the City*, and "Tangerine" in *Double Indemnity*, for example.[1] There is an assortment of big band numbers broadcast on a radio in *No Way Out* (Joseph L. Mankiewicz, 1950). "That Old Feeling" is heard over a crap game in *Where the Sidewalk Ends* (Otto Preminger, 1950). "I Remember You" is played over a segment of *The Glass Key* (Stuart Heisler, 1942). In general, *film noir* had little need for the kind of sound introduced by Elvis Presley, who by 1956 was beginning to make his own films.

Radio brought fame and opportunity to Welles, but it is doubtful whether his Mercury Theatre broadcasts could have rivaled the likes of the Everly Brothers, Paul Anka, the Platters, Connie Francis, Perry Como, Nat "King" Cole, and Chuck Berry. At this time, none of these popular singers would have deigned to perform a few numbers to warm up an audience awaiting the exhibition of a new film by Orson Welles. Even the elaborate orchestrations of Bernard Herrmann, whose music filled *Citizen Kane*'s soundtrack, were no match for the simple progressions and melodies sung by celebrated pop stars. Both Ricky Nelson and Dean Martin sing in Howard Hawks's *Rio Bravo* (1959). The baby-boom phenomenon commemorated by *Bye Bye Birdie* (George Sidney, 1963) was only a handful of years away. Furthermore, the iconography of *film noir* was already a subject of parody in the "Girl Hunt" sequence from *The Band Wagon* (Vincente Minnelli, 1953). The rhythmic congas and lively honky-tonk piano that are heard on the soundtrack in *Touch of Evil* undercut the dark and murky visual and narrative components of the film. A netherworld of crime and conflict clashes dialectically with driving, rhythmic percussion. The music tends to veer off in one direction, the dark visual compositions in another.

Everyone agrees that *Touch of Evil* is a puzzling film, with narrative loose ends, overlapping dialogue, vertiginous cinematography, and so much parallel action that one can easily follow the thread of one action and, as a consequence, lose track of another. Welles had no writer comparable to Herman Mankiewicz, who smoothed over transitions and fit disjunctive narrative segments neatly together in *Citizen Kane*. Dwight Macdonald thought that *Touch of Evil* was inferior to *The Maltese Falcon*, a film nearly two decades old. According to Macdonald, "*The Maltese Falcon* is my idea of a crime picture: logical, realistic, sardonic, humorous, fast, unpretentious. *Evil* is fast, but none of the other terms apply. Welles never knows where to stop. Motivations are nonexistent. Welles makes anything happen if he thinks it will be effective. . . ."[2]

Welles's *Touch of Evil* emerges as the culmination of a final trend in *film noir*, falling sharply away from the bland lucidity of semi-documentaries and moving toward exciting, arcane plots with jumbled spatial and temporal arrangements. Often they are quite unbelievable. When Mike Hammer is set loose in *Kiss Me Deadly* (Robert Aldrich, 1955), his incredible mission is to track down an atom bomb inside a plain box. Hammer follows obliquely in the tradition of Spade and Marlowe. But Ralph Meeker's sadistic interpretation of Micky Spillane's alter-ego did not precipitate the return to the screen of the private investigator, one of the foremost sacrifices engendered by the movement away from studio-based fiction and toward stories modeled as much as possible on real crimes.

Whenever possible, real methods of pursuing criminals, such as composite drawings (*He Walked By Night*), wiretapping (*The House on 92nd Street*), and the examination of income tax files (*The Undercover Man*) were shown in place of armchair ratiocination of the Sherlock Holmes kind. Films were even set in places where the events depicted actually occurred in real life (*Kiss of Death* and *The Wrong Man*, for instance).

In a related medium, Weegee advised amateur photographers "to feel a bond between yourself and the people you photograph . . . their laughter and tears. . . ."[3] Weegee's popular, nocturnal photographs had a certain grisly appeal that filmmakers sought to emulate. Not surprisingly, he had been influential as a technical adviser on several *films noirs*. Following his lead, a spate of semi-documentaries explored mostly urban environments and highlighted prosaic details that would never have materialized in studio films. As audiences became accustomed to the sights and sounds of bustling cities, instead of penetrating further, interest veered away from the true annals of crime and surged in favor of invention. The temporary affiliation between filmmaking and the indigenous flow of life in separate, distinct places gradually grounded to a halt.

To be sure, many malevolent aspects of the world, even in times of relative peace and prosperity, could have provided scenario after scenario for good *films noirs*. All kinds of cupidity, petty-mindedness, and injustice continued to flourish. But *film noir* relied more on its own textual reserves for replenishment. It became more conscious, self-reflexive, and indulgent in its use of shadows, stereotypical tough characters, and eschewal of ideals. Hence, films that emerge late in the cycle are often called baroque. *Touch of Evil*, which Paul Schrader has referred to as "film noir's epitaph,"[4] represents a quintessential instance of this phenomenon. One reviewer complains that "the exact course of the plot is almost impossible to follow." Instead of a linear exposition, the spectator is swamped with "up-from-the-floor and down-from-the-ceiling shots, distortions in frame, figure, light and shadow."[5] Only after a passage of time has the assessment that *Touch of Evil* "sums up almost everything there is to say about the film noir" come into vogue.[6]

Semi-documentary *films noirs* never quite progressed beyond a larval stage that produced maudlin tributes to hulking cities and powerful government agencies. Before 1950, Bryan Foy, presiding over Eagle-Lion studio, declared that "true-to-life stories produced on actual locales" threatened to change the Hollywood dream machine.[7] During this time, attention was focused on specific neighborhoods, buildings, and streets. Locations played a part in the determination of what could be said in the way of dialogue or happen in the way of action. Much depended upon what local denizens were like, how they spoke, and what they did.

But all too soon thereafter, location shooting—at least as far as *film noir* is concerned—moved into a period of decadence. It is unlikely that ten years earlier, in 1948, Welles would have tried to depict a Mexican village on location in Venice, California. He may have used back-screen projection in *The Lady from Shanghai*, but process shots of the San Francisco Aquarium serve as background for a scene that was actually shot right there on the premises. For a movie taking place in Mexico, he would have either shot his film in Mexico or built sets on a studio backlot.

As it was, the decision to exploit a suburb of Los Angeles had little to do with the merits of wedding Mexican and Texan decor to the environs of Southern California. By 1946, Henry Hathaway had shown with *13 Rue Madeleine* that Quebec could be handily used as a Normandy village and New York City, Boston, and Washington, D.C. could also be used to portray various parts of England. Despite this blatant trickery, a semi-documentary atmosphere could still be maintained. However, *film noir*'s strong emphasis on domestic settings generally held in check the temptation to indulge in international transformations like these.

According to Barbara Leaming, Welles first went to Tijuana to scout locations. Welles also planned to visit Nogales, below Arizona.[8] But Universal would not allow him to shoot anywhere in Mexico where the studio could not easily monitor his activities.[9] As a result, an agreement was reached to make a run-down Los Angeles suburb, already designed to look like an Italian city, have the appearance of a Mexican village on the Texas border. The whole disruption of the normal activity of the environment that is necessitated by such a maneuver is unlike what systematically occurs in the studio. Inside the studio, all that is needed is to dress up an empty stage. But places, unlike studio stages, already have an identity. This cannot entirely be obscured, even by the deft handling of Robert Clatworthy, who worked on set design for both *Touch of Evil* and, later, *Psycho*. Volumes of legally-binding contracts have to be read, signed, and notarized before

Hollywood can proceed to impose itself on an environment as it would in a studio. As with any transplant, the receptive organism naturally rejects at the same time it is forced to accept a foreign intrusion. Nearly fifteen years before, Hitchcock boldly shot *Shadow of a Doubt* (1943) in Santa Rosa, a small town near San Francisco. But outside the construction of a certain facade to accommodate lights, Hitchcock basically leaves well enough alone. The library, bank, church, and local tavern, in which scenes take place, remain as they are. In the case of *Touch of Evil*, one may well ask, "What kind of place is Los Robles?" Its arcades full of strip joints and rowdy boozers seem to suggest that it was patterned after Tijuana. But one has to distinguish between California and Texas borders with Mexico. It is the latter, not the former, that the film is concerned with.

Variety called *Touch of Evil* a "confusing, somewhat 'artsy' film." It "smacks of brilliance but ultimately flounders in it."[10] *The New York World-Telegram and Sun* complained that "the result is too uneven."[11] The film has also been described as "a manic vortex of time, space and energy."[12] Reviewers and critics routinely attribute confusion to *Touch of Evil*'s temporal inconsistencies. According to Leaming, *Touch of Evil*'s "murky angles and pictorial compositions—these posed no problems to the boys in the front office."[13] In her opinion, the main objection centered on the film's lack of linearity. Others concur that in the late 1950s, "*Touch of Evil* was widely criticized in terms of its non-sequential story line."[14]

Nevertheless, the film is unsettling from still another standpoint. Space is even more disconnected than time. There is no distinct border between Mexico and Texas, other than the makeshift station and the few officials seen at the beginning of the film. The whole geography of the film escapes one's imagination. As a rule, one cannot fathom where one place is in relationship to another. There are so few master-shots, smoothly broken down, with exteriors to acclimate the spectator to a change in setting and dissolves that unfold interiors already anticipated—a process familiar in classical Hollywood cinema. As a result, tension arises in the very compositions drawn from an environment that Hollywood virtually seized and converted to suit its own imperious needs.

Like *The Naked City*, *Touch of Evil* was made partially on location, and partially in the studio. Its primary location was Venice, an architectural eccentricity that approximates the famous Italian city. The Mirador Motel, from which Susan is abducted, was elsewhere, in Palmdale. The crew also shot exteriors in Santa Monica, where the house that served as the old brothel was discovered. Los Robles, the fictive border town where the drama unfolds, was in fact a "Kuleshovian" product of Welles's imagination. Outside the Immigration and Naturalization Station, built on one of the main thoroughfares in Venice, Welles hung a large sign, reading "Mexico" [Figure #7]. This streamlined appeal to the ancient authority of the printed word is practically all that establishes the setting.

It also constitutes an appeal to the authority of Hollywood. Welles once referred to this Dream Factory as "the greatest train set a boy ever had."[15] Now he labeled it "a

Figure 7. The Mexico-United States Border.

gold-plated suburb."[16] Indeed, Hollywood was any place
the filmmaking "power elite" wanted it to be. To accom-
plish this, numerous mundane business transactions had
to be finalized. For example, Universal's agents consulted
the Department of Water and Power in Venice to find out
the schedule for the operation of street lights.[17] They
entered into an agreement with an electric company for the
repair of neon lights as well as the generation of power to
extend the regular hours of arcade lights. They negotiated
the right to use park property.[18] They contacted the fire
department and agreed upon the amount of compensation
owed to the fireman who would have to stand by during
the tumultuous sequence following the explosion of Linnekar's convertible. Firefighting equipment had also to be
rented.[19] A policeman was hired to play himself.[20]

They canvassed the whole town to learn the name of
nearly every storeowner as well as the routine hours for each
store. Painstaking agreements made separately with each
owner kept stores open well past the normal closing hour.
For instance, on days when shooting took place within the
vicinity of the Venice Jewelry Store, the owner was promised $20. The St. Mark's Hotel, where the Vargases are
registered at the time of the car bombing, was thought more
vital. The proprietor was to be paid "$50.00 per day or
night," depending upon when Welles might have chosen to
film scenes on or around the premises of the hotel.[21] Signs
reading "teléfono público" and "oficina telegráfica" rein-
force the Mexican atmosphere. Anyone who has seen the
film knows how Welles literally "papered" exteriors with
billboards, notices, signs, posters, and floating debris.

These agreements were not strictly "business." By
leasing their stores, local businessmen entered into artistic
complicity with Hollywood filmmakers. However passive
and silent, they were partners to Welles, his superiors, and
underlings. Despite the glamor of moviemaking, not
everyone wished to get involved. Crew members were
warned to "expect trouble when photographing" around
Sylvia Semper's Dress Shop.[22] The belligerent owner of
Grady's Town House demanded a guaranteed sum of $300
for the use of his property. The studio obstinately re-

fused.[23] Tedium sometimes threatened to bog down
negotiations. Universal had to notify each customer of a
certain parking lot of the exact time of a particular shoot in
order to make sure the cars would be removed.[24]
Although filmmakers of *The Naked City* had difficulty
coping with the endless parade of New Yorkers throughout the city, they never attracted their ire. The biggest
antagonist was the persistently hazy weather. *Touch of
Evil's* story is different. Many residents of Venice felt they
had been either mistreated or shortchanged. The owner of
a vacant lot who expected to be paid a certain amount of
money was upset when the use of his property was
rejected. The grounds, which were to have served as a
parking lot, were deemed too soft.[25] The Location Manager
of the film, P. D. Nowell, had to placate someone who
blamed the crew for the disappearance of two light poles.[26]
Nowell predictably denied the accusation. A rankled
storeowner complained about what he thought was under-
payment for the use of his Used Clothing Mart. Nowell
wrote: "We sincerely hope that you and everyone in the
area will feel favorably toward us and our operation."[27]

The owner of a shoe store raged over the fact that Welles
ignored his establishment. Nowell explained: "From your
standpoint, we are sorry that we did not photograph your
store more frequently. However, our director's concept of
how these scenes in Venice were to be played resulted in
more action being photographed in some areas than in
others."[28] The owner of the Ritz Hotel, where "Pancho"
accompanies Mrs. Vargas to see his Uncle Joe Grandi,
wanted more money.[29] An annoyed shopkeeper surmised
that the filmmakers' presence discouraged patrons from
coming into his store. The Assistant Production Manager,
readily adopting Nowell's supercilious tone, argued that
"displays were put on the sidewalks in a manner not to
inconvenience anyone, but possibly on the contrary to draw
more traffic to the Windward area than is customary."[30]

The Windward area included the main boulevard down
which Heston and Leigh as the Vargases promenade on the
way to the American side of the border. In almost every
reply written to a disgruntled storeowner, a Universal

executive declared that he was "most grateful that the bulk of the merchants whom we were in contact with have accepted our work and payments received in a most cooperative and heartwarming manner."[31] Compared to the kinds of expenditures involved in the construction of sets, payments to the people of Venice amounted to a distinct bargain. An empty store rented for the modest fee of "$10.00 per photographing day," which entitled the filmmakers to both decorate and warehouse equipment as well.[32]

Whereas Dassin made use of a special van that permitted him to shoot candidly, unobserved by people on the street, Welles evacuated restricted areas before turning on the camera. Ruby Neil Vernon, co-proprietor of The Vernon Blind Workshop, appears as sole representative of the local population. Her blindness best symbolizes the role of the Venice citizenry in this production. In the film, she allows Vargas to telephone his wife, while Quinlan, Menzies, and Uncle Joe Grandi arrive at the flat across the street. To show such parallel action, Welles cleared the entire street, together with a cross street, of parked cars. The apartment, shared by Sanchez and Marcia Linnekar in the diegesis, was rented at the unusually large fee of $100 per day.[33]

Despite an illustrious cast, including Marlene Dietrich and cameos by Joseph Cotten and Zsa Zsa Gabor, little could be done to mitigate the probability of commercial failure. A year before the release of the film, *Newsweek* spoke of the "Return of the Prodigy."[34] But the weekly magazine completely ignored the film after it opened. *Touch of Evil* first appeared on the screen in neighborhood theaters all around New York City on Wednesday, May 21, 1958. In seven theaters in Manhattan, six in the Bronx, seven in Brooklyn, and four in Westchester, *Touch of Evil* topped a double bill with *The Unholy Wife* (John Farrow, 1957), starring Rod Steiger and Diana Dors. Together they were identified as "Two New Powerful Adult Dramas!"[35] Blurbs from the advertisement in *The New York World-Telegram and Sun* read, "How much could flesh stand?" and "How far was love willing to go!" *The New York Herald Tribune* seems to have stood alone in calling *Touch of Evil* a "personal *tour de force* of Orson Welles."[36]

One resourceful exhibitor in Texas created sensational publicity to attract patrons. He referred to Hank Quinlan as "the beast cop." The film was described as a "smashing expose of the border town beast-cops who trample the Mexicans and sell their wives into the sordid slavery of the perfumed houses." New Mexico and California had banned the film, possibly in response to "orders from someone above who wants to protect his billion dollar empire of sin." Welles was constrained to shoot *Touch of Evil* in Mexico because "they wouldn't let him film it in the United States." Only after a protracted struggle was it finally "filmed under the protection of the Mexican Minister of Public Safety."[37] The Dallas drive-in where these patently false claims brought in substantial audiences may have done well, but it was less than a week before *Touch of Evil* in New York City was superseded by "Two Brand New Shocking Hits!" These were *Girls on the Loose* and *Live Fast, Die Young* (both Paul Henreid, 1958). Both were billed as films made with "music in the mood of today's 'beat' generation."[38]

The passion to hear was displacing the desire to see. Edeson's prediction that the novelty of movies would eventually wear thin had some truth to it after all. Universal, controlled first by Decca Records before being bought by MCA, seems to have been prescient in this regard. During pre-production for *Touch of Evil*, Universal was in contact with Decca concerning the soundtrack, which had not yet been composed.[39] Howard Thompson, reviewer for *The New York Times*, seems to have had Henry Mancini in mind as much as Orson Welles when he singled out "the tempo" as "plain mercurial," and described how the "credits come on . . . to a sleepy, steady rumba rhythm."[40]

CAMERA

Whereas both *The Maltese Falcon* and *The Naked City* employ a balanced, classical camera, conscious of spatial integrity and temporary continuity, *Touch of Evil*'s cinematography is frenetic. There is a difference of opinion over whether *film noir* tended to favor "tightly framed shots that rigidly define the limits of the spectator's awareness,"[41] or "increased shot lengths and moving camera."[42] Both assessments, the one contradicting the other, apply with equal validity to *Touch of Evil*. It contains segments with excruciating long-takes and others with bewildering clusters of short takes. Despite its acrobatic finesse, Welles's camera is not an omniscient one. The first shot, which might have revealed the perpetrator's identity, is far too nebulous. The doubt concerning Sanchez's guilt that remains after the final shot is inconsistent with classical Hollywood cinema. It leaves the whole question of Quinlan's extra-legal methods open, while classical film would end in closure. Andrew Sarris is certainly correct in calling *Touch of Evil* "a strange movie by any standard," "too packed with privileged moments" and, in sum, "the kind of movie which makes you rethink what a movie should be."[43]

The ambiguity that lingers does more than deflect the matter of Sanchez's innocence or guilt, it also preserves the mystique surrounding Quinlan. Welles himself seems unable to decide if Quinlan is a monster or a saint. His game leg, which supposedly empowers him with unearthly intuitive skills, makes him anything but human. The cinematographic flirtation with extremes, either in terms of fluidity or rigidity, reflects this oscillation between the horror of great villains and awe of their capabilities.

It was Monday, February 18, 1957 when production on *Touch of Evil* began. Conscious of his lingering reputation as master of the long-take, Welles selected two shots, both of which amounted to approximately five minutes in length, without edits. The two shots comprised the scene during which Sanchez is booked for the murder of Rudy Linnekar. The crew consisted of the chief cinematographer, Russell Metty, a camera operator, a mixer, and two men working with a small crane. During the morning, from around 9:30 to lunch, a very small part of Universal's Stage #19, amounting to little more than a corner, served as the local police station. There, Welles directed Joseph

Calleia's Pete Menzies, Quinlan's honest subordinate. In this particular scene, Menzies, speaking over the telephone, asks Quinlan what to do about Sanchez, who is being held and charged with murder. Quinlan sneers, "Break him!"

About midday, a larger cast assembled and rehearsed all the way until six o'clock. After the application of make-up, shooting began in earnest at six-thirty.[44] The result was not merely a display of camera virtuosity, but also of brilliant *mise-en-scène* and skillful acting. The orchestration of actors milling about within such a claustrophobic space required the movement not just of people but of objects as well. Timing is especially relevant. One clearly hears Quinlan enunciate the word "dynamite" when Vargas accidentally overturns an empty shoebox in the bathroom. In a rhyming long-take, the incriminating evidence—two sticks of dynamite—appears inside the same shoebox.

At least some of Quinlan's fakery can analogously be considered that of filmmaking. Of course, nothing is on the screen unless it has first been planted there. To be sure, these shots could only have occurred within a studio with furniture placed on wheels and "wild" walls sliding conveniently away on cue. One expects such manipulation behind the scenes in studio compositions. But locations suggest authenticity. By definition, locations are places not designed explicitly for the sake of the camera. Their manipulation in *Touch of Evil* contributes in large part to the film's reputation as insolubly ambiguous. There is no key to understanding the film as either a studio production or a semi-documentary, both of which it is not. In fact, it is a corruption of both, insofar as it treats locations as if they were sets, and sets as if they were a natural extension of locations. Whereas *The Maltese Falcon* is a studio film and *The Naked City* a film whose impact derives mostly from location shooting, *Touch of Evil* can only be considered a studio-*like* production, making use of locations as *sets*.

Welles's first two shots in the can lead directly to the initial shattering of Quinlan's Mephistophelean power. At the same time, an unsubdued conspicuous camera serves to puncture the film's illusionism. Like Menzies, the spectator begins to see the premeditation that mingles with artistry of any sort. That Welles is absorbed by questions of authenticity in art becomes more evident years later with *F for Fake* (1975). In *Touch of Evil*, a certain inflection of camera position is all that registers Welles's condemnation of the deceptiveness of Quinlan.

Much of the shooting in the long-takes mentioned above occurs with a low-angle orientation. Welles used the same technique to bolster the character of Charles Foster Kane. In *Kane*, little overhead light was used and microphones were placed above ceilings made from porous muslin.[45] To introduce the subject of Kane's downfall, Welles has Kane shot in deep-focus with a high-angle. Boss Jim Gettys, Kane's nemesis, looms large in the foreground. Kane appears almost microscopic in the background. This occurs just after Kane's campaign speech and prior to the scene in which Gettys threatens to expose Kane's illicit affair. Similarly, after exaggerating Quinlan's arrogance and obesity with low-angle cinematography, a distinctive high-angle shot focuses attention on a more diminutive and submissive Quinlan. Consumed by thoughts of revenge, Quinlan is shown drinking his second bourbon, while his fellow conspirator, a local gangster, selects a record from the jukebox.

Stefan Sharff warns against the "fallacy in the assignment of fixed meaning to certain camera angles or graphic compositions."[46] In both *Kane* and *Touch of Evil*, the high-angle construction does not signal the demise of a certain character's power to inspire fear and command respect or even adoration. Welles cannot quite bring himself to repudiate Quinlan as much on the screen as he later did in interviews about the film. The final segment of the film involves a potpourri of abruptly edited shots, as little as three feet in length, and rarely more than twenty feet. This pastiche entails a tremendous variation in camera angle and distance from subject. Close-ups of Menzies, Quinlan, and Vargas are interspersed with close-ups of the tape recorder, usually shot from a high-angle. A great deal of dialogue is heard while the camera hovers just above the tape recorder's speaker. A series of low-angle close-ups reveal the derrick rigging in which Vargas hides. Many of the close-ups, especially those having to do with the recording device, are also moving camera shots, which make it difficult for the spectator to adjust to any particular perspective. According to Sharff, one of the chief purposes of multiangularity is to obscure the dominance of single points of view. Multiangularity is "an all-enhancing *composite view* of things, through the use of a criss-crossing network of observation points."[47] But instead of lucidity accompanying such a comprehensive treatment, what emerges is a great deal of confusion. As a result, there are almost as many interpretations of *Touch of Evil*'s resolution as there are reviewers and critics who have written about the film.

A crane provides a number of medium close-ups of the perambulation of Quinlan and Menzies toward and on the catwalk. Underneath, Vargas maintains a steadfast vigil. After Quinlan shoots Menzies, there is a close pan shot, twelve feet in length, of the piling near the bridge, shown at a skewed angle. A close, tightly-framed shot, five feet in length, shows Vargas on one of the river's banks beneath the bridge. A fast cut, enduring a mere two feet in length, shows the recorder from a high-angle. Another fast cut, also two feet in length, shows the Mexican end of the bridge from a low-angle. They are all situated at this point along what Andre Bazin, in his analysis of the Western, calls the mythic "borderline between good and evil, which also happens to be the Mexican border."[48] Another two-foot shot shows Menzies in close-up, his face agonizingly twisted by the realization that he has been mortally wounded. A low-angle two shot, lasting nine feet in length, shows Quinlan and Menzies in the same frame, facing each other in one final confrontation of conflicting morals and wills. A succession of very abrupt shots, all averaging about three feet in length, ensues.[49] In comparison, each of the pair of long-takes described earlier stretch beyond five hundred feet in length. Welles edits together nearly one hundred shots to take up the same amount of time on screen as is used by those two.

Russell Metty's camera has an incredible vitality. Often it slithers and darts about like a reptile. In one memorable movement, it slides into a local hotel, following the footsteps of a coterie of local dignitaries, and then, crouching in a corner, goes up an elevator to where Vargas is waiting with some important information. In another scene, it is strapped to the hood of a convertible, whizzing up and down narrow streets and alleyways. Heston recorded this ride in his journals, mentioning the revolutionary use of an extraordinary wide-angle, 18.5mm lens.[50] But the most remarkable shot that Welles and Metty accomplished appears at the very beginning of the film.

It was filmed sometime between four and six in the early morning hours of March 15, 1957, about a month into production.[51] Heston referred to it in his journals as "a complicated setup with the Chapman boom moving three blocks, angling down over buildings . . . through two pages of dialogue to a car blowing up."[52] It begins with an extreme close-up of the timing mechanism of a time-bomb and glides with exceptional grace over buildings and above the main street, alternately keeping both the ill-fated automobile and the Vargases in frame. Unfortunately, the decision was made to put the credits on the screen at the same time. These fritter away the shot's total impact.

WRITING

According to one unverifiable account, *Touch of Evil*'s producer, Albert Zugsmith, "and Welles became pals over a bottle of vodka, and Welles offered to direct the 'worst' script the producer had to offer"—the Paul Monash adaptation of Whit Masterson's novel, *Badge of Evil*.[53] To be sure, Welles must not have bestowed upon this pulp novel the same kind of reverence he lavished on Booth Tarkington's *The Magnificent Ambersons*. Yet it is a good enough guess that Welles perceived in this relatively trivial novel of police detection attractive formal elements and ideas he wished to develop.

The book was written by Robert Wade and H. Billy

Miller under the pseudonym of Whit Masterson. In early 1956 it was submitted to Universal and eventually read by Dick Whittle of the Story Department. Whittle wrote a favorable synopsis and recommended that the studio move to purchase the material.[54] An agreement for the acquisition of *Badge of Evil* was publicly announced a few months later in May.[55] Paul Monash subsequently worked for nine weeks devising a screenplay.

It was not until over a year later that the title of the film was changed from *Badge of Evil* to *Touch of Evil*, following a lengthy process of surveys and market analyses. Since filmmakers and booksellers had arranged a package deal wherein the book was to be released simultaneously with the movie, both should have had the same name. But Bantam Books conducted a test and found that *Badge of Evil* was popular chiefly among "frequent male moviegoers in the very young age brackets." This caused some reservations, as did the associative element due to a certain "Badge 714" television show. The title that seemed to attract the most interest at the time was "Little Tin God."[56] Other titles that were being considered included "Edge of Evil"; "Sign of Evil"; "Hangman, Hangman"; and "Pay the Devil."[57] In August, an executive at Bantam Books urged Universal to make a decision, saying, "We will be happy with Edge of Evil or Touch of Evil, but our time has run out."[58] Universal authorized Bantam Books to proceed with "Edge of Evil."[59] This choice was countermanded a month later.[60]

John Stubbs has painstakingly traced the evolution of the script to what ultimately became *Touch of Evil*.[61] In terms of the final product—the film—Stubbs rightfully credited Welles's contributions more highly than those by either the authors or the original screenwriter. Still, it is useful to remember that the framework out of which Welles ultimately carved the *Touch of Evil* screenplay consisted of imaginative ideas spun out by two novelists and a screenwriter. The fundamental sources for such a writing task were quite different from those of either *The Maltese Falcon* or *The Naked City*. The basic source material for *The Maltese Falcon* was Hammett's penetrating observations of San Francisco streets combined with his own Pinkerton experiences. *The Naked City* was built out of police detective files and documentation. Imagination plays a significant role throughout, but of the three films, only in *Touch of Evil* is it of paramount importance. Welles retained whatever he liked from either Wade and Miller's book or Monash's screenplay. From Wade and Miller, he saved all of the wordplay having to do with shoes and feet.[62] For instance, Sanchez says that he met Marcia Linnekar, "selling her shoes . . . and I've been at her feet ever since." Later, Quinlan tells Sanchez, "There was an old lady on Main Street last night picked up a shoe . . . and the shoe had a foot in it. We're going to make you pay for that, Sanchez." From Monash, Welles preserved the idea of making the framed suspect actually the guilty party.[63] In terms of originality, his most crucial addition seems to have been the construction of his own character. In formulating the role of Hank Quinlan, Welles made sure that his part was commensurate with his unique acting persona.

Except for a few sequences involving either the Vargases or the Grandis, Quinlan is always the focus of attention. Either he commands attention visually, or is the subject of conversation, as in Figure #8, from which he is absent. Unlike Bogart in *The Maltese Falcon* or Barry Fitzgerald in *The Naked City*, Welles is so much a product of make-up and costume that one has no idea what he really looks like. Not only did Welles use padding to enlarge the border cop's corporality, but he also made use of fake noses and gobs of extra make-up. "You're a mess, honey," says Marlene Dietrich's Tana. The grandiosity of Quinlan's bulky heap is expanded even further by means of a series of eerie close-ups taken by a wide-angle lens. Quinlan's position within the narrative is also of great magnitude. Menzies' idolization swells Quinlan into an almost unearthly superbeing. In Figure #8, Menzies is saying to Vargas, "I am what I am because of him." All in all, Quinlan is disproportionately large in terms of power and esteem. Along with the diminution in the relative importance of location, an element of realism in the portrayal of small-town justice is necessarily weakened.

Figure 8. Cops.

Welles himself found a place for his own pomposity, as well as that of his acting persona, in the villains he played. In the case of *Citizen Kane*, both Welles and Hearst could be said to have much in common, such as influence, prestige, and fame. Both were living legends co-existing with biographical half-truths. Hearst had been involved in filmmaking, mostly with the development of Marion Davies' career. Welles, in turn, had involved himself in the newspaper business, working briefly as a columnist for *The New York Post*. Both had political aspirations. In 1942, Welles served the United States in Brazil as a goodwill ambassador for the Office of the Coordinator of Inter-American Affairs. Both created panics: Welles with his "War of the Worlds" broadcast, and Hearst with his unscrupulous coverage of the Spanish-American War.

It was a different sort of model that Welles had in mind

for Quinlan. Paul Arthur has noted how *Touch of Evil* meditates "on the character of leading anticommunist crusaders of the postwar period, in particular Joseph McCarthy."[64] McCarthy's fall from grace had been both providential and precipitous. He died on May 2, 1957. To Arthur, Quinlan's "resemblances to McCarthy are too prevalent to be easily discounted."[65] Both have common, monosyllabic names—Hank and Joe. Both have an assortment of affectations. McCarthy used to limp, having faked a war wound to help get himself elected. In *Touch of Evil*, Menzies thinks that Quinlan really needs his cane, but Quinlan casually forgets it twice in the film. McCarthy and Quinlan are both overweight. By means of disheveled clothing and five o'clock shadows, each gives the impression of working ceaselessly without interruption. But both are alcoholics. As Arthur also points out, McCarthy died from sclerosis of the liver, while "Quinlan spends his last night getting drunk in Tanya's brothel."[66]

They share other traits as well. Both McCarthy and Quinlan are moral absolutists who randomly employ tasteless racial slurs. Both are inured to self-aggrandizing tactics designed to boost their careers, and predicated on the systematic condemnation of others. Both are xenophobic, repulsive bigots, yet are loved and respected. Both are indefatigable in the relentless pursuit of proving people culpable for crimes they more than likely did not commit. In short, Quinlan's personality amounts to a parody of McCarthy's feverish sanctimoniousness. On the way to the Mirador Motel, Menzies, a Roy Cohn-like assistant, admiringly points out to Susan how Quinlan "used to be a terrible lush, you know. But look at him now. No sleep, still at it." When Quinlan speaks, he even adopts McCarthy's nasal, trumpeting intonation.

Reverberations of anti-McCarthyism echo in Welles's personal assessment of Hank Quinlan, who "does not want to submit the guilty ones to justice so much as to assassinate them in the name of the law, using the police for his own purposes; and this is a fascist scenario, a totalitarian scenario, contrary to traditional law and human justice."[67] In a historical analysis, *The Politics of Fear*,

Robert Griffith's assessment of McCarthy's personality seems to apply with equal validity to Hank Quinlan. According to Griffith, McCarthy "demonstrated a ready willingness to disregard truth and to manipulate evidence to 'prove' his case."[68] Also, like Quinlan, McCarthy tended to drift "away from the law-making process, with its attention to tedious detail and its dependency upon others, and toward the investigative process, where the obstacles to notice and notoriety were fewer and more easily hurdled."[69] McCarthy rejected the practice of law as an effective tool to fight crime and prosecute criminals. In *Touch of Evil*, Quinlan abjures law, saying, "Lawyer! I'm no lawyer. All a lawyer cares about is the law!"

Despite the lives and careers he ruined, McCarthy remained throughout the witchhunt period "the genial and charming Irishman who wanted nothing more than to love and be loved."[70] Quinlan imploringly appeals for the same treatment. When he resigns in a histrionic fit of self-pity, he flings aside his shield, vowing not "to take back that badge until the people of this county vote it back."

In addition to the similarities between Quinlan and McCarthy, one should not overlook those between Welles himself and McCarthy. Both were of Irish descent and hailed from the state of Wisconsin, heartland of middle America. Both unsparingly attacked their ideological adversaries. McCarthy lashed out against liberals. Welles cleverly demeaned the character of Hearst, staunchly anti-Roosevelt and an iconic figure of conservatism. Both were inventive, egotistical and theatrical.

Predecessors to Quinlan, however, can also be found inter-textually within *films noirs* preceding *Touch of Evil*. In *I Wake Up Screaming*, an inspector—played by Laird Cregar, also a bulky actor—mercilessly hounds an innocent man for a murder he knows was committed by someone else. Another prototype for Hank Quinlan is Detective McLeod (Kirk Douglas) in *Detective Story* (William Wyler, 1951). McLeod is obsessed with the capture and conviction of suspects. Enjoying their anguish, he intimidates them until they confess. Dave Bannion (Glenn

Ford) in *The Big Heat* perfects the figure of the cop who
steps beyond the strict letter of the law in order to better
serve the law. Moreover, all three—Quinlan, McLeod and
Bannion—are motivated by a tragic, familial situation. All
avenge an irreversible, dark past: Quinlan, the murder of
his wife; Bannion, the murder of *his* wife; and McLeod, the
notoriety of his father, a criminal.

In addition to contributing the character of Hank Quinlan to the writing of *Touch of Evil*, Welles also introduced
the theme of racism. Stubbs points out how a vociferous
opposition to prejudice "had long been part of Welles's
social and political liberalism."[71] To Welles, Quinlan "is
hateful" and "a detestable man."[72] Nevertheless, as Thomas Schatz observes, "Welles's portrayal of the aging,
corrupt cop finally victimized by one of his own schemes is
so effective that Quinlan emerges as the film's most
sympathetic character."[73] Welles admits Quinlan is "sympathetic because of his humanity" and because "it's always
possible to feel sympathy for a son of a bitch."[74] Welles
insisted further that Vargas "speaks as a man of dignity,
according to the tradition of classical humanism, which is
absolutely my tradition as well."[75] But there is a discrep-
ancy between Welles's monolithic statements and his
artistic products. The latter resonate with rich contradictions. *Touch of Evil* is not so much a story about McCarthy
as a parable about him. As such, it has some curious lapses
in terms of political liberalism. Quinlan receives too much
reverence and Sanchez too little justice.

Anthony Perkins, recalling *The Trial* (Orson Welles,
1962), casts an interesting light on Welles's deeper, more
perplexing personality. According to Perkins, Welles's

> conception of Joseph K. was off-putting. His insistence
> that K. be this obsequious, apologetic, struggling-to-
> the-top type; it was horrible! I said, 'Orson, you can't
> mean this. Of all the things that symbolize the plight of
> the innocent—' and he said, 'he's guilty, he's guilty
> as hell!' I can hear him, he said, 'you're playing it
> too heroically. Remember, he's guilty, he's guilty as
> hell!'[76]

Perkins elaborated further on how guilt was the focus of attention for Welles, who "was much more interested in how guilty K. was, rather than how helpless he was."[77] Welles's philosophical approach to Kafka's masterpiece is a strange reflection of Quinlan's defensive response to Menzies, who asks, "How many did you frame?" Quinlan answers, "I told you . . . nobody! Nobody that wasn't guilty. Guilty! Guilty! Every last one of 'em . . . guilty."

DIRECTION

The most noticeable visual aspect of *Touch of Evil* is its ugliness. Screening *Touch of Evil* has been called "a seedy experience. Orson Welles drags us through the dirt, dust, and garbage of his characters' existence. . . ."[78] Not only is the enormous quantity of litter and debris a metaphor for moral decay, it is also an attack on the glamor-ridden facade of studio filmmaking in Hollywood. In retrospect, those backlot tenement sets of the Depression era have the appearance of whitewashed, quaint, even desirable places to live. They are fraught with the glowing warmth of a human element that is never corroborated by true fear-laden and impoverished city enclaves. Welles seems to have been eager to remedy the beauty of set designs with the repugnance of everyday eyesores, wherever possible. He was overjoyed by the discovery of "one of the hideous old buildings in downtown Los Angeles."[79] These are his own words as he instructed Universal to do away with the set—a cantina—for which the "hideous" building was supposed to have been substituted.

Heston recalls shooting in the middle of the night in a dilapidated Venice hotel. In the basement, Welles took an instant liking to all the pipes and the boiler. As a result, he decided to scrap a set already built and stage the scene in which Menzies shows Vargas an unambiguously incriminating piece of evidence—Quinlan's cane—against a backdrop of ugly fixtures.[80] The boiler-room, however, seems rather out of place next door to an isolated basement jail cell. The setting is almost surreal and not at all convincing. One can appreciate Welles's unsavory aesthetics and yet recognize its shortcomings as a criticism of a plastic Hollywood. The squalor depicted in the film literally has no referent, since Los Robles is a fictitious invention. So much rubbish is, in the final analysis, only so much tinsel, albeit of a different kind from Hollywood's more lavish version.

As complicated as the film is, *Touch of Evil* comes unraveled around the character of Hank Quinlan. Since Welles's filmography as an actor is so lengthy, the character of Hank Quinlan must not be perceived as an isolated case. Rather, it should be seen as a link in a chain of villainous roles. With Quinlan, Welles elaborated upon his continual propensity to play men with maniacal egos. Welles's direction may have attracted considerable criticism in the film industry, but his acting skills easily withstood the test of time. Universal hired him in January of 1957 at $12,500 per week, with a guarantee of at least ten weeks of work, to play the heavy according to Monash's original script of *Badge of Evil*.[81] Heston claims that his suggestion that Welles also direct the film, which struck him as "only a police-suspense story," was greeted with ridicule, "as though I'd asked to have my mother direct the picture."[82]

But Welles's credentials as someone inimitably suited to the playing of tainted Machiavellian men of importance were unquestionable. The proof was in the Hearst-like Charles Foster Kane; the immoral Nazi, Franz Kindler (*The Stranger*, 1946); the cruel industrialist, Arkadin (*Mr. Arkadin*, 1955); the corrupt police chieftain, Colonel Haki (*Journey Into Fear*, 1942); the con artist, Cagliostro (*Black Magic*, 1949); and the moody Macbeth (*Macbeth*, 1948). While *Touch of Evil* was in release, Welles also starred in *The Long Hot Summer* (Martin Ritt, 1958) as the father. A year later, he played the Clarence Darrow role in *Compulsion* (Richard Fleischer, 1959). Earlier, he appeared as a redneck sheriff in *Man in the Shadow* (Jack Arnold, 1957). In fact, this performance as a bigoted lawman led directly to the role of Quinlan in *Touch of Evil*.

Welles also stamped his presence into the vertiginous

camerawork, overlapping dialogue and general eccentricity of both plot and character development. Even the casting of Joseph Cotten, Akim Tamiroff, and Ray Collins, actors with whom he enjoyed a long and eventful association, further indicates a "Wellesian" project. Bazin may have been a champion of Welles, but Welles had his own egotistical designs apart from Bazinian humanism. His own, personal drive was certain to gain priority over humble self-effacements before reality, which are noticeably lacking in *Touch of Evil*. Yet, there is a fluidity and dynamism to Welles's creation, helped along by means of location cinematography, that is glaringly absent in the additional direction of Harry Keller, who finished production after Welles heatedly abandoned the film.

As a matter of record, Keller shot on Tuesday and Wednesday, November 19 and 20, 1957, more than half a year after Welles had begun shooting. Instead of Russell Metty, the cinematographer was Cliff Stein. Charlton Heston, Janet Leigh, Joseph Calleia, Mort Mills, and Valentine de Vargas (Pancho) were the actors summoned to Universal Studios to complete the job. To film the Vargases, as they pull to the side of the road on the way to the Mirador Motel, the crew used a small crane, a wind machine, and a moviola for backscreen projection. The romantic interlude was shot in a special "picture car" on Stage #21.[83] Keller also shot (1) Menzies, stepping into the car beside Susan as Mike goes dutifully along with Quinlan in the squad car; (2) Menzies, as he catches a glimpse of Grandi's car in the rearview mirror; (3) Schwartz, on a staircase, reaffirming to Vargas his willingness to seek proof of Quinlan's dishonesty; (4) the Vargases, exchanging some words in a hotel lobby; (5) Susan, aggravated by a menacing flashlight from an intruder across an alley as she puts on a sweater in the "privacy" of her room; (6) the Vargases, beginning their drive away from Los Robles; (7) Susan, reclining on a bed at the Mirador Motel, and (8) a reaction shot of "Pancho" to be inserted into the conversation sequence between Susan and Uncle Joe Grandi. Keller also shot exteriors of the police car, the Vargases's car and Grandi's convertible along a road in the Los Angeles area.[84]

The executives at Universal exhibited little patience with Welles, and he, in turn, could no longer endure the scrutiny of a vigilant front office. Three weeks into production, it was already obvious that Welles was going to go over budget.[85] Zugsmith tried to assure Welles that all he, as producer, wished for was "to help you the best of my ability to make an excellent photoplay." He told Welles that "all you have to do is ask me whatever you want done and usually it will be forthcoming."[86] But if nothing else, finances were too meager to sustain a consistently proficient work. The estimated budget, compiled as of mid-February, 1957, was a modest $832,780. In retrospect, it was an unrealistic amount. The wishful forecast included $125,000 for Welles, $55,000 for Janet Leigh, close to $9,000 for Zugsmith, nearly $15,000 for Metty, and Monash's $9,167.[87] Principal photography lasted twice as long as originally scheduled, beginning in the middle of February and stretching all the way to April. The sequence with the oil derricks took nearly ten days to shoot, approximately one day for every minute shown on screen. Fortunately, Heston settled for seven-and-a-half percent of the film's gross earning in lieu of a salary. He also agreed to help with publicity while in Europe, where *The Ten Commandments* (Cecil B. DeMille, 1956) was just on the verge of opening. In exchange, he asked Universal to pay his traveling expenses. There is no evidence to suggest that this deal was ever consummated.

Many minor actors and actresses were employed in *Touch of Evil*. Of these, quite a few were Hispanic. Their faces and Spanish accents serve as much as the proliferation of signs to identify the area as Mexican [Figure #9]. One Tina Menard, for instance, played the "lady with baby" who distracts Susan long enough to have her photographed alongside "Pancho."[88] Before Marlene Dietrich agreed to play Tana, one Pilar Arcos had been hired for the role.[89] Many uncredited Hispanic extras took part in street scenes, the barroom brawl and post-production looping. But like the location itself, they were not genuine inhabitants of the border between Texas and Mexico.

The power of Hollywood enabled it to build sets that

Figure 9. Signs.

could duplicate any place and to hire actors and actresses who could pose as anyone. Yet, just as the old saw says, nothing lasts forever; and not even a magician like the great Orson Welles could ultimately prevent an element of the counterfeit in filmmaking from eventually coming to light. The fact remains that as amazing as the film is, *Touch of Evil* should have been much better. It should also have been more *realistic*.

The Naked City used locations to penetrate the physical world—not necessarily in all its splendor. Still, its factual rendition of New York City did not lead to a deterioration in the relationship between residents and filmmakers the way *Touch of Evil* did in Venice. The acrimony engendered by this film was a logical response to the filmmakers' own peculiar "touch of evil." Like spirits casting a spell, they transmogrified Venice. A great lover of films and filmmaking, Welles always found Hollywood moviemaking objectionable. When he was younger, he regarded Hollywood contemptuously as a toy train set, but by the time he was middle-aged the toy had already succeeded in crushing his enthusiasm. With *Touch of Evil*, Welles was forced to become a frustrated cog in the overwhelming machinery of the mass-entertainment industry. The future belonged not to the lone wolf artist, but to the corporate-minded director. Word-of-mouth history has it that Welles did not see the film all the way through post-production to completion.

The use of locations in *Touch of Evil* represents a final tendency in *film noir* that distorted the physical world. It did not accurately reflect reality. In fact, if anything, it concealed reality. According to *New York Times* critic Howard Thompson, "the lasting impression of this film is effect rather than substance." Without a grounding in careful location shooting, even the narration loses its overall coherence. Why, queries Thompson, does a tough, redneck cop like Quinlan "buckle when a tourist calls his bluff?" Moreover, why does Vargas "pick the toughest little town in North America for a honeymoon?"[90]

Certainly, Welles was not the author of this new tendency. He is in no way to be held responsible for a collective trend set in motion by forces more powerful than the sum of all individual, artistic visions. Furthermore, this trend had more to do with film industry infrastructure than with questions pertaining to art. In any case, from this point on, *films noirs* became scarce and finally disappeared. Welles could not have seen that even strong, capable, talented leadership would not overcome the more fatuous needs and wants of spectators and producers alike. Without totally reverting back to the embryonic stage of the studio, filmmaking—philosophically, not technically—regressed. If all the world was once a stage, now it was—for all practical purposes—a studio.

NOTES

1. Porfirio: 227.
2. Dwight MacDonald, *Dwight MacDonald on Movies* (Englewood Cliffs, N.J.: Prentice Hall, 1969): 144–45.
3. Weegee, *Naked City* (New York: Essential Books, 1945): 243.

4. Schrader, "Notes on Film Noir": 12.
5. Review of *Touch of Evil, Cue,* 10 May 1958: 8.
6. Robert Ottoson, *A Reference Guide to the American Film Noir: 1940–1958* (Metuchen, N.J.: Scarecrow Press, 1981): 183.
7. Harold Heffernan, " 'Factual' Film Cycle Launched By Studios," *The Long Island Daily Press,* 19 March 1948: 18.
8. William Gordon, Inter-Office Memo to Gilbert Kurland, undated, Universal Collection, USC Cinema-Television Library and Archives of Performing Arts.
9. Barbara Leaming, *Orson Welles, A Biography* (New York: Viking, 1983): 421.
10. "Ron," Rev. of *Touch of Evil, Variety,* 19 May 1958: 16.
11. William Peper, "Welles Back in Old Villainy," *The New York World-Telegram and Sun,* 22 May 1958: 18.
12. Eric M. Krueger, "*Touch of Evil:* Style Expressing Content," *Cinema Journal,* Fall 1972: 58.
13. Leaming: 425.
14. Jeff Rovin, *The Films of Charlton Heston* (Secaucus, N.J.: Citadel Press, 1977): 92.
15. David Thomson, *America in the Dark: Hollywood and the Gift of Unreality* (New York: William Morrow, 1977): 127.
16. Orson Welles, quoted in "Return of the Prodigy," *Newsweek,* 29 April 1957: 108.
17. Venice Location Information, Universal Collection, USC Cinema-Television Library and Archives of Performing Arts: 1.
18. Ibid.: 2.
19. Ibid.: 3.
20. Day Player Agreement with Dave Sharpe, 14 March 1957, USC Cinema-Television Library and Archives of Performing Arts.
21. Venice Location Information, Universal Collection, USC Cinema-Television Library and Archives of Performing Arts: 4.
22. Ibid.: 8.
23. Ibid.: 13.
24. Ibid.: 25.
25. P. D. Nowell, letter to Mr. R. A. Michaels, 19 April 1957, Universal Collection, USC Cinema-Television Library and Archives of Performing Arts.
26. P. D. Nowell, letter to Mr. Malcolm J. La Rue, 30 April 1957, Universal Collection, USC Cinema-Television Library and Archives of Performing Arts.

27. P. D. Nowell, letter to Mr. Walter Carlson, 30 April 1957, Universal Collection, USC Cinema-Television Library and Archives of Performing Arts.
28. P. D. Nowell, letter to Mr. Jerry Sale, 13 May 1957, Universal Collection, USC Cinema-Television Library and Archives of Performing Arts.
29. P. D. Nowell, letter to Mr. Dave Butler, 15 May 1957, Universal Collection, USC Cinema-Television Library and Archives of Performing Arts.
30. P. D. Nowell, letter to Mr. Allan Sempers, 4 June 1957, Universal Collection, USC Cinema-Television Library and Archives of Performing Arts.
31. Ibid.
32. Venice Location Information, Universal Collection, USC Cinema-Television Library: 13.
33. Ibid.: 32.
34. "Return of the Prodigy," *Newsweek*, 29 April 1957: 108.
35. *The New York Daily Mirror*, 25 May 1958: 63.
36. Paul V. Beckley, *The New York Herald Tribune*, 22 May 1958.
37. R. N. Wilkinson, letter to Mr. Chas. Simonelli, Home Office, 26 June 1958, Universal Collection, USC Cinema-Television Library and Archives of Performing Arts.
38. *The New York Daily Mirror*, 25 May 1958: 63.
39. John A. Granara, at Universal, Memorandum to Sonny Burke, at Decca Records, 4 February 1957, Universal Collection, USC Cinema-Television Library and Archives of Performing Arts.
40. Howard Thompson, "Orson Welles Is Triple Threat in Thriller," *The New York Times*, 22 May 1958: 25.
41. Terry Comito, "Welles's Labyrinth: An Introduction to *Touch of Evil*" in *Touch of Evil, Orson Welles, director*, ed. Terry Comito (New Brunswick, N.J.: Rutgers University Press, 1985): 43.
42. Porfirio: 235.
43. Andrew Sarris, *The Village Voice*, 9 February 1976: 109.
44. *Badge of Evil*, Daily Production Report, 18 February 1957, USC Cinema-Television Library and Archives of Performing Arts.
45. Gregg Toland, A.S.C., "Realism for *Citizen Kane*," in *American Cinematographer*, February 1941: 54.
46. Stefan Sharff, *The Elements of Cinema, Toward a Theory of*

Cinesthetic Impact (New York: Columbia University Press, 1982): 32.
47. Ibid.
48. Bazin, "The Western" in *What Is Cinema?* Volume II: 146.
49. *Touch of Evil*, Continuity Script, Motion Pictures Division, State Education Department, Albany, New York.
50. Charlton Heston, *The Actor's Life, Journals 1956–1976*, ed. Hollis Alpert (New York: E.P. Dutton, 1976): 21.
51. *Badge of Evil*, Daily Production Report, 14–15 March 1957, USC Cinema-Television Library and Archives of Performing Arts.
52. Heston: 21.
53. Comito, "Interview with Orson Welles,": 201.
54. Dick Whittle, Synopsis of *Badge of Evil*, 23 February 1956, Universal Collection, USC Cinema-Television Library and Archives of Performing Arts.
55. Contract Brief between Universal and the Jaffe Agency, 1956, Universal Collection, USC Cinema-Television Library and Archives of Performing Arts.
56. Clark Ramsay, Inter-Office Communication to Ed Muhl, 23 July 1957, Universal Collection, USC Cinema-Television Library and Archives of Performing Arts.
57. Clark Ramsay, Inter-Office Communication to Marion Pecht, 1 August 1957, Universal Collection, USC Cinema-Television Library and Archives of Performing Arts.
58. Saul David, Telegram to David A. Lipton, 9 August 1957, Universal Collection, USC Cinema-Television Library and Archives of Performing Arts.
59. David A. Lipton, Telegram to Saul David, 9 August 1957, Universal Collection, USC Cinema-Television Library and Archives of Performing Arts.
60. William Gordon, Inter-Office Communication to All Department Heads and Others Concerned, 5 September 1957, Universal Collection, USC Cinema-Television Library and Archives of Performing Arts.
61. John Stubbs, "The Evolution of Orson Welles's *Touch of Evil* from Novel to Film," *Cinema Journal*, Winter 1985: 22.
62. Ibid.
63. Ibid.: 24.
64. Arthur: 161.
65. Ibid.: 167.
66. Ibid.: 168.

67. Orson Welles, "Interview with Orson Welles," in Comito: 206.
68. Robert Griffith, *The Politics of Fear, Joseph R. McCarthy and the Senate* (Lexington: University Press of Kentucky, 1970): 16.
69. Ibid.: 26.
70. Ibid.: 15.
71. Stubbs: 183.
72. Orson Welles, "Interview with Orson Welles," in Comito: 204.
73. Thomas Schatz, *Hollywood Genres: Formulas, Filmmaking, and The Studio System* (Philadelphia: Temple University Press, 1981): 144.
74. Orson Welles, "Interview with Orson Welles," in Comito: 204.
75. Ibid.: 205.
76. Anthony Perkins, "Inside Anthony Perkins." With Robert O'Brian, *RockBill Magazine*, July 1986.
77. Ibid.
78. Krueger: 57.
79. Orson Welles, Memorandum to Production Department, 3 February 1957, Universal Collection, USC Cinema-Television Library and Archives of Performing Arts.
80. Charlton Heston, Interview with James Delson, "Heston on Welles," in Comito: 221–2.
81. Jack Bauer, Inter-Office Communication to Albert Zugsmith et. al., 22 January 1957, Universal Collection, USC Cinema-Television Library and Archives of Performing Arts.
82. Heston: 18.
83. *Badge of Evil*, Daily Production Report, 19 November 1957, Universal Collection, USC Cinema-Television Library and Archives of Performing Arts.
84. Ibid.: 20 November 1957.
85. Picture Cost Report, Production Budget Department, 8 March 1957, Universal Collection, USC Cinema-Television Library and Archives of Performing Arts.
86. Albert Zugsmith, Inter-Office Communication to Orson Welles, 5 February 1957, Universal Collection, USC Cinema-Television Library and Archives of Performing Arts.
87. Budget for *Badge of Evil*, Universal-International, compiled as of 18 February 1957, Universal Collection, USC Cinema-Television Library and Archives of Performing Arts.
88. Day Player Agreement for Tina Menard, 22 February 1957, "Lady with baby," for $100 per day and $500 per week.

Universal Collection, USC Cinema-Television Library and
Archives of Performing Arts.
89. Day Player Agreement for Pilar Arcos, 8 March 1957, as
"Mother Lupe," at $150 per day and $750 per week.
Universal Collection, USC Cinema-Television Library and
Archives of Performing Arts.
90. Thompson.

V COMPARISONS

Comparisons among the three selected films, and the trends they subtend, reveal a certain bifurcation. In terms of the presentation of visual reality, *film noir* was consistent with the state of the industry at large. But it went to greater extremes in its preference for hard light over soft, for shadows and unusual light sources. The bleakness of *film noir*'s compositions was also in line with the moody *mise-en-scène* of war films, domestic melodramas, and psychological westerns. But in this category, too, *film noir* again outdid the genres that it competed against at the box-office. Their cinematographic components were often dark, but *film noir*'s camerawork was darker. Their philosophical tone was often melancholic, but *film noir*'s metaphysical orientation was more pessimistic. Their narratives were often harsh, but *film noir*'s stories were harsher.

In order to sustain such a serious lack of sentimentality, *film noir* incorporated a greater element of realism. Without enough realism to match the additional darkness, the films lacked a sense of balance. If one examines the stories of most *films noirs*, one finds that there are many sequences that strain credulity. An element of realism helped to bolster the credibility and artistic integrity of films that required such a boost. If nothing else, an element of realism sometimes made them seem more banal, and therefore less artistic, less contrived. Automobile traffic, pedestrian traffic, storefronts, alleys, streets, and houses were items that existed outside a director's jurisdiction. Their existence preceded the existence of the film that made use of them. The film would have to play out its drama around them, and not the other way around, as in a studio.

New economic strictures may have made location work all but imperative at some theoretical point in the 1940s, but *film noir* filmmaking took to the streets with special alacrity. Only so much could be done in a studio, by way of moving props and arranging camera positions, to create shadows and ominous settings. Outside studios, there were limitless possibilities. It would have been an unimaginative *film noir* filmmaker indeed who could not have made use of the modern landscape to do naturally what the diligent placement of shadows did artificially inside the studio. *Film noir* took advantage of power plants, warehouses, train yards, diners, department stores, amusement parks, and highways to spell out its message of despair even before its characters spoke or acted. In the urban maze, but also in certain rural locales, *film noir* found the physical correlative of its psychological disposition.

Film noir did not shy away from the environment with tight shots designed to blot out the surroundings, as is done in many of today's period films. The employment of wider lenses, the increase in the average length of shots and greater depth of field were all part of the same trend in cinema to pack more of the physical world into the frame. Not only did this trend target more space, it also sought to utilize more *time*, in terms of greater contemporaneity. Ultimately, even the frame widened, changing the Academy Ratio from 1.33:1 to 1.85:1.

Although Ronald Reagan, President of the Screen Actors Guild, attributed the decline in movie attendance to "censorship, discriminatory taxation and government harassment," television, as the main beneficiary, provided a strong impetus.[1] But its success at the expense of the film industry did not help define a strategy for films to stage a comeback. The medium itself chose to rally behind more serious films, using low-key cinematography and locations. Its concomitant experimentation with color, expanded screen size, and socially relevant subject matter was another way of perpetuating an ongoing dialogue with physical, political, economic, and societal realities in artistic representation.

The second world war caused a complete turnaround in

the attitudes of filmmakers toward reality, as something that had to be respected rather than manipulated. Responsibility for the war was in part ascribed to a universal lack of vigilance. It was only natural that Hollywood be made to shoulder some of the blame for drawing popular attention away from larger, more urgent topics. Miscreant film artists were constrained to gaze upon the earth with greater scrutiny. Schooled by the hard facts of war, spectators had little tolerance for the same old balderdash. Filmmakers would no longer permit themselves to make the same kinds of films. Blind faith in a bright future lost a great deal of its former luster. It is not surprising that as films grew more realistic, the studio system faltered. The dream factory sputtered and broke down, its commercial sanctum successfully undermined by a more informed, more world-weary breed of filmmaker. Visual reality became the cornerstone of a new, more sober outlook. This was the film medium's contribution to a wide-ranging artistic process already in motion. According to George J. Becker, it has always been the case that "American realism has had as its main point the refutation of traditional optimism."[2]

Unfortunately, such an edifying position is difficult to sustain. Today, even the worst horrors of World War II have become a subject of debate. A new, sinister imagination has firmed its grip on the young and the poorly educated. *Film noir*'s metaphysical pessimism seems to have anticipated an inevitable development in a less than perfect world, partly characterized by periodic, self-serving losses of memory. In *films noirs*, things go smoothly from bad to worse. Yet, even in a setting defined by purposelessness and impersonal materialism, drained of religious glory and mythological grandeur, *film noir* made room for the occasional act of heroism, character of nobility, and situation of hope.

This perspective is best expressed by a passage extracted from a French novel published in the middle of the *film noir* cycle, Albert Camus's *The Plague* (1948). During the heat of an epidemic, a character stricken with plague miraculously recovers. Another character is skeptical. If someone recovers from the plague, then it could not have been plague, since no one recovers from it. He expresses his disbelief to the doctor in charge. " 'You know as well as I do, once you have plague your number's up.' " The doctor replies, " 'True enough as a general rule. . . . But if you refuse to be beaten, you have some pleasant surprises.' "[3]

In the middle of its cycle, *film noir* seemed headed in a similarly euphoric direction. It is difficult, and perhaps even useless, to speculate as to what might have happened had it not collapsed into a baroque black hole. There is more than a coincidental connection between existentialist fiction and *film noir*. Camus was influenced by the tough-minded fiction of American authors, who also gave so much sustenance to *film noir*. It is difficult to separate the novels of writers such as Camus and Sartre, hardboiled American novels, and *films noirs*. All seem part of the same process, the same attempt to illuminate and alleviate the modern condition, characterized by meaninglessness. For the existentialist anti-hero, as well as protagonists of *film noir*, overtly futile, Sisyphean effort can sometimes avert the unspeakable. Even when it occurs, men and women under sentence of spiritual death can still redeem themselves through a full realization of their fatal mistakes.

Such is the case with Walter Neff (*Double Indemnity*), Frank Chambers (*The Postman Always Rings Twice*), Harry Fabian (*Night and the City*), Jeff Bailey (*Out of the Past*), and Thelma Jordan (*The File on Thelma Jordan*). Some are given a second chance: John Forbes (*The Pitfall*), George Taylor (*Somewhere in the Night*), and Leonora Eames (*Caught*). Only an acquaintance with evil on an intimate plane can prepare *film noir* characters for the clarity of vision they achieve in their final moments. Only a complete change of direction can save the ones whose expiation clears away the moral rubble to allow them a new start. In this sense, *film noir* can be thought of loosely as a metaphor for the war, which killed many but gave survivors an opportunity to rebuild a world community on a more solid footing.

But *film noir* was a metaphor for things more subtle, less visible, and possibly more sinister than war. It dealt with the underlying attitudes and dispositions that resulted in a world war. As such, *film noir* was as complex as the catastrophic events to which it indirectly alluded. Other kinds of films desperately clung to American platitudes, tailor-fitted to volatile political circumstances. For instance, in *Mission to Moscow* (Michael Curtiz, 1943), Hollywood depicted an avuncular Joseph Stalin, harassed by anarchic Troskyites. The Right had strategic reasons for whitewashing Stalin's image. In the middle of the war, Stalin was a staunch ally, regardless of his cruelty and connivances. But the Left remained permanently appalled. Stalin could do nothing to compensate for his betrayal of its confidence in his collusion with Hitler over the fate of Poland at the start of the war.

He could do nothing, nor did he wish to. The Popular Front alliance of international intellectuals and artists was deliberately sacrificed for the sake of military gain. Many of the European intellectuals and artists who were fortunate enough to have emigrated to the United States eventually found out that America was not the fulfillment of their European idealism. In its dark intonation, *film noir* documents the slide from hopefulness into despair, in recognition of the bitter realities of a world governed not by inspiring paradigms, ideals or great ideas, but by avaricious, self-serving interests.

Metaphorically, *film noir* expresses the disenchantment of a Left wounded and dispersed by political events that failed to vindicate its most cherished principles. This accounts for a good deal of *film noir*'s figurative darkness. It also helps account for the early demise of *films noirs* insofar as the disenchantment of a certain, time-bound constellation of leftists could not permanently sustain a type of filmmaking in the way that general fears and phobias could offer indefatigable support to horror films and science fiction.

-2-

Out of the ashes of old philosophies new ones arise. It would be difficult to underestimate the influence of *film noir* on today's films even though it has been about thirty years since a genuine *film noir* has been produced. It was very specific historical vectors that gave impetus to *film noir*. It was never simply pessimism. Pessimism pervades the arts during busts and dissipates during booms. It has a cyclical, if unpredictable, nature. Moreover, pessimism can only come about when events thwart more hopeful expectations. It takes some time to build up expectations again. *Film noir* seems to have taken the ephemeral nature of mood into account. It is never totally anarchic and atheistic. It nurtures an awareness of a larger picture where even hopelessness is doomed to fail. There are some interesting similarities to be found in early- and mid-1800s American literature. In a collection of essays entitled *American Realism* (1982), Jane Bernardete notes that "Nathaniel Hawthorne (1804–1864) and Herman Melville (1819–1891), had explored a darker side of the human spirit and the less reassuring aspects of American history. Yet they, too, worked within the idealistic conception of life. . . ."[4] An idealistic framework also surrounded *film noir*.

This idealism is perhaps more evident today than it was at the time. Contemporary reviewers almost always perceived *films noirs* as realistic. Quotations from their reviews were plentiful in the three analyses of representative works in order to emphasize this antiquated viewpoint. One has to preserve the context in which *films noirs* were originally screened in order to detect their movement toward greater visual integrity. This movement is especially reflected in the use of real events, rather than fictional stories, shot in the actual locations in which they occurred, rather than on sets. *Canon City* (Crane Wilbur, 1948) made use of the Colorado State Penitentiary, where the events depicted in this film actually took place. *Kiss of Death* (Henry Hathaway, 1947) made use of an assortment of New York locations, including "Sing Sing," the Penitentiary in Ossining, and a cell in the Tombs. Alfred Hitchcock painstakingly recreated the events of a tragic case of mistaken identity in New York City in *The Wrong Man* (1956).

Fictional *films noirs* also respected the use of locations

conforming to the actual settings of the story. The story for *Sorry, Wrong Number* (Anatole Litvak, 1948) takes place in New York City and the film contains location work shot in Staten Island and along Riverside Drive in Manhattan. *Killer's Kiss* (Stanley Kubrick, 1955) documents the seedier side of New York City in the mid-1950s. These films, and others like them, accurately reflect the nature of the environments in which they were filmed. Indirectly, they are exposés of big city loneliness and paranoia. Today, films that take place in New York but are filmed in Toronto, for instance, are commonplace. City buildings and streets may be interchangeable in the minds of directors and producers, but to the people who live in one place or another, the most similar blocks are sharply different from one another.

A wave of films that invested a great deal of their impact in location work exploded onto the screen in the years immediately following the close of the second world war. It was not long before their numbers abated. To be sure, there were more and more films being shot on location than before, but the kind of veneration for the world as it is found—which is such a large factor in the works of Rossellini—became scarcer and scarcer. The kind of respect for reality which was shown for New York City's diversity in Hellinger's production of *The Naked City* also became rare. But these films testify to a movement that culminated in such seminal films. It was a movement destined to capitulate to the needs of more commercial concerns. Location work continued, but without the revival of awe for the world as it exists that many *films noirs* reflect.

Even in the movement's final decadent form, bizarre *films noirs* maintained a surprisingly vigorous standard of visual realism. John Belton speaks of how *The Big Combo* "begins with a fragmented, spatially disorienting chase in the corridors of Madison Square Garden."[5] Other contemporary films shot on location showed signs of being manufactured in the image of painterly studio products. Changing the backdrop to a Hollywood film from a panorama to a city street seemed more and more like a vaudeville character changing hats to effect a new personality. Without the conscious intention to be as realistic as possible, and the deliberate attempt to actualize that intention, location shooting was just another controlled variable.

This is not to say that *films noirs* were *realistic*. For not only did they go further than other genres in the depiction of dark themes, they seemed also to depict a world much darker than it appeared in fact. They tended to highlight contrived situations pervaded by a thick, choking, melancholic atmosphere that probably few members of an audience, drawing upon a lifetime of experiences, recognized. Despite a panoply of fresh fears, stemming from the advent of nuclear power, Soviet domination in Eastern Europe, a bloody conflict in Korea, and a revolution in China, Americans were much less paralyzed by fear than their representative *film noir* protagonists might suggest. Few Americans could say that they were "all dead inside," in accordance with some of *film noir*'s more solemn litanies. Fewer still ever found themselves ensconced in a *"Dark Corner."* There probably never were a substantial number of movie patrons who in all sincerity ever echoed the sentiment of Johnny Kelly—played by Gig Young, himself a suicide—who says, in *The City That Never Sleeps*, "I feel like I'm in a cement mixer." Amid a rising GNP, low inflation, and a stable dollar, the fire and brimstone sermons from the 1930s were barely discernible. Although they were often perceived as such, *films noirs* were not especially realistic. But there is an element of realism involved in their rejection of the fairy-tale morality that pretty much dominated the general market.

As important as it is to take account of this element of realism, most evident in mid-cycle *films noirs,* it is equally important to see how transitory it was. Not long after the end of the second world war, interest in the cinematographic component of realism all but evaporated. Less than a decade before, *Citizen Kane* introduced this somewhat arcane subject with great esprit. Throughout the 1940s, cinematographers addressed issues relating to the illusionism of Hollywood. They sought to bring into

practice a more pristine camera, less polluted by the base
requirements of glamorization. They sought ways to rely
less heavily on gauze, diffused lighting, make-up, and the
repetitious employment of over-the-shoulder shots.
James Wong Howe, A.S.C., assailed the shot/reverse-
shot as "a screen convention that has no significance
whatsoever."[6] He also urged his colleagues to pare down
"shots from impossible angles," a spatially disorienting
device used rather frequently near the end of the *film noir*
cycle.[7] Robert Surtees, A.S.C., was proud of the fact that
he shot a feature film that dispensed with heavy make-up.
He boasted of how little "of any kind was used on any
member of the cast" of *Act of Violence* (Fred Zinnemann,
1948).[8] Joseph LaShelle, A.S.C., cinematographer for two
of Otto Preminger's *films noirs*, *Laura* (1944) and *Fallen
Angel* (1946), criticized liberties routinely taken with
camera positions and angles. According to LaShelle, "I
always try to keep the camera within the walls of the set
during shooting . . . so that the audience will catch the
feeling of actually being on the scene of the action."[9]

Progressive thoughts on the nature and obligations of
feature film cinematography were applied throughout the
mid- to late 1940s. Their applications form a basic component of an element of realism in *film noir*. It is of special
interest that there is an international dimension to the
whole debate on the function of the camera. Concerns
such as those cited above coincide chronologically with the
release of *Open City* in the mid-1940s. The Italian film's
world-wide reception caused many Hollywood filmmakers to rethink their values and strategies.

But a decade later, their break with the lax, irresponsible
wizardry of Hollywood illusionists appeared less clean.
With some notable exceptions, the 1950s have been characterized as the most juvenile period of American filmmaking.
Indeed, this was the decade during which the teenager rose
to prominence as the focus of popular, artistic production.
Filmmakers were getting ready to mount an attack on the
babyboomer's dollar. The late 1950s and early 1960s cashed
in on trends begun by Mickey Rooney, Judy Garland, and
Deanna Durbin during the late 1930s.

Somewhat disheartening to proponents of realism in cinema is the backsliding that occurred at this time. Directors, writers, and cinematographers repudiated ideas fashioned earlier during more tempestuous times. The same people who once advocated fundamental changes now held antithetical notions. For example, in the late 1950s Dassin recanted all of his emphatic views on the use of locations exemplified by *The Naked City*. He confided to a journalist that "in my ignorance, I imagined that one had to shoot inside real cafes or real skyscrapers. All that did was to limit the movements of the camera and, consequently, the staging of the scene."[10] Not a trace of the idealism that motivated a director to accept a bold new project seemed to survive. If this were just the case of one disillusioned director, there would be nothing more to add. But this is not an isolated case. Dassin speaks with a universal voice when he repudiates the idealism that made him want to direct actors in natural exteriors and shoot inside natural interiors. Now that location shooting and independent production had become routine, the film industry once again contracted. It restored the insulation it lost when the studios were broken up.

More than the studios and the studio system of production was disintegrating. A whole way of codification—of looking at things, seeing the world, interpreting its events, deciphering its meanings, and ascertaining and representing its difficult relationships—had reached an end. Especially devastated was the economic, political, intellectual, and artistically creative Left. Whereas it resolutely entered the second world war against fascism, it exited in a state of mass directionless confusion.

It is impossible to analyze the films of the 1930s, '40s and '50s without acknowledging the influential role of a crescent and decrescent Left. It helped catalyze the movement that resulted in location shooting. To the Left, filmmaking had the potential to transcend the crass mercantile level of Hollywood. The influence of the Left cannot be factored out of the downbeat atmosphere of *film noir*, which dovetailed nicely with a political philosophy that accused capitalism of creating a demeaning, lawless society. What the Left probably had not foreseen was the virtual apolitical acceptance by audiences of abject descriptions of life as something aesthetically pleasing. While not approving the conditions themselves, they were appreciative of Hollywood's new, more realistic orientation. They were aware that before *film noir* they were treated like children. Finally, Hollywood had taken off the kid gloves. Those accustomed to escapist fare looked favorably upon portrayals of a world as illogical and imperfect as the one they were acquainted with. This 180-degree transformation was welcomed for its own sake. Although in literature critical views of life have been a perennial staple, movies feared the slightest deviation from the most neutral, uncontroversial, and massively acceptable perceptions. Through *film noir* and other genres, the pleasures of the critical gaze of literature were transferred to the film medium.

Commenting upon the Spartan philosophy deftly woven into the fabric of the novels of James M. Cain, Joyce Carol Oates observes, "It is the fact that such pessimistic works are entertainment that fascinates. No happy endings, no promise of religious salvation, not even the supposition that society has been purged of evil—society is always worse than Cain's victims! Nothing is handed out to the reader; no obvious wish is fulfilled."[11] Hardboiled literature and *film noir* alike deny plenitude. Instead, they emphasize precariousness as the governing element of a life that in truth doles out no dependable moral compensation for unjust, violent actions. The Left was motivated to promote contrary viewpoints such as this, perhaps not fully realizing that while art is a great critical mechanism, it is a deficient one for staging a rally on behalf of alternate political systems. No matter how ugly and unfair *film noir* painted the world, nothing in it could persuade people to think that a socialist framework was preferable to a capitalist one.

Although people rejected the solutions that the Left devised, they did not totally dismiss the critiques that were offered. Withholding information and downplaying the significance of catastrophes and conflicts are the earmarks of totalitarian regimes. Different points of view are always to some extent welcome in a society that is characterized by sharp divergences. However, they are unfamiliar in a format that adopts a view of life that squirmingly avoids either contradiction or endorsement. Hiding problems has never yet made one go away. To the extent that cinema confronts the world we live in, there is a great deal to be said—from many people and from many angles.

D. W. Griffith once stated that his primary aim in filmmaking was to make audiences "see." To Griffith, the function of cinema was to show, not to conceal. It is a simple statement, but one worth considering. No one has ever succeeded in escaping the world through a diegetic corridor. There is no passageway to a beyond, as there is through a kiva in a Hopi legend that Louis L'Amour expands upon in his novel, *The Haunted Mesa* (1987). There is truly no way out, though fascist films have tried to skillfully rive art and reality into separate and distinct categories. It is no accident that *Triumph of the Will* and all of Cinecittà's "white telephone" movies are so shorn of details that might have documented the struggle to survive during the truculent 1930s.

Many filmmakers who were politically remote embraced documentary and semi-documentary techniques that had been brought to prominence by radicals. Filmmakers credited the work of artists who were politically progressive without giving support to their political beliefs. For instance, Mark Hellinger approved of *The Naked City* project only after he acquired the services of Albert Maltz. Certainly, Maltz was not hired because of his involvement in the communist party. But the skillfulness of Maltz's writing, that Hellinger so admired and sought to avail himself of, had been sharpened and refined because of the writer's alliance with an anti-establishment organization.

Alfred Hitchcock provides another example. According to Joseph A. Valentine, A.S.C., while shooting *Shadow of a Doubt* Hitchcock tried to emulate "the realistic effects the Russians get by filming so many of their pictures against actual locations rather than sets, and every-day people, rather than professional extras, moving through scenes."

Hitchcock was not interested in the underlying principles that fueled Soviet experimentation with documentary techniques. He knew that "They do it because they have to." But after filming in a Santa Rosa bank, Western Union telegraph office, and cocktail lounge, he was satisfied that location shooting created "an atmosphere of actuality that couldn't be captured in any other way."[12] Valentine also noted the lack of interchangeability between studios and locations: "Not only have we given our picture its background on a scale that couldn't satisfactorily be reproduced in studio-made construction; we've captured a note of realism which also can't be reproduced in a studio."[13] A primary influence at the time were Soviet documentaries, in which great dramatic intensity was accomplished without embellishments, editorial sleight-of-hand, intense close-ups, ethereal superimpositions, inserts, or gut-wrenching music.

-3-

Not only radicals and aestheticians of the camera but also purveyors of mass entertainment saw early on an alternative market in shooting done outside the confines of a studio. The newsreel was developed by such entrepreneurs. As Raymond Fielding points out, the subject matter of a newsreel might be topical, but its substance "belonged to show business rather than to journalism."[14] Any hint of disputatiousness was thought to have been detrimental to the whole film industry. Martin Quigley, owner of the leading trade publication, the *Motion Picture Herald*, criticized *The March of Time* for stirring up controversy.[15] Opposition to contention was mulilateral. "Roxy" Rothapfel excoriated the screening of anything of a controversial nature in his theatre.[16] Fox also maintained a policy of not exhibiting a film or newsreel if it was the least bit disquieting to the status quo. General American spectators embraced the neutral point-of-view of theatre owners, but did not unconditionally accept as newsworthy the images that were foisted on them. They did not necessarily appreciate the sugar-coating done supposedly on their behalf. Liberal patrons were known to jeer and sometimes picket Hearst's *News of the Day*, released by MGM, for pandering to the Right.[17] Furthermore, it is doubtful that, given the opportunity, the Right would have defended Hearst's propaganda as a beacon of truth.

In such a historical context, it is not surprising that the portrayal of the darker aspects of contemporary life on film should be funneled into fictional channels. Feature films have the rare privilege of being able to explore the dark recesses of the human soul in places where even hidden cameras are unlikely to go. *Film noir* heralded a new era of confrontation with serious matters like urban violence, racism, abuse of authority, class friction, and harmful power struggles in elite inner circles. The use of locations helped *film noir* attain its goal of making films in the places where such injustices actually occur. As such, it was following the lead of much of the literature upon which it based so many of its stories. Filmmaking had to come out of the studio just as mystery writing had to lift its stories out of the parlor.

Commenting upon the *Black Mask* school of pulp fiction, Philip Durham points out that "Hammett went to the American alleys and came out with an authentic expression of the people who live in and by violence."[18] Raymond Chandler expressed his gratitude to Hammett by describing how he "gave murder back to the kind of people who commit it for reasons, not just to provide a corpse; and with the means at hand, not hand-wrought pistols, curare and tropical fish."[19] *Film noir* capitalized on this new tough-mindedness in its adaptations and spin-offs. According to Jon Tuska, "what most appealed to [Edward Dmytryk] about filming the Chandler milieu was that it allowed him to break with a number of traditions. First, detective films had been formerly preoccupied with crimes committed among the rich; this story [*Farewell, My Lovely*—retitled, *Murder, My Sweet*] permitted the camera to venture among the lower levels of society where crime was far more commonplace, even a product of the milieu itself; second, where before right and wrong had always been black and white, now it was possible to conceive of the world as gray."[20]

Film noir was especially fascinated by the lower depths. One of the leading characters in The Woman in the Window (Fritz Lang, 1945) describes an almost stereotypical femme fatale, Alice Reed (Joan Bennett), as "the bottom of the barrel." However, a portrait of her idealizes her. Analogously, film noir treated the most decrepit vistas as though they were riveting treasures for the eye. Film noir exploited numerous unsightly locations such as a squalid section of Chicago in Call Northside 777 (Henry Hathaway, 1948), the Monterey cannery in Clash by Night (Fritz Lang, 1952), Albuquerque's Armor Meat Plant in Gun Crazy, Los Angeles drainage ditches in Roadblock (Harold Daniels, 1951), and an unfinished stretch of highway leading away from San Francisco's Sutro's Museum in The Lineup (Don Siegel, 1958).

Street scenes shot on location occur as early as 1941 in I Wake Up Screaming (H. Bruce Humberstone). Mean streets became an essential element of films noirs, just as outdoor scenes were a vital aspect of impressionism nearly a century before. Throughout the film noir cycle, location shooting often emerges unexpectedly in films shot predominantly inside a studio (e.g., While the City Sleeps and The Enforcer). This is not to say that studio replications were ineffective. Quite the contrary. For example, in the early 1950s Simone de Beauvoir observed that New York City in actuality was very much like its depiction in movies: "what worried me was that these studio sets, which I had never believed in, should be so real."[21] They appeared "fake by association" on the screen because the films themselves were not as carefully cut from the fabric of life.

Only a concerted effort could significantly reduce the role of fakery in cinema. Despite burgeoning concern about how detached Hollywood productions were from real life, discontent was far from unanimous among spectators or filmmakers. The shift to location shooting and independent production did not automatically signal a halt in cinematic prestidigitation. The magic show continued, unabated, even stronger than before. But location shooting and freedom from the dominance of a corporate mentality were essential conditions, if anything was to be gained in the direction of realism.

It is the way in which locations were used that is crucial, just as it is what independent filmmakers did with their independence that is crucial. Research shows that it was more difficult for Hellinger et al. to shoot *The Naked City* than it was for Welles to shoot *Touch of Evil*. Hellinger's crew could not "rent" streets, stores, blocks, and houses, as did Welles's. With all his clout, Hellinger could not disrupt the daily grind of New Yorkers as much as Welles could prevail upon the citizenry of Venice. Yet *The Naked City* remains the more realistic of the two, while *Touch of Evil* is approachable only with the most arcane allusions to psychoanalysis and linguistics.

The Naked City provided as good a vindication as any of von Stroheim's radical notion that even invisible elements are reflected on film. Studio facilities lacked more than simply the means to duplicate skyscrapers. They lacked the ability to reflect the mindlessness, impersonality, and randomness of the great cities. They would always come up short. This was not a matter of improving technology. For a similar reason, Bazin dismissed *Scott of the Antarctic* (Charles Frend, 1948) as "proof enough that the documentary-film-by-reconstruction is dead."[22] According to Bazin, "studio reconstructions reveal a mastery of trick work and studio imitation—but to what purpose? To imitate the inimitable, to reconstruct that which of its very nature can only occur once, namely risk, adventure, death."[23]

In some documentaries, shots are not just taken, they are won by means of hard effort and luck. It was the visible reflection of hazardous, life-threatening circumstances that compelled Bazin to call the documentary *Kon-Tiki* (1958) "an admirable and overwhelming film."[24] Ezra Goodman, writing for *American Cinematographer*, mentions how documentaries made from 16mm war footage, "taken under the most trying conditions, have put Hollywood's professional 'realism' to shame."[25] This is not to diminish the role of technology, in combination with ingenuity. For instance, Welles's opening *tour de force* crane shot for *Touch of Evil* has rightfully achieved a legendary status. Without detracting from this privileged moment in cinema, one must note for the sake of analysis that Welles obtained this lengthy shot under favorable circumstances. He had complete mastery of the environment. Nothing impeded his movement through it. In contrast, *The Naked City*'s crew operated with considerably less authority. As a result, its candid shots of New York City during a sweltering heatwave in the summer of 1947 are much less fanciful. Welles's opening shot for *Touch of Evil* is many things, but one thing it is not is a slice of life.

Michelangelo is thought to have said that he saw works of art embedded within shapeless stones. As an artist he chiseled out works of art that were already fully formed therein. His task was not to invent, but to gaze into an amorphous mass and tease out the object within. His craft required perception and skill, but not invention. It would be more logical if filmmakers could see in specific environments stories in search of authors—or auteurs. But most filmmakers start with a personal brainstorm and then strive to make the material world conform to it, rather than the other way around. It was an idea that motivated Welles in *Touch of Evil*—or perhaps at times it was less an idea and more an emotion. In a word it was abhorrence—abhorrence of totalitarianism, fascism, dogmatism, police states. No one can say that it was not a worthy idea, or that Welles was not fully capable of bringing it to the screen. What he required was the complicity of a more precise location, one that fit the needs of the story rather than the budget of the financiers.

Welles knew that his idea needed fertile soil if it was to germinate into something real and palpable. There is no question but that Welles wanted to shoot on location along the U.S.-Mexico border. In such a situation, the environment itself, and the reality of the subject material he was dealing with, would have influenced the actual outcome of the film. It would have been less cryptic, more accessible, and altogether harder-hitting. He might have settled for Arizona rather than Texas, the actual setting of the story. But the front office forced him to make do with a suburb of

Los Angeles, already an oppressive restraint. Welles had little choice but to resign himself to the unartistic wishes of the film's financial backers. However, wherever possible, he negotiated a piece of location shooting that had not been originally planned for. Welles was especially fascinated by the squalor and decrepitude he discovered in late 1950s Venice. With each new discovery, he abandoned sets built or about to be built at Universal. As interesting as these backdrops are, they are simply wrong for the story. One has only to think of how *The Naked City* might have looked if large chunks of it had been filmed in Toronto, as is sometimes done today. The illusion of reality in movies is elastic, but it can be stretched only so far before it will snap.

To reduce location shooting in the aftermath of World War II to a set of new economic factors governing filmmaking activity in Hollywood is to miss out on the aesthetic ramifications of the period. To be certain, changes in vital business relationships go a long way toward explaining the emergence of widespread location shooting. According to William Lafferty, the use of locations ultimately became an economic imperative. In 1946, controls on prices were lifted, ending the enforced rationing of filmmaking equipment. Major suppliers like Kodak and DuPont raised their prices significantly. Postwar inflation added to the escalation in costs. Persistent labor disputes provided further aggravation undermining the equilibrium of the old Hollywood.[26]

To reiterate a statement already articulated, what filmmakers did with location shooting is a more crucial topic of concern than the fact that they began to shoot on location during the mid- to late 1940s. Even pushing this distinction aside, the metamorphosis of location shooting from the cocoon of studio filmmaking cannot be attributed wholly to economics. Filmmaking has always consisted—from "before the beginning"—of multiple interests. Monetary obstacles to the resumption of steady studio production were never at any point insurmountable. In fact, despite the termination of autonomous studios, studio-type filmmaking never completely ground to a halt. It continued to phase out gradually for decades, never quite approaching the brink of obsolescence. Today, studios are still very much an integral part of filmmaking.

But since the advent of location shooting in the 1940s they have never regained the power they once wielded. Francis Ford Coppola's and Zoetrope's blunder, *One From the Heart* (1982), was an elaborate attempt to stoke the ancient fires of dominant studio filmmaking. It proved in a roundabout manner that studio filmmaking is not so much unfeasible as undesirable. While indispensible, the role of finance is but one among several elements in a very complex process. There is little question but that money is the bottom line. Nevertheless, if money were all that mattered, the capital of the film industry might still be in the East, closer to New York banks than to California sun.

Raymond Williams provides an enlightening parallel to the switch from studio to locations in filmmaking in his treatment of the introduction of rooms in theatre. This took place "during the nineteenth century in a wide area of the European theatre." According to the traditional explanation, technological developments, such as gas lighting, carpentry, and a variety of improvements having to do with the stage brought about this intriguing transmutation. But Williams points out that although these advances were indeed important, they are subordinate to something else. They helped support a more fundamental change in aesthetic consciousness. Interpretations to the contrary place the horse before the cart. To Williams, "the production of the room on the stage was a particular reading both of the natural centre of dramatic action in terms of social extension and the emphasis on the contemporary."[27]

Similarly, the shift from studio films to films made on location entailed a correlative change in dramatic orientation. At least in the beginning, rarely was a studio film interchangeable with a film shot on location. The aesthetic approach of one was never commensurate with that of the other. Speaking about Italian cinema, David Bordwell and Kristin Thompson stress economic considerations to account for the changeover from studio to location. Bordwell and Thompson point out that Cinecittà was so heavily damaged during the second world war that location shooting became an urgent necessity. For that reason, "Neorealist mise-en-scène relied on actual locales, and its photographic work tended toward the raw roughness of documentaries."[28] This is to suggest that neorealism could just as easily have crystallized from within the painted walls, facades, and ceiling-less rooms of stage set-ups— and this is absolutely untrue.

-4-

Fundamental transformations of a particular medium's form of expression demand other, ancillary alterations as well. Appeals to a higher plane of visual realism and a greater fidelity to the physical environment need to be bolstered by different, more serious, and more meaningful themes. A self-regulated industry to begin with, Hollywood policed itself throughout this period of transition. A significant adjustment that the film capital made in order to better accommodate location work was to distance itself from the platitudinous myths it formerly propagated. Hollywood developed a new obligation, beyond the likes and dislikes of its patrons, to bring its film products more in line with the source from which they were derived— reality, in all its visual, moral, and social complexity. This movement is evident in the way *film noir* discredited the happy ending, which always rings false when it occurs, like an antique that has been touched up to look as though it were new. The connoisseur sees through the deception, knows that it was the result of a commercial ploy, and understands that the true value of the piece—be it furniture or film—lies underneath.

When Malvin Wald wrote the treatment for *The Naked City*, he did not know he was writing a *film noir*. He wanted to write a tough, uncompromising, unmitigated crime drama that took place in New York City. Moreover, he intended all along for it to be filmed in New York City and to not transgress against the truth in the name of art. His research revealed that contrary to "the movies," which "keep telling that the police don't know how to solve" crimes, no murders of record were ever solved independent of the police. As a result, there is no Private Eye in the film. The semi-documentary strove for further accuracies in the depiction of the investigation. When Tom Polhaus (Ward Bond) shows Spade the murder weapon in *The Maltese Falcon*, it is wrapped inside a handkerchief. In *The Naked City*, professional investigators loop a string around a material clue. Wald's research further revealed that crime detection is not only more laborious than its representation in movies, but that it is also much more frustrating. According to Wald, "the New York police report that they haven't found a set of five good fingerprints on a gun in the last twenty years."[29]

Not every film artist agreed with the principle of truth for its own sake. Leon Shamroy, A.S.C. [*Leave Her to Heaven* (John Stahl, 1945)—arguably a *film noir* shot in color] cautioned filmmakers against the threat of " 'ultra-realism,' which can mean jeopardizing large investments." In 1947, while the semi-documentary was ascendant, Shamroy clung to the age-old assessment of cinema as "a welcome escape from the everyday trials and tribulations." According to this philosophy, movies should be painted with thick, bold strokes. Heroes should be "youthful, handsome and virile." Heroines should be "young and beautiful, complete with smooth, silken complexions."[30]

Hal Rosson, A.S.C., who shot the consummate product of this kind of thinking, *The Wizard of Oz* (Victor Fleming, 1939), was also a staunch defender of a conservative studio system of filmmaking. Indeed, many of the best auteurs flaunted reality. For instance, Hitchcock's innocents on the lam run away from the police as much as they do from the bad guys. In reality, people ordinarily seek the assistance of the authorities. To Hitchcock, if characters in trouble go to the police, the result is a movie that is boring. Hitchcock's longevity in a capricious industry testifies to the wisdom of this assumption.

John Ford, another director who triumphed over the vicissitudes of fickle taste and fashion, jumbled and re-arranged historical facts and figures to fit the grid of his own personal logic. According to Ford, strict adherence to historical minutiae can actually produce a paradoxical aura of incredulity: "There have to be some compromises with historical fact and accuracy in all movies. The public will simply not accept things which seem strange to them, true as they may be."[31] An edification of this type of thinking is expressed by *The Man Who Shot Liberty Valance* (John Ford, 1962), in which the printed legend exceeds the value of the unprinted truth.

If *film noir* did not actually change the pro-fictional stance of Hollywood into pro-factuality, it at least introduced greater flexibility. This is especially evident in regard to roles. Because of *The Maltese Falcon*, Bogart metamorphosed his constricted stock villain screen persona into one that is far more complex. As has been shown, Bogart's Sam Spade was interpreted by contemporary reviewers as a realistic character. Similarly, although Mary Astor failed to rise to the expectations of some of these reviewers, they still understood from her performance that her character far outdistanced any female protagonist they had hitherto seen, in terms of feminine villainy.

Other actors and actresses also underwent reverse face lifts that made them uglier, hiding the cloying goodness of their former acting personae. Dick Powell's conversion from a smooth-complexioned singer, hoofer, and bubbly romancer to an ill-shaven, acidic cynic is probably the most famous. But the list also includes Fred MacMurray in *Double Indemnity* (Billy Wilder, 1944), Robert Montgomery in *Ride the Pink Horse* (Montgomery, 1947), Robert Young in *They Won't Believe Me* (Irving Pichel, 1947), and William Holden in *The Dark Past* (Rudolph Mate, 1948). Transmogrifications such as these in *film noir* benefited numerous actresses who were normally condemned to playing roles bound by prudish standards. Two good examples are Ann Sheridan and Joan Bennett.

A parody of this process can be read into nearly the first half of *Dark Passage* (Delmer Daves, 1947). In this mid-cycle *film noir*, Bogart plays an escaped convict by the name of Vincent Perry. Perry first appears wrapped in bandages after undergoing plastic surgery following a prison escape. A picture printed in a newspaper reveals what he looked like before. It shows that he had straight, even features but when the bandages come off he is left with Bogart's more distinctive mug.

Film noir created roles that provided acting debuts for Kirk Douglas and Burt Lancaster, and sustained the careers of Dan Duryea, Thomas Gomez, and Elisha Cook, Jr. It also helped liberate cinematographers from the onus of having to repetitiously shoot monotonous eye-level, evenly-lit set-ups. During this time, progressive film-makers marshaled industry opinion against the dominance of brilliantly-lit compositions. Writing in *American Cinematographer*, Herb A. Lightman deemed *Blood on the Moon* (Robert Wise, 1948)—starring *film noir* regular, Robert Mitchum—a "low-key picture, a quality that sets it apart from the usual sun-drenched western."[32] Another writer for *American Cinematographer*, Arthur E. Gavin, lauded Charles Lang, Jr.'s shooting for *Wild Is the Wind* (George Cukor, 1957) as "realistic." Lang did not go "overboard on fill light and arty effects" and achieved "an effective pictorial balance by keeping the light on background walls down to the minimum."[33]

Gavin also singled out Sam Leavitt's "low-key treatment" of *The Defiant Ones* (Stanley Kramer, 1958).[34] In general, it is unwise to assign a definite meaning to any particular visual variable. But in the context of *film noir*, low-key cinematography served a dual purpose. First, it set a pessimistic tone. Second, it was perceived as realistic. It was emptied of the frivolity sometimes associated with brighter compositions. An early experiment with location shooting, *The Dark Corner*, was often literally as dark as its name implies. *The Naked City* did not require such an embellishment. It proved that the existential texture of *film noir* is due to more than the use of artifice, expressionistic devices, and horror film techniques. It also had to do with the way in which it fictively interpreted the real world, contingent upon the use of an element of realism.

Many *films noirs* sought the corroboration of various authorities as testimony to their verity. For example, *The*

House on 92nd Street employed footage showing Fifth Column spies, FBI agents, and the latter's office space in Washington, D.C. A written prologue stated that the film used classified information only recently released by the FBI in the wake of the bombing of Japan. In its preliminary stages, *The Naked City*'s publicists strove to emphasize the film's affinity with "such pictures as 'Boomerang,' 'Kiss of Death,' and 'House on 92nd Street.' "[35] All of these films took pains to stress the fact that they depicted actual events, shot as much as possible in the settings where the events actually occurred.

The Phenix City Story (Phil Karlson, 1955) began with voice-over, documentary news footage and an emcee. The latter holds a microphone and addresses the camera. He explains the basis for the story, the vice trade that infiltrated a middle-American locale, and the heroic resistance of plain citizens who refused to give in to it. He goes on to interview people who would be dramatically portrayed by actors and actresses in the film shortly to follow. In this heavy-handed fashion, the filmmakers assured the audience that what they were about to see was timely as well as based on a true story. Also, it was on the side of the "people," the silent majority, and against the parasitical purveyors of gambling, immorality, and corruption.

There are subversive elements in *film noir*, but they are displaced by the need to please rather than offend the status quo. *The City That Never Sleeps* is obsequiously and pompously "dedicated to the police and police departments of America—a brave army of men and women who form our first line of defense in preserving our sacred principles of personal liberty and justice." *The Lineup* ends with an expression of gratitude to the San Francisco Police. Such expressions were common. *Thunder Road* (Arthur Ripley, 1948) pays tribute to the Alcohol and Tobacco Tax Division, the Internal Revenue Service, and the Treasury Department. In a sort of mock tribute to this procedure, Luis Buñuel's *Los Olvidados* commences with a similar acknowledgment: "This film is entirely based on actual incidents and all characters are authentic." Hitchcock explains in person at the outset of *The Wrong Man* that his semi-documentary film was based on a true miscarriage of justice.

It seems that as *films noirs* became more reliant on facts, figures, and documents, they also became more apologetic. None of the films analyzed in this study begin with a sanctimoniously written prologue, but the difference between the opening shot of *The Maltese Falcon* and that of *The Naked City* reveals a great deal about the patriotic flourish that came about during *film noir*'s middle period. In *The Maltese Falcon*, the image of the jewel-encrusted figurine, supposedly concealed underneath a layer of black enamel, emerges just after the Warner Bros. logo. The music swells as the credits are shown in an animated sequence. They "magically" shrink and dissolve, like verbal mirages. The imperious statuette and the dazzling music, together with the snaky lettering, combine to produce an aura of mystery, suspense, and escapism. They hold at bay the unwanted intrusion of sad, world-weary truths and personal sorrows. Like the worthless piece of lead shaped in the guise of an invaluable black bird, the studio promises only the diaphonous substance of dreams.

This introductory segment is artful and deftly controlled. Its chief purpose is to jolt the spectator out of reality (or vice versa) and prepare him or her for a substitute reality, an *unreality* that is more profluent, focused, exciting, and entrancing. The spectator can be reasonably sure that no allusions to the real world left behind will threaten to disturb the fabulous pleasure that awaits. But, as the analysis of *The Maltese Falcon* has shown, Huston's pessimism provides a very hospitable conduit for the real world. Intimations of the universal insecurities of existence are everywhere apparent. An element of realism is piped in, sight unseen.

In contrast, shown without the distraction of credits, the first image of *The Naked City* is the Statue of Liberty. Shot from an airplane, this incipient visual construction is qualitatively different from the stock footage that perfunctorily sets *The Maltese Falcon* in San Francisco. *The Naked*

City's distant, night-for-night shot appears in conjunction with narration by Mark Hellinger, who died just months before the initial release of the film. The shot conjures up an eerie, reverential tone. In fact, all of the location footage to follow will evoke a range of nostalgic and other piqued responses to historically-bound images that studio-created films could rarely, if ever, attain. Hellinger himself speaks not as a representative of Universal, but as one of the anonymous eight million.

He speaks proudly of his city's diverse culture and ethnic mix without the reassuring imprimatur of the studio. This is an independent production motivated by independent thought. The narration is spoken in a language different from the stilted wording of most semi-documentary prologues. Sadly, he could not have known that the independence with which the film was so finely crafted would be bulldozed by the distributor. He could not have anticipated the change in climate that would undermine independent thinking and filmmaking. As independent production replaced studio filmmaking, independent filmmaking began to resemble studio filmmaking in terms of the suppression of an element of realism— the true reality *noir* behind this *film noir*.

NOTES

1. "Don't Blame TV for Film Woe—Reagan," *The Denver Post*, 23 May 1957: 40.
2. George J. Becker, *Realism in Modern Literature* (New York: Frederick Ungar, 1980): 92.
3. Albert Camus, *The Plague*, trans. Stuart Gilbert (New York: Vintage Books, 1971): 148.
4. Jane Benardete, Introduction, *American Realism*, ed. Jane Benardete (New York: G. P. Putnam's Sons, 1972): 10–11.
5. John Belton, *Cinema Stylists* (Metuchen, N.J.: Scarecrow Press, 1983): 203.
6. Ezra Goodman, "Post-War Motion Pictures," *American Cinematographer*, May 1945: 176.
7. James Wong Howe, A.S.C., "The Documentary Technique in Hollywood," *American Cinematographer*, June 1944: 32.

8. Robert Surtees, A.S.C., "The Story of Filming 'Act of Violence'," in *American Cinematographer*, August 1948: 282.
9. Herb A. Lightman, "Exponent of the Moving Camera," in *American Cinematographer*, November 1948: 394.
10. Jules Dassin, "I See Dassin Make 'The Law'," interview by John Lane, *Films and Filming*, September 1958: 28.
11. Joyce Carol Oates, "Man Under Sentence of Death, The Novels of James M. Cain," in *Tough Guy Writers of the Thirties*, ed. David Madden (Carbondale: Southern Illinois University Press, 1968): 85.
12. Joseph A. Valentine, A.S.C., "Using an Actual Town Instead of Movie Sets," in *American Cinematographer*, October 1942: 462.
13. Ibid.: 440.
14. Raymond Fielding, *The American Newsreel, 1911–1967* (Norman: University of Oklahoma Press, 1972): 225.
15. Ibid.: 222.
16. Ibid.: 223.
17. Ibid.: 248.
18. Philip Durham, "The *Black Mask* School," in *Tough Guy Writers of the Thirties*: 53.
19. Chandler: 530.
20. Jon Tuska, *Dark Cinema: American Film Noir in Cultural Perspective* (Westport, Conn.: Greenwood Press, 1984): 177.
21. Simone de Beauvoir, *America, Day by Day* (New York: Grove Press, 1953): 14.
22. Bazin, "Cinema and Exploration," in *What Is Cinema?* Volume I: 156.
23. Ibid.: 158.
24. Ibid.: 161.
25. Goodman: 160.
26. William Lafferty, "A Reappraisal of the Semi-Documentary in Hollywood, 1943–1948," in *The Velvet Light Trap*, Summer 1983: 24.
27. Raymond Williams, "A Lecture on Realism," *Screen*, Spring 1977: 66.
28. David Bordwell & Kristin Thompson, *Film Art: An Introduction* (New York: Alfred A. Knopf, 1986): 371.
29. Malvin Wald, "Cops and Writers," *The Screen Writer*, March 1948: 25.
30. Leon Shamroy, A.S.C., "The Future of Cinematography," *American Cinematographer*, October 1947: 358.
31. John Ford, "The Old Horseman Rides Again: John Ford

Talks About Westerns," Interview with Bill Libby in *My Darling Clementine*, ed. Robert Lyons (New Brunswick, N.J.: Rutgers University Press, 1984): 139.
32. Herb A. Lightman, "Low Key and Lively Action," *American Cinematographer*, December 1948: 411.
33. Arthur E. Gavin, *"Wild Is the Wind* Is Realistic!" in *American Cinematographer*, January 1958: 56.
34. Arthur E. Gavin, *"The Defiant Ones*—Ultimate in Mood Photography," in *American Cinematographer*, August 1958: 484.
35. *A Publicity and Advertising Campaign for "The Naked City,"* 2 February 1948, The Mark Hellinger Collection, USC Cinema-Television Library and Archives of Performing Arts: 2.

VI AN ELEMENT OF REALISM IN FILM NOIR

-1-

As can be seen by the analyses of *The Maltese Falcon*, *The Naked City*, and *Touch of Evil*, nearly every element that contributed either figuratively or literally to the darkness of *film noir* served a secondary function as well. It also caused *films noirs* to be perceived by contemporary audiences as more realistic than the kinds of films they were acquainted with. Audiences were already familiar with various crime scenarios, images of bloodshed, and sad tales of betrayal of one sort or another in the context of thrillers, action films, and mysteries. However, *film noir*'s tough-mindedness, violence, cheerlessness, and dim cinematographic constructs put the cycle securely in a class of its own. *Film noir* emerged full-blown, an entirely separate species. Its homologies were omnipresent, alluding to a host of ancestral lines of descent, but its ability to convey an acute sense of impending doom kept it at least one evolutionary stage removed.

An element of realism was part of the darkness, and therefore part of what distinguishes *film noir* from other films. If *films noirs* today appear laden with style, it is because our eyes are schooled in other presentations, groupings, and sequencings of images. One of the reasons *films noirs* were received as more transparent than opaque is that they are reinforced by anti-Hollywood intonations (*The Maltese Falcon*), location shooting (*The Naked City*), and contemporaneity (*Touch of Evil*). It is difficult to disentangle the dark component of *film noir* from an element of realism in *film noir*. It is like trying to make out the outline of a dark object against a dark background.

Only in its early stages of development did *film noir* move, by fits and starts, in the direction of greater visual realism. This movement culminated in a peak period of faithful visual realism. It was during this period that Hollywood explored the use of location shooting in the context of feature films. The semi-documentary changed the whole focus of Hollywood away from invention and imagination. Hollywood responded more and more to topicality, refining its portrayal of characters and situations to fit more squarely into the actual scheme of things. *Film noir* rode this crest, releasing the best semi-documentaries of the bunch. But the raw stimuli of the outside world ceased to retain the interest of the camera eye, representing the interests of the moviegoing community. The result was the final, most bizarre stage of *film noir*, of which *Touch of Evil* is a fine example.

In the baroque phase of *film noir*, an element of brooding darkness continued to flourish, but with the attenuated support of an element of realism. The studio mentality gradually assumed a renewed, reinvigorated position of dominance. Even without studios, it was still possible to prettify, doctor, and adulterate locations. It is practically a truism that people do not see clearly and think deeply enough for such violations to matter. By means of a studio mentality, based on antiquated studio filmmaking, Hollywood surmounted the obstacle of location shooting, which seemed to suggest an entirely new set of values and rules.

In retrospect, the "golden calf" built on the morning of liberation should not be surprising. To paraphrase something Jean-Paul Sartre was fond of saying, freedom is a condemnation. It entails great responsibility, vigilance, and attention to what is, rather than what might, should, or could be. *Film noir* broke loose from the tethers of studio filmmaking, guided in part by progressive ideas and left-leaning tendencies. It is hardly coincidental that the failure of the Left to regroup in any viable manner following the second world war coincided with the eventual diminution of the influence of documentary filmmaking. The role of imagination in moviemaking, which had suffered some during the semi-documentary period, resurged with post-war, red-menace paranoia. *Film noir* received a dividend from this shameful, irrational episode in American history in Samuel Fuller's *Pickup on South Street* (1953) and Robert Aldrich's *Kiss Me Deadly* (1955). These are good *films noirs,* but their depictions of communist conspiracy border on the ridiculous.

A thin veneer of parody and self-mockery blurs the contours of the endmost *films noirs.* The advent of war and the gravity of revelations in its immediate aftermath produced a blunter and more realistic *film noir* in the early and middle stages of the cycle. Certain profound truths were reluctantly acknowledged that contradicted the desires and wishes of a whole generation. Among these was the death of idealism.

Richard H. Pells points out how George Orwell "assumed at the outset of the war that the Allied nations would have to move to the left in order to survive, that victory and revolution were inseparable. Now he conceded with some amazement that, while winning the war, the Allies had not embraced any form of socialism."[1] Dwight Macdonald was "equally bewildered by the effects of World War II on American life."[2] One by one, radicals relinquished their ideals, renounced their hopes, and ended their dedication to counter-culture and oppositional thinking. According to Pells, following the 1945 armistice, "almost every intellectual announced his disenchantment with the values and objectives of prewar radicalism."[3]

The dissolution of the American Left undermined the hidden but vital force that gave birth to and sustained the documentary movement. As has been indicated, it was the simultaneity of the advent of *film noir* and the increasing prestige of documentary that elevated an element of realism in *film noir* to a position of prominence. Without the continued support of the Left, the continued position of strength of an element of realism in such films was jeopardized. It was bound to abate, in terms of importance, and ultimately collapse under the weight of other, secondary variables in *film noir*—contrived narratives, angular shots, and perverted characters.

Since the filmmakers themselves changed, so did the

films. For those who harbored radical sentiments and anticipations of a new, leftist era for such a long span of time, the gradual eating away at these expectations must have been unpleasant. It is traumatic for an individual to lose a set of beliefs. For a world-wide coterie of intellectuals and artists, it is a dark, frustrating process. It is a *film noir* on a large scale.

Many of the leading personalities who fostered the trend that culminated in semi-documentary *films noirs* were at least at one time steeped in radical political philosophy. It was not for nothing that the Right concentrated on Hollywood in its effort to break the power of potential, leftist adversaries. It is equally not surprising to find the presence of some prominent diehard radicals involved in the production of even the few films selected for analysis in this study. The three that come readily to mind are: Dashiell Hammett, Albert Maltz, and Orson Welles.

In each case, dedication to the causes of the Left was undercut by doubt, reticence, and personal vacillation. Hammett, Maltz, and Welles oscillated within a dialectical quandary, shifting restlessly between blind loyalty to a collective fate and individual integrity. According to Pells, lack of tenacity is indigenous to the American intellectual community. Its manner of wavering between idealism and pragmatism was exploited by McCarthy and HUAC. In this miasma, proponents of the Left were unprotected, tragic figures, each vulnerable and abandoned by the others.

It is easy to see how the despair of the Left is mirrored in the early and middle stages of *film noir*. Almost all *films noirs* describe idealism gone awry. They are exercises in disillusionment, in coming to terms with a world in which there is no redemption and no possibility for improvement. In *Double Indemnity*, for instance, a passionate relationship seems to justify the death of an unsympathetically portrayed capitalist. Their love seems at first to transcend even the crass mercantile component of the premeditated murder. Ultimately, the true character of their partnership emerges. They are no better—in fact, worse—than the man they kill. In *Sunset Boulevard*, two characters make an attempt to rise above the level of insensitivity that engulfs their tattered lives. In the end, they also fail.

In the final stage, the connection between the end of idealism and the beginning of new, bitter rivalries is undermined by oversimplifications. It is not surprising to find the role of fantasy given a boost in the fascistic *films noirs* of Samuel Fuller. Moreover, Fuller's films shy away from locations. They abound with dream sequences (*Shock Corridor* and *The Naked Kiss*) and strive more for the verisimilitude of studio filmmaking (*Pickup on South Street* and *Underworld U.S.A.*) rather than the raw and rudimentary visual realism of location work. A good example of how locations could be manipulated and doctored can be seen in *The Naked Kiss*. As the leading character, played by Constance Towers, arrives in a small town, *Shock Corridor* is visible on a theater marquee just outside the bus station.

Whether fascistic or hard-line Marxist, the result is the same. Good ideas cannot thrive for long when they are divorced from bitter realities. Whether a thousand-year Reich, the dictatorship of the proletariat, or a chicken in every pot, no inflated slogan can endure. Similarly, superior films must be grounded in locations, or in some sense preoccupied with matters appertaining to locations. And a manifesto of this notion can be intuited from *film noir*.

According to Pells, World War II signaled "the death of optimism, rationality and the assumption that there were certain moral limits nations would not dare to exceed even in war."[4] This was especially poignant amid the aftermath of the war. It is important to note that the particular strain of despair that is so epidemically rampant in *film noir* was not exactly caused by the war alone. The war did not change things so much as give a final, devastating expression to changes already immanent.

World War I provides a good analogy in the context of Thomas Mann's *Doctor Faustus*. The narrator of the story morosely observes that "carelessness, this indifference to the individual's fate, might appear to be the result of the four years' carnival of blood just behind us; but appearances were deceptive. As in many another respect here too the war only completed, defined, and drastically put in practice a process that had been on the way long before and had made itself the basis of a new feeling about life."[5] It was the loss of meaning and moral perception that preceded war that necessitated a closer look at the world. Location shooting was a way of helping to restore the alienated to the world, shorn of intervening myths and slogans, propaganda and profiteering. *Film noir* did its part to disabuse the spectator of many pre-war illusions.

Paul Arthur contends that *film noir* was catalyzed by the Cold War rather than the Second World War. Accordingly, *film noir* did not emerge in 1941, but later, around 1944-1945.[6] Similarly, to Philip Kemp, the primary impetus behind *film noir* stemmed from "the years of the great anti-Communist witch-hunt of HUAC (House Committee on Un-American Activities), McCarthy and the blacklist."[7] Good arguments can be made to connect *film noir* to all three—World War II, the Cold War, and the red scare. In terms of the traditional conception of the development of *film noir*, the Cold War and anti-communism reach their greatest pitch of paranoia after the middle point of the cycle. In light of the discussion at hand, it is interesting to note that cold war hostility and red hysteria were so dependent upon states of mind, propaganda, stereotypes—in short, fiction. World War II was a time of action and the elimination of belligerent mythologies. In its aftermath, the Cold War and a resurgent Right gave birth to new, prejudicial mythologies.

-2-

The more significant question deals less with the multiple influences on, and antecedents of *film noir*, and more with the mystery of its relatively early demise. On the basis of the discussion at hand, it appears that as an element of realism was wrested from the films, the cycle grew increasingly moribund. The eventual dearth of realist aspirations is most appropriately attributed to the collapse of the American Left. Looking once again at the three most probable "causes" of *film noir*—WWII, the Cold War, and the communist witchhunts—one notes that all helped destroy the potentiality and cohesiveness of the Left.

In a finicky sort of way, one can actually speak of a classical *film noir*, in which location shooting and other contributions to an element of realism were thrust against stylish lighting and contrived narratives to create a mutually supportive dialectical tension. As an element of realism gradually weakened, a proliferation of bizarre compositions created a state of imbalance throughout the 1950s. Imaginative flights of fantasy displaced the restraint inherent in semi-documentary shooting. One even finds strange overlaps between the two, contradictory approaches. *Killer's Kiss*, for instance, contains great location footage of New York City. But some of its key scenes, such as a fight involving the use of an ax and a spear amidst hundreds of manikins, is nearly surrealistic—quite obviously the outcome of a screenwriter indulging his overactive imagination.

At this time, interest in documentary steadily declines not only in *film noir*, but throughout American cinema. Once a topic of considerable magnitude, documentary ceased to command the attention of mainstream filmmakers. With it went all the values it supported, including "appeal to the logic of men's minds" and "realism . . . in camera angles, lighting, natural settings, and the absence of make-up."[8] While location shooting became more and more vital to feature filmmaking, the loss of the influence of documentary would have devastating results on an already ravaged element of realism in Hollywood films.

Not only documentary, but other vibrant movements, ideas, and trends contingent upon radical thought also evaporated. In a sense, *film noir* turned against itself. In the above-mentioned *Killer's Kiss*, the protagonist believes that he has been betrayed by "the girl." Two-faced *femmes fatales* were a familiar threat in *film noir*. But in defiance of this pattern, she turns out to be a faithful, good woman. At least one narrational factor had come full circle, entailing a setback to the liberation that the deceptive female achieved for female roles in *film noir*.

More than obliterate many of the subversive gains *film noir* achieved for itself as well as the entire industry, this aesthetic turnaround canceled out a whole, robust trend in filmmaking. While the documentary influence was still being felt, *film noir* paralleled Italian neorealism in some important respects. According to George A. Huaco, the first of a list of attributes defining neorealism has to do with "The use of nonprofessional actors in major dramatic roles." Whereas the exact same cannot reasonably be said for *film noir*, it is true that several *films noirs* make use of nonprofessionals in secondary roles. For example, Hitchcock's *Shadow of a Doubt* makes use of many of the local inhabitants of Santa Rosa, California. *Canon City, The Phenix City Story, Boomerang,* and almost all of the semi-documentaries employ nonprofessionals in some capacity. They are ubiquitous in the backdrops throughout *The Naked City*. Numerous street scenes in diverse *films noirs* used the anonymous masses in lieu of extras.

However, it is true that among the professional actors who were cast in major *film noir* roles, many were of far less than star stature. Among them were those who either had never acted in films before or did so very infrequently. *Film noir* can boast of many inductions and debuts. For new actors and new directors alike, it became a testing and proving ground that helped forge illustrious careers. For instance, Burt Lancaster and William Holden each benefited a great deal from *films noirs*. Some of Marilyn Monroe's first parts were in *films noirs*. To be sure, non-actors never advanced as far in *film noir* as they did in neorealist films, but they were certainly more visible than in more controlled Hollywood films. Even if *film noir* does not duplicate neorealism in terms of Huaco's first attribute, it at least approximates it.

Second, neorealism entailed the "Rejection of studio sets and documentary use of 'real life' settings." This is more or less the crux of the issue of *film noir*'s limited resemblance to neorealism. Whereas neorealists deliberately chose locations over studio sets, this being an integral element of the genre, the same documentary consciousness informed decisions on both sides of the Atlantic. Along divergent paths, both movements arrived at the same aesthetic milestone almost simultaneously. Both opposed the feathery philosophy that lightly brushed Hollywood films. Both are grim, moody, heavy, and hard-hitting—qualities that owe a lot to the use of locations instead of studios. Locations not only made the films seem more real, but they established a connection between the film and the audience that a studio-made film never could. After all, locations are shared by spectators and the films shot there.

Third, neorealists employed "Naturalistic photography using the 'available-light' approach (e.g., the use of real sunlight instead of artificial light, the shooting of night scenes at night instead of faking them with a red filter and so on)." Because of the liberal use of low-key cinematography, the *film noir* cycle's equally generous use of naturalistic shooting is often overlooked. Low-key lighting was by no means exclusive to *film noir*. Many other kinds of films flaunt funereal low-key embellishments. Moreover, *films noirs* could dispense with low-key exaggerations altogether, as in *The Naked City*, or begin with a shadowiness that is later abandoned, as in *The Big Clock* (John Farrow, 1948). Natural sunlight probably plays a much larger role in *film noir*'s cinematographic strategies than is generally recognized. Even *Touch of Evil*, with its highly expressionistic devices, makes ample use of sunlight. But the biggest area of comparison with neorealism in terms of natural lighting has to do with night-for-night shooting. As has already been mentioned, night-for-night shooting without filters was commonplace in *film noir*.

Huaco's fourth attribute of neorealism has to do with "The use of individual heroes who are, however, nonidealized and frequently isolated." Generally, this description is equally applicable to *film noir*'s Private Eyes and assorted protagonists. As a rule, they are vulnerable, morally ambiguous, and sometimes, as is often the case with Mike Hammer, not even very bright. Many of them are crafty, even talented, but rarely exceptional. For the most part, they are average in every respect. Trouble comes "for no good reason" when they try to break loose from the confines of a mediocre existence, as is the case with the drifting pianist, Al Roberts (Tom Neal) in *Detour* (Edgar G. Ulmer, 1945). If they succeed in sustaining a distinguished life and career, they are ultimately brought back to earth with a vengeance, and soundly defeated—as is the case with Hank Quinlan in *Touch of Evil*.

Fifth, "Detailed psychological characterization of major and minor characters" is a broad enough category to include *film noir*. A scan of all the characters, major and minor, who populate *films noirs* would reveal a thorough cross-section of 1940s and 1950s Americans. In fact, one of the main, artistic goals of *The Naked City* was to bring to the spectator's attention the rich ethnic plurality of the melting pot. Absent are the smooth-jowled, superhuman characters that have no real-life counterparts. Their absence serves to enhance the vitality and believability of the unenviable, imperfect characters.

Lastly, the neorealist "camera technique presents the environment by an accumulation of small, concrete details."[9] Neorealism was emphatic and precise in this regard. The neorealist camera boldly probed villages and impoverished rural communities, unheedful of the spectator's craving to vicariously experience wealth and well-being. But the *film noir* camera was also observant and just as prone to reveal a great deal of minutiae that could never have found its way into a studio no matter how often the art department worked overtime. The *film noir* camera was often more flexible than it is credited to have been; it has received short shrift the better to accentuate the concomitant expressionistic tendencies of *films noirs*.

According to George J. Becker, the perception of *un monde noir* that is endemic to neorealist literature "is traceable in large part to social causes. During the forty years of the Fascist regime it was impossible to tell the truth."[10] For very different reasons, Hollywood also suppressed the truth. Whether by governmental decree or because of commercial pressures, the outcome is the same. Both neorealist films and *films noirs* share common concerns during a key historical period of artistic liberation. Neorealist films are especially noted for their descriptions and comments upon moral penumbrae which in turn, constitute such a large part of an element of realism in *film noir*. Neorealism addressed contemporary problems. *Film noir* was less direct, but its metaphor of crime to represent various societal ills is but thinly disguised. To Huaco, the negativity of neorealist films can be ascribed to "poverty, unemployment, hunger."[11] The atmosphere of decay that permeates *film noir* is more attributable to opportunism and greed. To a contemporary audience they are worlds apart. But the spectator today, seeing the two distinct kinds of cinema out of each's time boundaries, can unite them under a single banner of bleak despair. The problems that set the stage for both neorealism and *film noir* are timeless and ineradicable. If anything, discrepancies in terms of wealth and poverty (neorealism) are still widespread, and crime (*film noir*) has expanded exponentially. The two cinemas did not vanish because the problems they inscribe went away.

Historically, the Left strove to give art more of a free hand in the marketplace of truth than the Right allowed. It did so not because of altruism but for an ulterior motive: it wanted art to vindicate its anti-establishment views. Unfortunately, neither neorealism nor *film noir*—nor any work of propaganda, for that matter—has ever truly justified such faith in artistic representation. No film has ever presented truth as transparently and as "ambiguously" as Bazin dreamed it might some apocalyptic day. The best any film can achieve in the way of transparency is to include a textual element of realism, subject to interpretation and re-interpretation. In recognition of this weakness, the Right also produced documentaries that made a mockery of the Left's original intent. In a relatively safe process of acculturation, the Right did itself no damage and helped neutralize a potentially subversive tool.

According to Richard Meran Barsam, the *This Is America* series was "an unsatisfying reminder of the function of mass-appeal entertainment." It was superficial, glossing over topics of concern. Instead of trying to involve the spectator, it encouraged docility and passive allegiance. *This Is America* segments were like quarterly reports of companies with flagging profits, hiding the bad news in a barrage of sugarplum language. The sanguine nature of such films stemmed "from an optimistic vision of America, the vision of a producer and of directors, writers, and photographers who looked for the best in life around them and who tried to present it attractively—and with as little controversy as possible."[12]

This Is America was indefatigable in its dedication to the status quo and never disappointed viewers. No matter what cataclysm its cameras focused upon, it "always found plenty within its subject matter to suggest that a good future would come out of an uncertain present."[13] Instead of impending doom, the Right disseminated a feeling of imminent solution. This is not to say that the Right had a monopoly on what amounts to an emotional disposition. The blacklisted filmmakers who made *The Salt of the Earth* (Herbert Biberman, 1953), a semi-documentary dealing with exploitation and racial injustice, also found reasons to be cheerful. But their optimism was the result of faith in concerted effort, resistance to the status quo, and the ultimate triumph of the human spirit, not in comatose passivity.

-3-

According to Paul Arthur, at least twenty-one *films noirs* "commence with some type of documentary or pseudo-documentary introduction—and most of these contain intermittent passages which continue the documentary thrust."[14] As previously indicated, documentaries created by the Left made a dismally small impact upon the masses. Even during the darkest hours of the Depression, the great majority of Americans simply took no interest in radical panaceas. Documentary took root in the public conscious-ness via war footage. Gradually, documentary passages were absorbed into feature films.

In the context of *film noir*, they were very well-received. Though by now it has lost its timeliness, *The Naked City* was an extremely popular film. The same people who would not sit still for the most uplifting documentaries avidly watched shots not unlike those in travelogues of buses arriving at curbsides, the working force trudging along narrow sidewalks, and passengers packed like sardines in subway trains trekking to Queens. The ready availability of documentary images to *film noir* automatically suggests an indissoluble link between negativity and an element of realism, the subject of this treatise. The success of films utilizing realistic imagery in negative contexts indicates a kind of popular endorsement of this un-Hollywood-like point of view.

Furthermore, not only documentary passages, but every dissociation from the mindless machinery of escapist production was greeted with warm enthusiasm. Crowther called *Double Indemnity* a work characterized by "a realism reminiscent of the bite of past French films."[15] *The Lost Weekend* was "shatteringly realistic."[16] The camera revealed "the grim relation of the individual to the vast, unknowing mass."[17] Crowther's colleague at *The New York Times*, Thomas M. Pryor, deemed *Sunset Boulevard* a "segment of life."[18] Commentary like this, that attaches great value to realism, reflects a spectatorship with unusually high standards.

Indeed, its craving for a more realist cinema was left unsatisfied by the *March of Time* and *This Is America* serials. Unmoved by films produced by *Frontier Films* and *The Workers Film and Photo League*, spectators responded with greater alacrity to an element of realism in *films noirs*. Furthermore, the fact that Wilder's work could be singled out for realist touches shows that a trend set in motion by left-wing endeavors was very successful even if its progenitors were not. Although his films testify to a condition of endless corruption in capitalism, Wilder's work is still politically uncommitted. Corruption is rampant, but no more insidious than animal predators, providential disasters, and other facts of nature—human or otherwise.

Filmmakers on the Left quite logically seized on the idea of location shooting, but could not always achieve results in their own best interests. In the context of *film noir*, locations are overdetermined, saturated with significances tangential to the narratives. A studio set, duplicated from a particular reading of a location, becomes meaningful only in terms of a guiding narrative and what the filmmakers choose to do with their pre-planned constructions, every inch literally accounted for. Locations, on the other hand, are not so easily packaged. They are stratified with layers of histories. They are an integral part of numerous lives. They are integrated with other locations.

The resonance of true locations is too easily frittered away by filmmakers who arrogantly impose their own fantasies and quests for personal glory upon them. Filmmakers practically choke the life out of places with trucks, cables, generators, cams, bureaucrats, security personnel, actors, crew, gophers, and extras. Sophisticated dream machinery produces sophisticated dreams, and an element of reality gets lost in the shuffle. Therefore, filmmakers can use locations in either of two distinct manners. Either they can enter into complicity with them or seal them off like closed sets.

A wide range of locations was used in various *films noirs*. From these films, one can ascertain a sense of life throughout the 1940s and 1950s. Location work in *film noir* brings sharp contrasts into focus: gaudiness and tawdriness; glamor and deprivation; excitement and tedium; cities (*Panic in the Streets*, et al.), suburbs (*The Reckless Moment*), and countryside (*Out of the Past*). Location shooting in *film noir* included things big and small, famous and obscure: the gates and grounds of Paramount Studio (*Sunset Boulevard*); Jerry's Market (*Double Indemnity*); Hartford's Supermarket and Walter's Music (*Kiss Tomorrow Goodbye*); the Los Angeles storm sewers (*He Walked By Night*); a cannery in Monterey (*Clash by Night*); a public swimming pool (*I Wake Up Screaming*); the Silver Fox Cafe of London (*Night and the City*); the 16th Precinct, 43rd St. Hotel, and Washington Heights (*Where the Sidewalk Ends*); and Chicago's loop (*Nightmare Alley*).

Film noir presents a fairly thorough geographic survey of urban America. *The Scar* or *The Hollow Triumph* (Steve Sekely, 1948) and *The Blue Gardenia* (Fritz Lang, 1953) make extensive use of Los Angeles. New York provides backdrops for *The Window* (Ted Tetzlaff, 1949), *Where the*

Sidewalk Ends (Otto Preminger, 1950), and *The Sweet Smell of Success* (Alexander MacKendrick, 1957). In *Sudden Fear* (David Miller, 1952), Jack Palance's Lester Blaine chases Joan Crawford's Myra Hudson through deserted, hilly San Francisco streets in the middle of the night. Edmund O'Brien's Frank Bigelow dashes through the busy streets of San Francisco by daylight in *D.O.A.* Chicago, New Orleans, and many other cities as well provided settings for *films noirs*.

On the surface, it might appear that location shooting and semi-documentary passages in *film noir* are tantamount to a searing critique of American society. To be certain, subversive undertones occur throughout the *film noir* cycle. Insofar as attention is shifted from opulent or idealized sets to seedy city streets strafed by capitalist greed, organized crime, and petty feuds, *film noir* owes a debt to Marxist thought. But *film noir*'s purview of society lacks the teleological component of Marxism, and hence its optimistic outlook, too. As a result, radical thinkers could not unconditionally claim the support *film noir* seemed to offer. At the same time, stalwart defenders of the status quo could not fully condemn a cinematic enterprise that painted a less than flattering picture of contemporary social conditions.

For similar reasons, Marxists could not condone the tough-minded novels that helped launch the *film noir* cycle, despite their subversive ideological content. To one Marxist literary critic, "The principal resource of the bourgeois novel and drama was an interesting plot. Crimes, adventures, questions of money, adultery, in short all the patterns of a decadent and rotten world were what kept it moving. But these plot devices are not appropriate in a literature whose mission is to reflect and contribute to the advancement of a society that has rid itself of all the vices inherent in the bourgeois order."[19] For reasons of their own, Marxists—like Hollywood capitalists—sought to separate negativity from an element of realism in art.

The core communist party line flatly rejected the defeatism that prevails in *film noir*. According to David Caute, in

1947, the French Communist leader, Maurice Thorez, "told the Party Congress at Strasbourg: 'To decadent works of bourgeois aesthetes, partisans of art for art's sake, to the pessimism without solution and the retrograde obscurantism of the existential *philosophers* . . . we have opposed an art which should be inspired by socialist realism . . . an art which would aid the working class in its struggle for liberation.'"[20] In short, Hollywood denied the severity of socioeconomic problems, while Marxists practically wallowed in the presentation of the defectiveness of life under capitalist regimes. However, Marxists made sure that such exposés should always be coupled to the prescribed solution. *Film noir* neither ignored the modern malaise nor grandstanded for the opposition.

As has already been noted, many of the cinematographers, writers, directors, and others connected with the production of *film noir* were in favor of the creation of a cinema at odds with Hollywood. They may have disagreed on questions of methodology—how to change and virtually invert a whole industry. They may have had strong reservations about the likelihood of ever bringing such a cinema into existence. But they were united in the wistful longing to make American films as realistic and intellectually compelling as European and Soviet films. They may have contributed on a large scale to the systematic production of films that skillfully skirted the issues, avoided controversy, and ducked out of confrontation, but they themselves were aware and often quite vociferous in the espousal of dissident, left-wing notions.

Nevertheless, even in their most contentiously self-righteous moods, they were never prepared to follow a prescribed artistic policy. Each artist had his own individual ideas, irradiating singular nuances and subtleties. Lacking among radicals was a core philosophy, due in large part to the fact that Americans have never experienced a mentor on par with a Marx, a Lenin, or a Gramsci. Their position along the political spectrum was as open and undefined as it was vulnerable to attack, both from the hardliners of the Left and from the witchhunters of the Right. The commitment of American artists to left-wing ideals had to have been ambiguous and dubious to begin with to cave in so rapidly when it did, in the very middle of the *film noir* cycle.

This divestiture of idealism was a dramatic episode in the history of artists in America. Nothing quite this traumatic has to date ever been repeated. With the dissolution of the Left, the movement toward a more realist American cinema reached an impasse. Glimmerings of a new cinema are everywhere apparent in the state of disharmonious tension with which *film noir* existed vis-à-vis status quo viewpoints and mythologies. But ultimately, nothing permanent flourished. Detached from its historical underpinnings, *film noir* would come to symbolize paranoia and pessimism, darkness and godlessness. But it was never this abstract, never this timeless, never this pure. To the contrary, it was very much integrated into the specificity of its own time frame and contemporary cultural manifestations. It was and remains as simple and as complex as the era during which its films were released.

Semi-documentary *films noirs*, like *The Naked City*, are testimonial monuments that commemorate a certain potential abandoned by Hollywood and neutralized by television. Although far from the first semi-documentary *film noir*, *The Naked City* was a key instigator in the movement in location shooting that thrust conspicuously against the grain of traditional Hollywood filmmaking. Ironically, the strength of its influence became a major source of its undoing as television surpassed filmmaking in terms of the sheer number of weekly programs shot on location. Television's diversity went unchallenged by a much less prolific film industry.

According to David George, after the emergence of *The Naked City* "the moment came when all that remained was to turn the whole thing over to television and the ultimate never-never world of *Dragnet*."[21] The dominance of television in the competition for entertainment and leisure dollars has often been cited as a significant factor that helped shape the pessimistic tones, overtones, and undertones of *film noir*. The usurpation of the mesmerizing power of cinema over a massive, loyal audience is thought to be present in the downbeat, self-reflexive nature of *film noir*. This is certainly true, as far as it goes. Yet the ascendency of television was more than a simple, fickle change in allegiance from one medium to another. It also symbolizes the victory of conservative forces in terms of the mass consumption of artistic products.

Similarly, despite the breakdown of the studio system, independent filmmaking did not ultimately lead to independent thinking. Independence of thought became a luxury that the film industry—regardless of its vertical and horizontal organization—could ill-afford. Topicality no longer remained a province of the film industry. The dark, philosophical camera lens that shot so many of the *films noirs* was wrested from the filmmaking community. Like location shooting, independent filmmaking fell more and more under the command of conservative, moneymaking interests.

It certainly did not help matters any that artists with ostentatious ties to the Left were so ignominiously cut loose. Commercial considerations aside, an atmosphere of fear could not have been conducive to originality and artistic freedom. *Film noir* could not therefore have come about in reaction to the decimation of left-wing artists in Hollywood. It was an anomalous type of filmmaking that came about because of the vague but prophetic intimation of an imminent disaster. It did not even come about consciously. It seems to have arisen from the reservoirs of a collective subconscious, like a bad dream whose undesirable meaning somehow manages to escape even though it is not supposed to.

Without the Left, independent filmmaking reverted to the same commercialized aesthetics that propelled the Hollywood of old. It is well known that *film noir* is not a genre. Among other reasons, that is because it does not fit squarely into the dream factory machine. It exists somehow in orbit around Hollywood, under its gravitational pull, but never fully within its grasp. Without a sustaining independent spirit, *film noir*, too, was doomed to fail. It could never have become a genre. It could never have become a part of Hollywood, new or old.

-4-

So the mystery of *film noir* is also in part the mystery of the American Left, whose decline is an enormous topic in itself. However, the decline of the Left among Hollywood artists seems to have been assured by its inability to conjure and sustain long-standing conviction. Hammett, Maltz, and Welles were all fervid advocates of the Left, yet none of them fully surrendered his individuality to a common cause. Each yoked his fate to the fate of the radical commonality, yet none just left it at that. Throughout the turbulence of the 1940s and 1950s, each maintained a strong measure of reserve. Each found niches in the radical community that allowed them to turn out highly complex works of art while existing, on a much more fundamental plane, safely within the fold.

In 1949, Hammett, along with Howard Fast, publicly refused to play the role of informer and would not tell the government the names of the members of the Civil Rights Congress. The Civil Rights Congress raised money to pay bail for communists who had to appear in court. To HUAC and McCarthy, it was a communist front organization. How Hammett was connected to the Civil Rights Congress would require a great deal of research. According to Victor S. Navasky, an authority on the subject, Hammett had "no interest in or knowledge of the membership list that he refused, on principle, to turn over to the state."[22] He courageously held his ground, not so much because he had something to hide, but because he did not want to demean his life before his accusers by pretending to be on their side.

As a result, Hammett incriminated himself. American Communists could not have hoped for greater assistance from a fellow traveler. But Hammett's motives remain unclear. His silence says nothing about whether or not he condoned the activities of the fund-raising organization he protected. His admirable, unshakable resolve before HUAC straddles the line between party politics and Hemingway grace under pressure. To this day, Hammett's participation in or with the American Communist Party remains at least partially a topic of speculation. No one has ever proven that he was ever at any time a *bona fide* member.

Nevertheless, Hammett certainly developed a lifelong habit of flirting with the idea of belonging to the radical fringe. This proclivity is evoked by his *oeuvre*, which Steven Marcus sums up as a "proto-Marxist critical representation of how a certain kind of society works."[23] The novel that Hammett wrote that most nakedly supports this notion is *Red Harvest* (1929). Although a flawed novel, especially in comparison to *The Maltese Falcon*, *Red Harvest* contains a good depiction of a chaotic, unjust, and violent social matrix presided over by a corrupt capitalist figure.

Maltz's novels more overtly address and explore the shortcomings of capitalism. Maltz himself enjoyed being considered America's foremost political writer, next to Clifford Odets—before Odets left the communist party. Despite his status among radicals, he was constrained to toe the party line. When he tried to break free, he got involved in an imbroglio that helped bring his career down from the Left even before the Right delivered the *coup de grace*. Hammett had the good fortune to have made his mark in the literary world and the movie industry years before the communist witch trials. But the tempestuous political scene ultimately ruined any chance Maltz had of fulfilling the promise his brilliance as a writer seemed to hold out.

Maltz is a perfect example of a prominent left-wing artist of the 1940s who wrestled against the low standards of realism that prevailed in Hollywood. Later, Maltz admitted that he compromised his own personal principles because of the size of the paychecks he received from the studios. He knew just how remote was the possibility of bringing about a morally and visually realist cinema in the United States, but he remained committed, plodding onward. Unfortunately, during a crucial period of confrontation—with documentaries impacting on feature films and *film noir* permitting dark scenarios—Maltz was forced to withdraw from the business.

As he did, so did others. But Maltz was one of the

hardest hit among the artists and intellectuals who were ostracized during this sad chapter in American history. Simultaneously, he was harshly criticized by both the Left and the Right. As though in fear of suffering the same unenviable fate, radicals who might otherwise have taken up the cudgel in defense of change, did not. Bold, new thinking shrank until it was again overcome by the narrow mentality that caused Hortense Powdermaker to entitle her study of Hollywood, *The Dream Factory*. André Bazin once remarked that the addition of sound to cinema did not constitute a revolution in terms of the way films were being made. Similarly, the evolution of a mechanically primitive cinema to one that is technologically sophisticated has not significantly altered cinema's basic orientation toward the real world as something to be dominated, manipulated, and controlled—either duplicated inside a studio, or disguised on location.

Maltz was drawn to Marxism by reason of its devotion to humanitarian causes, egalitarianism, and civil rights. Like thousands of novelists, playwrights, and artists all over the world, he joined the communist party not to spite the capitalist system but to expand upon the role of human rights. In his own life, Maltz responded positively to capitalist incentives, while maintaining a position of leadership within the radical community. During this era, dual existences such as this were entirely credible. The party enhanced one's life in a mercurial world. It provided a *modus operandi*, an international movement in favor of people rather than governments, which seemed more promising than the slow wheels of parliamentary and democratic legislation.

But Maltz never adjusted to the political infrastructure of the American Communist Party, which eventually caused him a great deal of discomfiture. To be sure, his association with progressive thinkers made him look good, even in the eyes of artists who were independent of the Left. Maltz enjoyed a great deal of prestige as a novelist firmly embedded within a socialist framework. He had talent and he had convictions. On erudite panels addressing the latest issues, he spoke out against injustice and inequality. In left-wing journals, he published topical articles and

editorials. He was a consummate American artist, supreme defender of the faith—free speech, freedom of the
press, and independence of mind.

Despite his brilliance, Maltz just could not grasp the
Realpolitik underlying the concerted effort of radicals to
sustain a viable, political alternative. Maltz fought for
beauty and truth, not political power and domination.
Ultimately, art and politics, at cross-purposes, would have
to part company. Like Phillip Raven (Alan Ladd), the
protagonist of his first screenplay, *This Gun for Hire*, Maltz
appears now in retrospect to have been an outsider with an
important, special talent—a hired gun. He was probably
never as integral a part of the communist organization as
he perhaps believed himself to be. For Maltz, the situation
was one of doing all the right things, but winding up
wrong. He joined the communist party to fight oppression, but wound up under its heel, himself a victim of
oppression. In his writing, he expressed his solidarity with
the working class, but he was ultimately unable to bridge
the gap between the middle-class affluence of the writer
and the material and spiritual impoverishment of the
underclass being written about.

In right-wing *films noirs*, like *The Woman on Pier 13*,
communists are commonly portrayed as perverse thugs.
They are fanatical in their anxious attempts to undermine
society, gain power, and set themselves up as rulers in the
name of abstract, arcane double-talk. But Maltz was
nothing like this. D. Angus Cameron, an editorial consul-
tant for Alfred A. Knopf, publisher of Maltz's novels,
described him as "a very pure man." To Cameron,
"Albert's apparent goodness was such that it was embarrassing; you had a feeling that there was a halo there that
you were feeling the heat from."[24] Maltz's commitment to
the Left motivated him to work for half a year inside a
factory in California. In his own words, he wrote for the
same reason he joined the communist party, to benefit all
mankind: "The history of literature is largely dominated by
writers distinguished in their lives and work by their
compassion for people and their love of people—rather
than by their cynicism; distinguished further by their

partisan espousal of those social movements in their time that were forward-looking, often radical."[25]

Maltz wrote the original script for *The Robe* (Henry Koster, 1952). In true saintly fashion he received no credit for this spectacular CinemaScope film. In late 1946, not long before working on *The Naked City*, Maltz picked up a hitchhiker who became the model upon which *The Journey of Simon McKeever* was based. He published this study of an old, itinerant California worker in 1949. It was immediately sold to 20th-Century Fox, but a year later, was withdrawn from production.[26] By that time, any production was doomed to failure that was associated with the name of one of the Hollywood Ten, who were sent to jail after refusing to testify before the House UnAmerican Activities Committee.

But Maltz's notoriety as one of the Hollywood Ten is something that is well-known. What is seldom mentioned is that he was also the victim of left-wing intolerance. His problems with the Left stemmed from his inability to reconcile the policy of socialist realism, a.k.a. Zhadanovism, with his own individualistic artistic impulse. In defiance of this set of inflexible strictures, he penned an article in condemnation of the treatment of art as a political tool. To draw boundaries around art was to put it in "a straitjacket."[27] To Maltz, art was not "a weapon, like a leaflet, serving immediate political ends, necessities and programs." Apart from ideological concerns, art was not "worthless or escapist or vicious."[28]

Despite the lucid rationality of such a point-of-view, it amounted to a searing rebuttal of a political policy that superseded everything else, including all of the finer, more charitable projects with which American communists were associated at the time. Because of his innate goodness, Maltz could not have anticipated the pigheadedness of politicos who directed campaigns against the very things he hated—inequality, oppression, and cupidity. He could not have foreseen how slyly one injustice could substitute for another. Maltz was so sincere and well-intentioned in his plea on behalf of the freedom of the artist that he could not have been prepared for the backlash his article would ultimately bring about.

In a strange case of publish and perish, Maltz totally lost his credibility among radicals. And when he retracted his statements, not wanting to fight, he lost his credibility among mainstream sympathizers who were certain that he was right, that the Left was too narrow-minded about art. Having lost the support of the Left, it did not tax the energies of the Right to find a way to break him. Despite his elegant appeal for the independence of the artist working within a political framework of increasing complexity, "What Shall We Ask of Writers?" met with disheartening criticism.

In brief, the argument focused on Frederick Engels' admiration for Honoré de Balzac, a reactionary monarchist. While Engels had to condemn a political formation headed by a monarch seated upon a throne, scepter in hand, he praised Balzac's literature. Specifically, he appreciated the way it contained accurate descriptions of the decadent Aristocracy in the early part of the 19th century in post-Napoleonic France. It was also the tone of Balzac's novels that impressed Engels. Compared to Zola, Balzac was much less negative. Negativity fostered resignation, a disposition that is not useful to a revolutionary.

Maltz used the phenomenon of Engels' acceptance of an artist with backward political ideas as the foundation for his argument. He stressed the fact that Balzac "was a Royalist, consistently and virulently anti-socialist, anti-communist in his thinking." He went on to say that "an artist can be a great artist without being an integrated or a logical or a progressive thinker on all matters."[29] The drawback of prescribing how writers should write, painters paint, or filmmakers film is that prescriptions compromise the integrity of both the artist and the artistic product. The result is a portrayal of "life, not as it is, but as [the artist] would like it to be."[30]

Innocent as this expression of an artist's inalienable rights may appear, American Communists received it with unmitigated scorn. Howard Fast reviled Maltz's thesis as "liquidationist—and by virtue of that, anti-progressive—and in its final form, reactionary."[31] Fast went on to reprimand Maltz for writing favorably about *Studs Lonigan*.

The author of *Studs Lonigan*, James T. Farrell, had been a Trotskyite. To the American Communist during the reign of Stalin, Trotskyism was heresy. Still, Fast exalted the general American Left, despite Trotskyism and other misinformed divergences, for the sustenance it gave to diverse writers from "Jack London to young Arthur Miller."[32]

With righteous indignation, Alvah Bessie proclaimed that "the artist and the man are inseparable."[33] Bessie emphasized the fact that Balzac "loathed, hated, and despised the power of money *and* the corruption of his own beloved aristocracy."[34] To show how vital Marxism was to writers, Bessie cited the case of Clifford Odets. According to Bessie, Odets' work noticeably atrophied after the playwright lost his Marxist ideals, stopped being loyal, and veered away from party concerns.

Maltz caved in to his critics, who were also his friends and colleagues. He entitled his unconditional recantation, "Moving Forward," but it was in effect a step backward. He conceded to his detractors that his "one-sided, non-dialectical treatment of complex issues—could not . . . contribute to the development of left-wing cultural movement."[35] More than a recantation, it was an incantation, an attempt to magically restore that blissfully naive state of blind faith in the wisdom of the party. But Maltz's first article had shattered the innocence. The writer was indeed at odds with the party, and in deep trouble as a result. In a similar fashion, in its final stage, *film noir* could no longer recover the innocence of its earlier stages. It too, became self-conscious.

However, Maltz never lost faith in reality as the true arbiter of artistic policy, rather than an oligarchy of demagogues—which is what it all came down to. At the same time that he apologized, Maltz eloquently urged artists to continue the exploration of the reality of contemporary American existence:

> We have in America today the opportunity for a flowering of a profound art, one that will deeply enrich the great tradition we inherit. If this flowering

comes to pass, it will be based upon a passionate, honest rendition of the real, mutual relations in society; it will be a true art based upon the real lives, the disappointments, struggles, aspirations, of the American people. Such an art, being realistic, will be socially critical; this follows as night follows day. But by being tied to life as the source of true artistic inspiration, it will not substitute slogans for rich events, or substitute mechanical selectivity for a description of real mutual relations in society. Marxism will be the interpretative guide; the raw material will be the facts of life, faced absolutely, with burning honesty.[36]

Maltz's downfall marks the end of an era. From this point on, one seldom encounters arguments dealing with the role of art in a dynamic society or, simply, art as a microscope illuminating the intricacies of a particular geopolitical landscape. In fact, it seems as though at this point in time, history, politics, economics, and even culture are factored out and entertainment factored in. The whole issue of location shooting in cinema is reduced to a question of mechanical technique. Movie clichés are no longer avoided, but refined until they become more palatable. True, documented stories no longer sustain interest unless beefed up with action, excitement, and spectacle. It is as if the industry tacitly understood that realism bore the stamp of radicalism—and that meant trouble.

As an element of realism in *film noir* grew faint, *films noirs* became almost surrealistic, all effect and very little substance. That the realist discourse of previous *films noirs* should start to gradually vanish from the screen so soon after it reached its peak should come as no surprise. The same could be said about Albert Maltz, whose career dropped off sharply and suddenly from the heights. It is when a trend is most conspicuous that it is likely to become a target. And nothing is quite as conspicuous as success. Had *The Naked City* not been a hit, had Albert Maltz not been famous, and had *film noir* been inaccessible to the

public at large, then an element of realism in *film noir* might
have endured. But this was not the case.

Perhaps only those who crave dark stories not as
campfire anecdotes but as corroborations of the pessimistic
vision of life will ever fully appreciate *film noir* as an
interpretation of human experience. One sees only what
one wants to see, and *films noirs*, except as nostalgic
oddities, are no longer desiderata. Those who detest the
status quo will find *film noir* a source of inspiration because
of its subversiveness. Those content to live in harmony
with the status quo will delight in the conservative nature
of *film noir*. But neither will ever wish to see *film noir* as
reality rather than fantasy. Curiously enough, it takes
quite a bit of imagination to see *film noir* fantasy as reality.
To see *film noir* exclusively as imaginary is to suppress this
fascinating visual aid—one's own imagination. Maltz was
only half-right when he denied that art is a weapon. It is a
weapon. But it can only be triggered by the spectator's
complicity at a deep level of interpretation.

-5-

Like Hammett and Maltz, Welles's relationship with the
Left was ambiguous. *New Masses* gave his *chef-d'oeuvre*,
Citizen Kane, a good write-up, calling it "biography without
the benefit of Tyrone Power."[37] The communist publication lauded Welles for making a movie that was so bold
and original. Indeed, the Welles who made perhaps *the*
quintessential American film was a bit of a rebel, a
provocateur, and a realist. But Welles was no revolutionary. With *Citizen Kane*, Welles could not reasonably have
hoped to destroy Hearst, only to show him that he was his
equal. Hearst took the challenge seriously. He already had
a good grasp of how damaging mass media could be,
independent of the truth, having already manipulated the
news himself to sell newspapers. Although a work of
fiction, the connection to William Randolph Hearst in
Citizen Kane was obvious. Welles's fiction was just as fuzzy
as his politics.

At the time, Welles planned to make a groundbreaking anti-Hollywood film, "which will deal with a *real* Mexican story and use *real Mexican* characters."[38] Already, more than fifteen years before he shot *Touch of Evil*, Welles was making plans to shoot a film about Mexicans. He emphasized shooting the film with real Mexicans, rather than Hollywood extras. He intended for the narrative to be about real Mexicans, rather than based on a screenwriter's wild imaginings. He must also have meant to shoot the film on Mexican soil, to make it even more authentic. From his study of *Stagecoach*, he no doubt saw the value of locations in John Ford's use of Monument Valley. His own film was speculatively entitled *Mexican Melodrama*, but it was never produced. The closest he got to a "Mexican story" was *Touch of Evil*. By that time, Welles's vision had been tempered by years of disappointment, his aesthetics had changed to accommodate low-budget financing, and his position within the filmmaking community was several notches lower than it was before. He no longer commanded the awe he once did, no longer had the ambition to make a groundbreaking anti-Hollywood film, and no longer had the requisite backing even if he wanted to.

Perhaps because of his encounter with misfortune early in his filmmaking career, Welles never became the threat he might otherwise have posed to the Right. Then, too, Welles was always a leader, rarely a follower, and he would not have made a good cipher in the radical movement.

However, like Maltz and Hammett, Welles consistently defended liberal causes he felt worthy of his support. While never blacklisted, *Red Channels*, the blacklister's bible, did feel obliged to designate him as "dangerous."[39] Employers were warned to regard Welles with caution, but it is certain that he never joined the Communist Party. Welles was not against capitalism so much as against conservatism. As such, he shared with communists a common enemy. With *The New York Post*, Welles found a forum with which to lash out against conservative forces and personages.

The columns he wrote for what was then a more

reputable newspaper than it is today could not be mistaken for radical verbiage by the loosest standards of interpretation. Welles combines humor with humanitarian views to create his own, personal, entertaining, yet compassionate ideology. Clearly, he delighted in championing causes that were vital to the underprivileged. While by no means as compelling as his films, Welles's writing is rather precise and gives a clue as to the identity of the auteur behind the films. Welles obviously wanted to achieve in the humanitarian fields of endeavor the kind of grandiosity that mostly only demagogues seem to have achieved in the 20th century. Welles saw in the villains he lambasted a reflection of the grandeur he probably wanted for himself—and in some measure brought about. In *Citizen Kane*, Welles pits Charles Foster Kane against Adolf Hitler in doctored stock footage, but the American giant doesn't have the wherewithal to match in kindness what the Nazi Fuehrer was in cruelty.

It would take a colossal effort to accurately sort out Welles's multisided personality, but there seems to be a great deal of agreement between the man and the artist. Many of the opinions Welles expressed in the *Post* column in 1945 are confirmed in *Touch of Evil*, some thirteen unlucky years later. For instance, through directed characters and written words alike, Welles cautioned his readers against idealism, which "can bring on quickly the sense of defeat, of cynicism—the deterioration of hope that gives the peace-killers their green light."[40] In *Touch of Evil*, Quinlan warns Menzies along a narrow catwalk spanning the Rio Grande not to turn into "one of these here starry-eyed idealists." Although Quinlan, the villain of the story, is about to succumb to a "starry-eyed idealist," he is an ambiguous bad guy. Things are not black and white, and Welles's words seem to intimate that idealism might not provide the safest means for opposing evil. In fact, there is in the line a faint suggestion that idealism may in fact contain the seeds of a new, even stronger evil than the one it seeks to destroy. Says Quinlan, "They're the ones making all the real trouble in the world. Be careful. They're worse than crooks."

In another column, Welles expressed the hope that one

day nations will embrace one another. It is an age-old hope, perhaps best expressed in film in the euphoric ending to *Birth of a Nation*. It is not enough, Welles seems to be saying, that people should leave the hope of peace to political or artistic leaders. Neither governments nor artistic media can perform the role of ambassador. People themselves have to depart from their native lands, travel, and address foreigners in their own voices, using their own words: "The miracles of our modern communication systems are useless magic tricks unless we move as many people as possible across as many borders. The common man's ideas must be exchanged. He is his own spokesman, and what he wants to hear and see won't always be found on his television set. He must have the time and opportunity and freedom to go calling as much as he pleases."[41]

Here Welles's journalism most resembles words spoken by Vargas, the other protagonist in *Touch of Evil*. Like Quinlan, Vargas is a character almost entirely invented by Welles. On the winding drive to the Mirador Motel, located on the American side, the Mexican Vargas tells his American wife how "one of the longest borders on earth is right here between your country and mine. An open border. Fourteen hundred miles without a single gun emplacement."

Like Maltz, Welles dreamed of a better world. But Welles seems to have differed from Maltz in his greater understanding of the futility of idealism, no matter how well-intentioned. He also seems to have rid himself of the notion that the film medium has redemptive powers. In disproportionate ways, *films noirs* allude to these discrepancies—between how things are and how things might have been, but never are. Somewhere in between the soft lies of cinema and the harsh truths of reality, there exists an element of realism in *film noir*.

NOTES

1. Richard H. Pells, *The Liberal Mind in a Conservative Age, American Intellectuals in the 1940s and 1950s* (New York: Harper & Row, 1985): 48.

2. Ibid.: 49.
3. Ibid.: 181.
4. Ibid.: 41.
5. Thomas Mann, *Doctor Faustus, The Life of the German Composer Adrian Leverkuhn as Told By a Friend,* trans. H.T. Lowe-Porter (New York: Vintage Books, 1971): 365.
6. Paul Arthur, *Shadows on the Mirror: Film Noir and Cold War America, 1945–1957,* unpublished Ph.D. dissertation, New York University, 1985.
7. Philip Kemp, "From the Nightmare Factory, HUAC and the Politics of Noir," *Sight and Sound,* Autumn 1986: 266.
8. Joseph V. Noble, "Development of the Cinematographic Art," *American Cinematographer,* January 1948: 26.
9. Huaco: 16–17.
10. Becker: 128.
11. Huaco: 17.
12. Richard Meran Barsam, " 'This Is America: Documentaries for Theaters, 1942–1951,' " *Nonfiction Film Theory and Criticism* (New York: E.P. Dutton & Co., 1976): 134.
13. Ibid.: 118.
14. Arthur: 336.
15. Crowther, *The New York Times Reviews, A One-Volume Selection, 1913–1970:* 214.
16. Ibid.: 218.
17. Ibid.: 219.
18. Ibid.: 259.
19. Henri Arvon, *Marxist Esthetics,* trans. Helen R. Lane (Ithaca, N.Y.: Cornell University Press, 1977): 90.
20. David Caute, *Communism and the French Intellectuals, 1914–1960* (London: Andre Deutsch, 1964): 327.
21. George: 15.
22. Victor S. Navasky, *Naming Names* (New York: The Viking Press, 1980): 37.
23. Steven Marcus, "Introduction," in Dashiell Hammett, *The Continental Op,* (New York: Vintage Books, 1975): xii.
24. D. Angus Cameron, Interview by Louis Sheaffer, *Popular Arts Project* (1977), Oral History Research, Special Collections, Columbia University: 263.
25. Albert Maltz, *The Writer as the Conscience of the People* (Hollywood Arts, Sciences and Professions Council of the Progressive Citizens of America, 1947): 5–6.
26. Jack Salzman, *Albert Maltz* (Boston: Twayne, 1978): 115.
27. Navasky: 298.

28. Albert Maltz, "What Shall We Ask of Writers?" *New Masses,* 12 February 1946: 19.
29. Ibid.: 20.
30. Ibid.: 21.
31. Howard Fast, "Art and Politics," *New Masses,* 26 February 1946: 6.
32. Ibid.: 8.
33. Alvah Bessie, "What is Freedom for Writers?" *New Masses,* 12 March 1946: 9.
34. Ibid.: 8.
35. Albert Maltz, "Moving Forward," *New Masses,* 12 March 1946: 9.
36. Ibid.
37. Howard P. Ryan, *New Masses,* 12 January 1941: 28.
38. Ibid.
39. Pells: 307.
40. Orson Welles, *The New York Post,* 5 April 1945: 44.
41. Ibid.: 9 May 1945: 40.

SELECT BIBLIOGRAPHY

In the following bibliography, I have included certain entries not cited in *Autopsy*. These helped me grapple with the larger, philosophical question of art and reality that surrounds the topic of realism in *film noir*. In fact, the subject of art and reality is sufficiently ponderous so that virtually any cultural artifact is bound to have an impact on it. As a result, *not* included are many of the novels of both the 18th and 19th centuries that also helped shape my thinking. Such a listing might have appeared so eclectic and diverse—lumping Balzac, Zola, Flaubert, Tolstoy together with the likes of Cain, Burroughs, Woolrich, and Spillane—as to deflect away from the focus of this study.

Advertisement for *The Maltese Falcon*. *The New York Daily News*, 3 Oct. 1941: 58.

Advertisement for *The Maltese Falcon*. *The New York Sun*, 1 Oct. 1941: 31.

Advertisement for *The Maltese Falcon*. *The New York Tribune*, 3 Oct. 1941: 17.

Agee, James. *Agee on Film*. 1958. New York: Beacon Press, 1964.

Ager, Cecelia. "Drama and Film Critics See the Stage and Screen's Function as Vivid in War." *Variety*, 7 Jan. 1942: 25.

———. "Hellinger Film Is a Love Song to NYC." *PM Daily*, 5 Mar. 1948: 15.

Alexander, William. *Film on the Left: American Documentary Film From 1931 to 1942*. Princeton, N.J.: Princeton University Press, 1981.

Alloway, Lawrence. *Violent America: The Movies 1946–1964*. New York: Museum of Modern Art, 1971.

Amberg, George, ed. *The New York Times Film Reviews: A One-Volume Selection, 1913–1970*. New York: Arno Press, 1971.

Appel, Alfred, Jr. *Nabokov's Dark Cinema*. New York: Oxford University Press, 1974.

Arnheim, Rudolph. "Fiction and Fact." *Sight and Sound*, 8.32 Winter 1939–1940: 136–7.

Arthur, Paul. "Shadows on the Mirror: Film Noir and Cold War America 1945–1957." Diss., New York U., 1985.

Arvon, Henri. *Marxist Esthetics*. Trans. Helen R. Lane. Ithaca, N.Y.: Cornell University Press, 1977.

Astor, Mary. *A Life on Film*. New York: Delacorte Press, 1971.

Auerbach, Erich. *Mimesis: The Representation of Reality in Western Literature*. Trans. Willard R. Trask. Princeton, N.J.: Princeton University Press, 1974.

Bakhtin, M. M. *The Dialogic Imagination: Four Essays*. Ed. Michael Holquist. Trans. Caryl Emerson and Michael Holquist. Austin: University of Texas Press, 1987.

Barker, Virgil. *From Realism to Reality in Recent American Painting*. Lincoln: University of Nebraska Press, 1959.

Barlow, John D. *German Expressionist Film*. Boston: Twayne, 1982.

Barnes, Howard. Review of *The Maltese Falcon*. *The New York Herald Tribune*, 4 Oct. 1941: 6.

———. Review of *The Naked City*. *The New York Herald Tribune*, 4 Mar. 1948: 17.

Barnouw, Erik. *Documentary: A History of the Non-Fiction Film*. London: Oxford University Press, 1979.

Barrett, William. *Irrational Man: A Study in Existential Philosophy.* Westport, Conn.: Greenwood Press, 1977.

Barsam, Richard Meran. " 'This Is America': Documentaries for Theaters, 1942–1951." *Cinema Journal,* 12.2 Spring 1973: 22–38.

————, ed. *Nonfiction Film Theory and Criticism.* New York: E. P. Dutton, 1976.

Baxter, John. *Hollywood in the Thirties.* New York: A. S. Barnes, 1980.

Bazelon, David T. "Dashiell Hammett's Private Eye." *Commentary Magazine,* May 1949: 469–471.

Bazin, André. *Jean Renoir.* Trans. W. W. Halsey II and William H. Simon. New York: Simon & Schuster, 1973.

————. *Orson Welles: A Critical View,* trans. Jonathan Rosenbaum. New York: Harper & Row, 1978.

————. *What Is Cinema?* Volumes I & II, trans. Hugh Gray Berkeley: University of California Press, 1967.

Beauvoir, Simone de. *America: Day by Day.* New York: Grove Press, 1953.

Becker, George J. *Realism in Modern Literature.* New York: Frederick Ungar, 1980.

Behlmer, Rudy. *America's Favorite Movies: Behind the Scenes.* New York: Frederick Ungar, 1982.

Belton, John. *Cinema Stylists.* Metuchen, N.J.: Scarecrow Press, 1983.

Benardete, Jane, ed. *American Realism.* New York: G. P. Putnam's Sons, 1972.

Benoit-Levy, Jean. "The Cinema Must Induce Universal Thought." *Screen Actor,* Sept. 1946: 7; 16.

Beresford, Maurice. "Realism and Emotion." *Sight and Sound*, Apr. 1945: 13–15.

Bessie, Alvah. "What Is Freedom for Writers?" *New Masses*, 12 Mar. 1946: 8–10.

Bessy, Maurice. *Orson Welles*. Trans. Ciba Vaughan. New York: Crown, n.d.

Biskind, Peter. *Seeing Is Believing: How Hollywood Taught Us to Stop Worrying and Love the Fifties*. New York: Pantheon Books, 1983.

Blanchard, Walter. "Aces of the Camera—I: William Daniels." *American Cinematographer*, Jan. 1941: 8; 38.

———. "Aces of the Camera—XXII: Arthur Edeson, A.S.C." *American Cinematographer*, Nov. 1942: 476; 490–1.

Boehnel, William. "Cycle of Melodrama Seems Due in Movies: 'Maltese Falcon' Paves the Way." *The New York World Telegram*, 4 Oct. 1941: 5.

Boorstin, Daniel. *The Decline of Radicalism: Reflections on America Today*. New York: Random House, 1969.

Borde, Raymond and Étienne Chaumeton. *Panorama du Film Noir Américain 1941–1953*. Paris: Les Editions de Minuit, 1955.

Bordwell, David. *Narration in the Fiction Film*. Madison: University of Wisconsin Press, 1985.

Bordwell, David and Kristin Thompson. *Film Art: An Introduction*. New York: Alfred A. Knopf, 1986.

Bordwell, David, Janet Staiger, and Kristin Thompson. *The Classical Hollywood Cinema: Film Style & Mode of Production to 1960*. New York: Columbia University Press, 1985.

Box Office Returns. *Variety*, Oct.–Dec. 1941; Mar.–Apr. 1948.

Cairns, Adrian. "We Are Such Stuff As Films Are Made On." *Sight and Sound*, 15.59 Autumn 1946: 92–3.

Cameron, Kate. " 'The Maltese Falcon': A Film With a Wallop." *The New York Daily News*, 4 Oct. 1941: 20.

———. " 'Naked City' Exhibits New York in the Raw." *The New York Daily News*, 5 Mar. 1948: 68.

Campbell, Russell. *Cinema Strikes Back: Radical Filmmaking in the United States, 1930–1942*. Ann Arbor, Mich.: UMI Research Press, 1982.

Camus, Albert. *The Plague*. Trans. Stuart Gilbert. New York: Vintage Books, 1971.

Caute, David. *Communism and the French Intellectuals: 1914–1960*. London: Andre Deutsch, 1964.

Céline, Louis-Ferdinand. *Journey to the End of the Night*. Trans. Ralph Manheim. New York: New Directions, 1983.

Ceplair, Larry and Steven Englund. *The Inquisition in Hollywood: Politics in the Film Community 1930–1960*. Berkeley: University of California Press, 1979.

Chambers, Sue. "What Hollywood Is Talking About." *The Milwaukee Journal*, Screen & Radio: 6.

Chandler, Raymond. *The Simple Art of Murder*. Boston: Houghton Mifflin Co., 1950.

Clarke, Charles G. "How Desirable Is Extreme Focal Depth?" *American Cinematographer*, Jan. 1942: 14; 36.

Coe, Richard L. "Hellinger Mixed Real Manhattan." Review of *The Naked City*. *The Washington Post*, 9 Apr. 1948: 24.

Comito, Terry, ed. *Touch of Evil: Orson Welles, Director*. New Brunswick, N.J.: Rutgers University Press, 1985.

Comolli, Jean-Louis and Jean Narboni. "Cinema/Ideology/Criticism." Trans. Susan Bennett. *Screen Reader I: Cinema/Ideology/Politics*. London: The Society for Education in Film and Television, 1977: 2–11.

Cook, Alton. "Intense 'Naked City' Bares Real New York." *The New York World Telegram,* 4 Mar. 1948: 30.

Corliss, Richard. "The Limitations of Kracauer's Reality." *Cinema Journal,* 10.1 Fall 1970: 15–22.

Cowie, Peter. *A Ribbon of Dreams: The Cinema of Orson Welles.* New York: A. S. Barnes, 1973.

Creelman, Eileen. Review of *The Maltese Falcon. The New York Sun,* 4 Oct. 1941: 6.

———. Review of *The Naked City. The New York Sun,* 5 Mar. 1948: 23.

Cross, Elizabeth. "Lighten Our Darkness." *Sight and Sound,* 14.54 Summer 1945: 52–3.

Davidman, Joe. Review of *The Maltese Falcon. New Masses,* 21 Oct. 1941: 28.

Deming, Barbara. *Running Away from Myself: A Dream Portrait of America Drawn From the Films of the 40's.* New York: Grossman, 1969.

"Don't Blame TV for Film Woe—Reagan." *The Denver Post,* 16 May 1958: 40.

Durgnat, Raymond. "The Family Tree of Film Noir." *Film Comment,* 10.6 Nov.–Dec. 1974: 6–7.

Dyer, Richard. *Stars.* London: British Film Institute, 1979.

Edwards, Tudor. "Film and Unreality." *Sight and Sound,* 15.58 Summer 1946: 59–61.

Eliot, T. S. *T. S. Eliot: The Waste Land & Other Poems.* New York: Harcourt Brace Jovanovich, 1962.

Ernst, Morris L. " 'Fight and You'll Win': Meaning Hollywood, Which Meekly Bows to Censors' Dictation." *Variety,* 7 Jan. 1942: 9.

Eyles, Allen. "The Maltese Falcon." *Films and Filming*, Nov. 1964: 45–50.

Fast, Howard. "Art and Politics." *New Masses*, 26 Feb. 1946: 6–8.

Feldman, Seth. "Cinema Weekly and Cinema Truth." *Sight and Sound*, 43.1 Winter 1973/4: 34–37.

Fell, John L. *Film and the Narrative Tradition*. Berkeley: University of California Press, 1986.

Ferguson, Perry. "More Realism From 'Rationed' Sets?" *American Cinematographer*, Sept. 1942: 390–1; 430.

Ferro, Marc. *Cinema and History*. Trans. Naomi Greene. Detroit: Wayne State University Press, 1988.

Fielding, Raymond. *The American Newsreel: 1911–1967*. Norman: University of Oklahoma Press, 1972.

———. "Hale's Tours: Ultrarealism in the Pre-1910 Motion Picture." *Cinema Journal*, 10.1 Fall 1970: 34–47.

Flaubert, Gustave. *Madame Bovary*. 1857. Trans. Mildred Marmur. New York: Signet, 1979.

Flinn, Tom. "Out of the Past." *The Velvet Light Trap*, Fall 1973: 38–43.

Frank, Nino. "Un Nouveau Genre 'Policier': L'Aventure Criminelle." *L'Écran Française*, 28 Aug. 1946: 8–9, 14.

Garbicz, Adam and Jacek Klinowski. *Cinema, The Magic Vehicle: A Guide to its Achievement, Journey One: The Cinema Through 1949*. Metuchen, N.J.: Scarecrow Press, 1975.

Gavin, Arthur E. "Rural Route for Realism." *American Cinematographer*, Sept. 1958: 552–3; 576–7.

———. " 'Wild Is the Wind' Is Realistic!" *American Cinematographer*, Jan. 1958: 24–5; 54–6.

George, David. "Film as Literature: Review of *The Naked City, A Screenplay by Albert Maltz and Malvin Wald.*" *The Jerusalem Post Magazine*, 8 Aug. 1980: 15.

"Giant Cycloramas Are Used in Pictures." *The Denver Post*, 7 Dec. 1941, Sec. 3: 6.

Goldman, Eric F. *The Crucial Decade: America 1945–1955.* New York: Knopf, 1956.

Gombrich, E. H. *Art and Illusion: A Study in the Psychology of Pictorial Representation.* Princeton, N.J.: Princeton University Press, 1960.

Goodman, Ezra. "A Cinematographer Speaks." *American Cinematographer*, Apr. 1945: 120–1; 132; 141.

———. "Post-War Motion Pictures." *American Cinematographer*, May 1945: 160; 176.

Gottfried, Robert S. *The Black Death: Natural and Human Disaster in Medieval Europe.* New York: The Free Press, 1983.

Gow, Gordon. "Cult Movies: *Touch of Evil.*" *Films and Filming*, Aug. 1976: 28–32.

———. "Style and Instinct: Interview of Jules Dassin." *Films and Filming*, Feb. 1970: 23–26.

Griffith, Robert. *The Politics of Fear: Joseph R. McCarthy and the Senate.* Lexington: The University Press of Kentucky, 1970.

Gundlach, Ralph H. "The Movies: Stereotype or Realities?" *The Journal of Social Issues*, 3.3 Summer 1947: 26–32.

Hammett, Dashiell. *The Continental Op.* 1923–1930. New York: Vintage Books, 1975.

———. *The Maltese Falcon.* 1929. New York: Vintage Books, 1989.

———. *Red Harvest.* 1929. New York: Vintage Books, 1972.

"Happy Endings Being Added to All New Films." *The Atlanta Constitution*, 14 Dec. 1941, Sunday Magazine and Feature Section: 9.

Harrington, Clifford G. "Rain, Fog nor Wind Ever Slows Location Shooting for 'The Lineup.'" *American Cinematographer*, June 1958: 362–3; 378–9.

Hartung, Philip T. Review of *The Naked City*. *The Commonweal*, 12 Mar. 1948: 546.

Hatch, Robert. "The New Realism." *The New Republic*, 8 Mar. 1948: 27.

Hays, Will H. "Motion Pictures and Total Defense." *19th Annual Report to the Motion Picture & Distributors of America, Inc.*, 31 Mar. 1941: 1–2.

———. "The Motion Picture in a World at War." *20th Annual Report to the Motion Picture Producers & Distributors of America, Inc.*, 30 Mar. 1942: 7.

Heffernan, Harold. "'Factual' Film Cycle Launched by Studios." *The Long Island Daily Press*, 19 Mar. 1948: 18.

Hellinger, Mark. Columns. *The New York Daily Mirror*. 1937.

"Hellinger, Mark." *Who's Who in America 1940–1941, Vol. 21*. Ed. Albert Nelson Marquis. Chicago: A. N. Marquis, 1940.

Herron, Don. *Dashiell Hammett Tour*. San Francisco: Dawn Heron Press, 1982.

Heston, Charlton. *The Actor's Life: Journals 1956–1976*. Ed. Hollis Alpert. New York: E. P. Dutton, 1976.

Higham, Charles. *The Films of Orson Welles*. Berkeley: University of California Press, 1970.

———. *Hollywood at Sunset*. New York: Saturday Review Press, 1972.

————. *Hollywood Cameramen: Sources of Light.* Bloomington: Indiana University Press, 1970.

————. *Orson Welles: The Rise and Fall of an American Genius.* New York: St. Martin's Press, 1985.

Hingley, Ronald. *Russian Writers and Soviet Society 1917–1978.* New York: Random House, 1979.

Hirsch, Foster. *Film Noir: The Dark Side of the Screen.* New York: Da Capo Press, 1981.

Hobart, John. Review of *The Maltese Falcon. The San Francisco Chronicle,* 12 Dec. 1941: 9.

Horton, Andrew. "Jules Dassin: A Multi-National Filmmaker Considered." *Film Criticism,* 8.3 Spring 1984: 21–35.

Houston, Penelope. *The Contemporary Cinema.* Harmondsworth, Eng.: Penguin Books, 1966.

Huaco, George A. *The Sociology of Film Art.* New York: Basic Books, 1965.

Hume, Kathryn. *Fantasy and Mimesis: Responses to Reality in Western Literature.* New York: Methuen, 1984.

"Inside Stuff—Pictures." *Variety,* 12 Nov. 1941: 18.

Isaacs, Hermine Rich. "The Movies Murder Illusion." *Sight and Sound,* 16.61 Spring 1947: 27–9.

Jarratt, Vernon. "Luchino Visconti's Ossessione." *Sight and Sound,* 17.65 Spring 1948: 25–6.

Jensen, Paul. " 'The Return of Dr. Caligari': Paranoia in Hollywood." *Film Comment,* 7.4 Winter 1971–2: 36–45.

Johnston, Eric. "Utopia Is Production." *Screen Actor,* Aug. 1946: 14–15.

Kaplan, E. Ann, ed. *Women in Film Noir*. London: British Film Institute, 1980.

Kracauer, Siegfried. *Theory of Film: The Redemption of Physical Reality*. London: Oxford University Press, 1979.

Krueger, Eric M. "*Touch of Evil*: Style Expressing Content." *Cinema Journal*, 12.1 Fall 1972: 57–63.

Lafferty, William. "A Reappraisal of the Semi-Documentary in Hollywood, 1945–1948." *The Velvet Light Trap*, Summer 1983: 22–26.

Langman, Larry. *A Guide to American Screenwriters: The Sound Era 1929–1982*. New York: Garland Publishing, 1984.

Lawson, John Howard. "Art Is a Weapon." *New Masses*, 19 Mar. 1946: 18–20.

———. *Film: The Creative Process, The Search for an Audio-Visual Language and Structure*. New York: Hill And Wang, 1964.

Layman, Richard. *Shadow Man: The Life of Dashiell Hammett*. New York: Harcourt Brace Jovanovich, 1981.

Leaming, Barbara. "Engineers of Human Souls." Diss., New York U., 1976.

———. *Orson Welles: A Biography*. New York: Viking, 1983.

Levitas, Louise. Review of *The Maltese Falcon*. *PM's Weekly*, 5 Oct. 1941: 19.

Leyda, Jay. *Kino: A History of the Russian and Soviet Film*. New York: Collier Books, 1960.

Lightman, Herb A. "*A Double Life:* The Camera Goes Backstage." *American Cinematographer*, Apr. 1948: 116–7; 132–3.

———. "Exponent of the Moving Camera." *American Cinematographer*, Nov. 1948: 376; 394.

———. *"The Lady From Shanghai:* Field Day For the Camera." *American Cinematographer,* June 1948: 200–1; 213.

———. "Low Key and Lively Action." *American Cinematographer,* Dec. 1948: 411; 424.

———. *"The Naked City:* Tribute in Celluloid." *American Cinematographer,* May 1948: 152–3; 178–9.

———. "New Horizons for the Documentary Film." *American Cinematographer,* Dec. 1945: 418; 442.

———. *"Sleep My Love:* Cinematic Psycho-Thriller." *American Cinematographer,* Feb. 1948: 46–7; 55.

———. "The Technique of the Documentary Film." *American Cinematographer,* Nov. 1945: 371; 378; 402.

———. *"13 Rue Madeleine:* Documentary Style in the Photoplay." *American Cinematographer,* Mar. 1947: 88–9; 110.

Llosa, Mario Vargas. *The Perceptual Orgy: Flaubert & Madame Bovary.* Trans. Helen Lane. New York: Farrar, Straus and Giroux, 1987.

Lowery, Harry. Review of *The Naked City. The Denver Post,* 14 Apr. 1948: 19.

Lukacs, Georg. *Realism in Our Time: Literature and the Class Struggle.* Trans. John & Neeke Mander. New York: Harper Torchbooks, 1971.

Lyons, Robert, ed. *My Darling Clementine.* New Brunswick, N.J.: Rutgers University Press, 1984.

McArthur, Colin. *Underworld U.S.A.* New York: The Viking Press, 1972.

McBride, Joseph. *Orson Welles.* New York: Viking Press, 1972.

McCoy, Horace. *They Shoot Horses, Don't They?* 1935. New York: Avon, 1970.

MacDonald, Dwight. *Dwight MacDonald on Movies*. Englewood
Cliffs, N.J.: Prentice Hall, 1969.

MacShane, Frank. *The Life of Raymond Chandler*. New York: E. P.
Dutton, 1976.

Madden, David, ed. *Tough Guy Writers of the Thirties*. Carbondale: Southern Illinois University Press, 1968.

The Maltese Falcon. Files. The Warner Bros. Collection. USC
Cinema-Television Library and Archives of Performing Arts.

———. Files. Warner Bros. Archive. Princeton University Libraries.

Maltz, Albert. "Moving Forward." *New Masses*, 9 Apr. 1946:
8–10; 21.

———. *The Writer as the Conscience of the People*. Hollywood Arts,
Sciences and Professions Council of the Progressive Citizens
of America, 1947.

———. Special Collections, Mugar Memorial Library, Boston
University.

Mann, Thomas. *Doctor Faustus: The Life of the German Composer
Adrian Leverkuhn as Told By a Friend*. Trans. H. T. Lowe-Porter.
New York: Vintage Books, 1971.

Marcus, Steven. Introduction. *The Continental Op*. By Dashiell
Hammett. New York: Vintage Books, 1975.

"Mark Hellinger's Last Picture Opens at the Capitol Theatre."
Review of *The Naked City*. *Cue*, 6 Mar. 1948: 16.

Marx, Karl and Friedrich Engels. *Literature and Art by Karl Marx
and Friedrich Engels: Selections from Their Writings*. New York:
International Publishers, 1947.

Meltzer, Milton. Review of *The Maltese Falcon*. *The Daily Worker*,
6 Oct. 1941: 7.

Mishkin, Leo. "Powerful 'Naked City' Will Stand As Lasting Memorial to Hellinger." *The New York Morning Telegraph,* 5 Mar. 1948: 2.

———. Review of *The Maltese Falcon. The New York Morning Telegraph,* 3 Oct. 1941: 2.

Mortimer, Lee. " 'Naked City' Is Top Mystery Thriller." *The New York Daily Mirror,* 5 Mar. 1948: 32.

———. Review of *The Maltese Falcon. The New York Daily Mirror,* 4 Oct. 1941: 17.

The Naked City. Files. Mark Hellinger Collection. USC Cinema-Television Library and Archives of Performing Arts.

Naremore, James. "John Huston and *The Maltese Falcon." Literature/Film Quarterly,* July 1973: 239–249.

———. *The Magic World of Orson Welles.* New York: Oxford University Press, 1978.

Navasky, Victor S. *Naming Names.* New York: The Viking Press, 1980.

"New York Is the Star of 'Naked City.' " *Cue,* 14 Feb. 1948: 15.

Nichols, Bill. *Ideology and the Image: Social Representation in the Cinema and Other Media.* Bloomington: Indiana University Press, 1981.

Nietzsche, Friedrich. *Beyond Good and Evil.* Trans. R. J. Hollingdale. Harmondsworth, Eng.: Penguin Books, 1987.

———. *Twilight of the Idols.* Trans. R. J. Hollingdale. Harmondsworth, Eng.: Penguin Books, 1984.

"No End Seen to Western Sagas." *The Denver Post,* 13 June 1958: 38.

Noble, Joseph V. "Development of the Cinematographic Art." *American Cinematographer,* Jan. 1947: 10–11; 26–7.

Nochlin, Linda. *Realism, Style and Civilization.* New York: Penguin Books, 1971.

Nolan, William F. *Hammett: A Life at the Edge.* New York: Congdon & Weed, 1983.

Ogle, Patrick L. "Technological and Aesthetic Influences upon the Development of Deep Focus Cinematography in the United States." *Screen Reader I: Cinema/Ideology/Politics.* London: The Society for Education in Film and Television, 1977: 81–108.

Ottoson, Robert. *A Reference Guide to the American Film Noir: 1940–1958.* Metuchen, N.J.: The Scarecrow Press, 1981.

Overbey, David, ed. and trans. *Springtime in Italy: A Reader on Neo-Realism.* Hamden, Conn.: Archon, 1979.

"Paramount Invites All to Rock-'n'-Roll Party." *The Denver Post,* 23 May 1957: 55.

Pells, Richard H. *The Liberal Mind in a Conservative Age: American Intellectuals in the 1940s and 1950s.* New York: Harper & Row, 1985.

Pelswick, Rose. " 'The Maltese Falcon' Moves Into Strand: Slick Melodrama Oozes Suspense and Mystery." *The New York Journal-American,* 4 Oct. 1941: 14.

Peper, William. "Welles Back in Old Villainy." *The New York World-Telegram and Sun,* 22 May 1958: 18.

Pike, Burton. *The Image of the City in Modern Literature.* Princeton, N.J.: Princeton University Press, 1981.

Place, J. A. and L. S. Peterson. "Some Visual Motifs of Film Noir." *Film Comment,* Jan. 1974: 30–34.

Plouffe, Paul Bernard. "The Tainted Adam: The American Hero in Film Noir." Diss., U of California, Berkeley, 1979.

Polan, Dana. *Power and Paranoia: History, Narrative, and the American Cinema 1940–1950.* New York: Columbia University Press, 1986.

Porfirio, Robert Gerald. "The Dark Age of American Film: A Study of the American Film Noir 1940–1960." Diss., Yale U., 1979.

Pratley, Gerald. *The Cinema of John Huston.* New York: A. S. Barnes, 1977.

Proctor, Kay. "Glamour Boy." *Screen Life,* Dec. 1941: 35; 50–1.

Reid, Larry. Editorial. *Motion Picture,* 62.6 Jan. 1942: 98.

"Report on a Motion Picture Research Project, Directed by Leo C. Rosten." *Screen Actor,* Apr. 1941: 7.

Review of *The Naked City. Look,* 16 Mar. 1948: 96–98.

Review of *The Naked City. The Milwaukee Journal,* 28 April 1948: 10.

Review of *The Naked City. Movie Life,* June 1948: 50.

Review of *The Naked City. Variety,* 21 Jan. 1948: 8.

Review of *The Maltese Falcon. The Atlanta Constitution,* 14 Dec. 1941, Sunday Magazine and Feature Section: 7.

Review of *The Maltese Falcon. Cue,* 4 Oct. 1941: 19.

Review of *The Maltese Falcon. Motion Picture Herald,* 4 Oct. 1941: 78.

Review of *The Maltese Falcon. Variety,* 1 Oct. 1941: 9.

Review of *Touch of Evil. Cue,* 10 May 1958: 8.

"RKOs Book Adult Fare." *The New York Mirror,* 21 May 1958: 36.

"R. M. D." "Reviewing the screen." Review of *The Maltese Falcon. The Milwaukee Journal,* 18 Jan. 1942, Section II: 4.

Rodgers, William F. "Vitamins E and U for Post-War Pix." *Variety,* 7 Jan. 1942: 16.

"Ron." Review of *Touch of Evil*. *Variety*, 19 Mar. 1958: 16.

Rose, Billy. " 'Escapology' Not the Answer; Showmen Must Sell Aggressive Americanism to Everybody." *Variety*, 7 Jan. 1942: 28.

Rousseau, Jean-Jacques. *Politics and the Arts: Letter to M. D'Alembert on the Theatre*. Trans. Allan Bloom. Ithaca, N.Y.: Cornell University Press, 1977.

Rovin, Jeff. *The Films of Charlton Heston*. Secaucus, N.J.: The Citadel Press, 1977.

Salt, Barry. *Film Style and Technology: History and Analysis*. London: Starwood, 1983.

———. "From Caligari to Who?" *Sight and Sound*, 48.2 Spring 1979: 119–123.

———. "Let a Hundred Flowers Bloom: Film Form, Style and Aesthetics." *Sight and Sound*, 43.2 Spring 1974: 108–9.

Salzman, Jack. *Albert Maltz*. Boston: Twayne, 1978.

Sarnoff, David. "Every Chance in the World." *American Magazine*, Apr. 1948: 135.

Sarris, Andrew. *The American Cinema: Directors and Directions 1929–1968*. New York: E. P. Dutton, 1968.

———. "Andrew Sarris Picks the Best of the Classic Cinema." Review of *Touch of Evil*. *The Village Voice*, 9 Feb. 1976: 109.

Schatz, Thomas. *Hollywood Genres: Formulas, Filmmaking, and The Studio System*. Philadelphia: Temple University Press, 1981.

Schlüpmann, Heide. "Phenomenology of Film: On Siegfried Kracauer's Writing of the 1920's." Trans. Thomas Y. Levin. *New German Critique*, 14.1 Winter 1987: 97–114.

Schrader, Paul. "Notes on Film Noir." *Film Comment*, 8.1 Spring 1972: 8–13.

Selby, Spencer. *Dark City: The Film Noir*. Jefferson, N.C.: McFarland, 1984.

Shamroy, Leon. "Future of Cinematography." *American Cinematographer*, Oct. 1947: 358.

Sharff, Stefan. *The Elements of Cinema: Toward a Theory of Cinesthetic Impact*. New York: Columbia University Press, 1982.

Sheridan, Bart. "Three and a Half Minute Take." *American Cinematographer*, Sept. 1948: 304–5; 314.

Shindler, Colin. *Hollywood Goes to War: Films and American Society 1939–1952*. London: Routledge & Kegan Paul, 1979.

Silone, Ignazio. *Bread and Wine*. 1937. Trans. Harvey Fergusson II. New York: Signet, 1963.

Silver, Alain and Elizabeth Ward, eds. *Film Noir: An Encyclopedic Reference to the American Style*. Woodstock, N.Y.: The Overlook Press, 1979.

Steinbeck, John. *The Grapes of Wrath*. New York: Random House, 1939.

Steinberg, Cobbett. *Reel Facts: The Movie Book of Records*. New York: Vintage Books, 1982.

Stern, J. P. *On Realism*. London: Routledge & Kegan Paul, 1973.

Stull, William. "Lighting Without Photofloods." *American Cinematographer*, Dec. 1942: 520; 534.

Sullivan, Kay. Rev. of *The Naked City*. *Parade*, 7 Mar. 1948: 22.

Sundquist, Eric J. *American Realism: New Essays*. Baltimore: Johns Hopkins University Press, 1982.

Surtees, Robert. "The Story of Filming 'Act of Violence.'" *American Cinematographer*, Aug. 1948: 268; 282–4.

Symons, Julian. *Dashiell Hammett*. New York: Harcourt Brace Jovanovich, 1985.

Tagg, John. *The Burden of Representation: Essays on Photographies and Histories*. Amherst: University of Massachusetts Press, 1988.

Talbot, David and Barbara Zheutlin. *Creative Differences: Profiles of Hollywood Dissidents*. Boston: South End Press, 1978.

Tank, Herb. " 'The Naked City': Good Job, Well Done." *The Daily Worker*, 5 Mar. 1948: 12.

"Technical Progress in 1941." *American Cinematographer*, Jan. 1942: 6–7; 45–6.

Telotte, J. P. "Film Noir and the Dangers of Discourse." *Quarterly Review of Film Studies*, 9.2 Spring 1984: 101–112.

"The Naked City Is *The Movie of the Month.*" *Motion Picture Magazine*, May 1948: 64.

Thompson, Howard. "Orson Welles Is Triple Threat in Thriller." *The New York Times*, 22 May 1958: 25.

Thomson, David. *America in the Dark: Hollywood and the Gift of Unreality*. New York: William Morrow, 1977.

Toland, Gregg. "Realism for 'Citizen Kane.' " *American Cinematographer*, Feb. 1941: 54–5; 80.

Touch of Evil. Files. Universal Collection. USC Cinema-Television Library and Archives of Performing Arts.

Tuska, Jon. *Dark Cinema: American Film Noir in Cultural Perspective*. Westport, Conn.: Greenwood Press, 1984.

Vardac, A. Nicholas. *Stage to Screen: Theatrical Method from Garrick to Griffith*. New York: Benjamin Blom, 1968.

Wald, Malvin. "Cops and Writers." *The Screen Writer*, Mar. 1948: 23–6.

Wald, Malvin and Albert Maltz. *The Naked City: A Screenplay*. Ed. Matthew J. Bruccoli. Carbondale: Southern Illinois University Press, 1979.

———. *The Naked City:* Continuity and Dialogue Script. New York State Archives, Albany, New York.

Warnke, Frank J. *Versions of Baroque: European Literature in the Seventeenth Century.* New Haven: Yale University Press, 1972.

Watts, Richard, Jr. "Drama and Film Critics See the Stage And Screen's Function as Vivid in War." *Variety,* 7 Jan. 1942: 25.

Wead, George. "Toward a Definition of Filmnoia." *The Velvet Light Trap,* Fall 1974: 2–4.

Weegee [Arthur Fellig]. *Naked City.* New York: Essential Books, 1945.

"W. E. H." Review of *The Maltese Falcon. The Denver Post,* 31 Dec. 1941: 19.

Wellek, René. *Concepts of Criticism.* New Haven: Yale University Press, 1963.

Welles, Orson. Editorials. *The New York Post,* Jan.–June 1945.

Willeman, Paul. "On Realism in the Cinema." *Screen Reader I: Cinema/Ideology/Politics.* London: The Society for Education in Film and Television, 1977: 47–54.

Williams, Roger L. *The Horror of Life: Charles Baudelaire, Jules de Goncourt, Gustave Flaubert, Guy de Maupassant, Alphonse Daudet.* Chicago: University of Chicago Press, 1980.

Winsten, Archer. " 'The Naked City': Hellinger's Best." *The New York Post,* 5 Mar. 1948: 24.

Wolfe, Thomas. *You Can't Go Home Again.* 1934. New York: Harper & Row, 1973.

Yates, Virginia. " 'Rope' Sets A Precedent." *American Cinematographer,* July 1948: 230–1; 246.

Yerrill, D. A. "The Technique of Realism." *Sight and Sound,* 17.65 Spring 1948: 23–4.

Young, Mahonri Sharp. *The Eight: The Realist Revolt in American Painting.* New York: Watson-Guptill, 1973.

Zola, Émile. *The Experimental Novel and Other Essays.* Trans. Belle M. Sherman. New York: Haskell House, 1964.

INDEX

Academy Ratio—153
Act of Violence—160
Amazing Dr. Clitterhouse, The—64
Anna Christie—93
Anna Karenina—93
Anthony Adverse—48
Appointment for Love—46
Arnheim, Rudolf—28
Asphalt Jungle, The—10
Astor, Mary—42, 55, 65, 68, 70, 173
Auerbach, Erich—26

Bad Men of Missouri—41
Bakhtin, M. M.—27
Balzac, Honoré de—203–4
Band Wagon, The—120
Barnouw, Erik—14, 16, 98
Barrett, William—32
Barthes, Roland—5
Bazin, André—4–5, 23, 27–8, 49, 65, 69, 80, 86, 94, 133, 143,
    167, 190, 200
Bennett, Joan—173
Bessie, Alvah—204
Big Clock, The—188
Big Combo, The—120, 158
Big Heat, The—56, 85, 140
Big Sleep, The—24
Birth of a Nation—209
Black Legion—99
Black Magic—142
Black Mask (journal)—24, 165
Blanke, Henry—42, 48

Collins, Ray—143
Communist Party of America—100, 107, 198, 200, 203, 207
Comolli, Jean-Louis—23
Compulsion—142
Confessions of a Nazi Spy—102
Cook, Elisha, Jr.—174
Coppola, Francis Ford—170
Corsia, Ted de—77, 91
Cortez, Ricardo—38
Cotten, Joseph—128, 143
Courbet, Gustave—25
Criss Cross—45
Crossfire—85, 106
Crossing Brooklyn Ferry (poem)—97
Crowther, Bosley—78, 99, 192
Cry Danger—45

D.O.A.—194
Daniels, Bebe—38
Dark Age of American Film, The (unpub. diss.)—11
Dark Corner—97, 159, 174
Dark Passage—45, 173
Dark Past, The—173
Dassin, Jules—2–3, 16–19, 50, 82, 95, 97–8, 103–4, 128, 164,
    167, 181–2, 186, 191–2, 199
Davies, Marion—137
Davis, Bette—40
Defiant Ones, The—174
Depression, the—14, 27, 29, 40, 141, 191
Detective Story—139
Detour—10, 119, 189
Devil's Passkey, The—94
Dieterle, William—40
Dietrich, Marlene—128, 136, 144
Dmytryk, Edward—165
Dr. Ehrlich's Magic Bullet—64
Doctor Faustus (novel)—184
documentary—2–3, 14–19, 50, 82, 95, 97–8, 103–4, 163–4,
    167, 175, 177, 181–2, 186, 191–2, 199; *see also* semi-
    documentary

Mitchum, Robert—174
Monash, Paul—134–6, 142
Mother—51
Murder My Sweet—10, 165

Naked City, The—3, 8, 76–116, 118, 127, 129, 131, 135–6,
    163, 167–9, 171–2, 174–6, 180, 187–9, 196, 202, 205
Naked Kiss, The—184
Nathan, George Jean—63
naturalism—23, 27
negativity—28, 192, 194, 203
neorealism—84–5, 171, 187–90
Nick Carter Detective Stories—63
Nietzsche, Friedrich—23, 32
Night and the City—10, 120, 155, 193
Nightmare Alley—193
1920s—58
1930s—8, 14, 16, 26, 81, 95, 100, 159–61, 163
1940s—33, 78, 85, 95, 153, 161, 170, 189, 193, 198
1950s—33, 85, 95, 160–1, 169, 189, 193, 198
1960s—8, 33, 160
Ninotchka—28, 93
Nixon, Richard M.—118
No Way Out—120

O. Henry—99
Oates, Joyce Carol—162
Odets, Clifford—100, 199, 204
O'Dwyer, William—77, 84
Olvidados, Los—175
One From the Heart—170
Open City—97, 160
optimism—2, 10, 21, 154, 184, 191, 194
Orwell, George—182
Out of the Past—10, 45, 155, 193

Panic in the Streets—85, 193
Panorama du Film Noir American—3
Paradine Case, The—49
Paramount—16, 94
Paramount Decision of 1948—11

Sullavan, Margaret—46
Sunset Boulevard—183, 192–3
Surtees, Robert—160
Swamp Water—50
Sweet Smell of Success, The—10, 120, 194

Tainted Adam, The: The American Hero in Film Noir
    (unpub.diss.)—27
Tamiroff, Akim—118, 143
Tarkington, Booth—134
Taylor, Don—76, 83–4
Ten Commandments, The—144
They Won't Believe Me—173
Thin Man, The—39
13 Rue Madeleine—123
This Gun For Hire—201
This Is America—190–2
Thunder Road—175
Toland Gregg—50–1, 118–119
Touch of Evil—3, 8, 117–151, 167–8, 180–1, 188–9, 207–9
tough-mindedness—180
Treasure of Sierra Madre, The—106
Trial, The—140
Triumph of the Will—163
20th Century-Fox—97, 164, 202

U.S.A. (novel)—97
Undercover Man, The—121
Underground Stream, The (novel)—99
Underworld U.S.A.—10, 184
Unholy Wife, The—128
Universal—8–9, 87, 91, 106, 109, 123, 127–30, 135, 141–2,
    144, 176–7
unreality—176

Valentine, Joseph A.—163
verisimilitude—5, 20, 39, 48, 66, 77, 184
Vertigo—118
violence—4, 8, 10, 27, 42–3, 68, 180

Index **247**